*For Kathy, Steve,
and Anne*

# Preface to the Third Edition

In its recent development, American bureaucracy has been the victim of two very strong anti-bureaucratic trends. The first trend has been the growing effort to repoliticize the executive branch by bringing the decisions and actions of career bureaucrats under more intensive political control. From small beginnings in the late nineteenth century, as Stephen Skowronek shows, American bureaucracy became more and more professionalized.[1] The spoils system was put to rout and power gravitated to skilled administrators.

During recent decades, however, that trend has been reversed. Presidents as diverse as Dwight Eisenhower, John Kennedy, and Ronald Reagan have made strenuous efforts to reestablish the primacy of elected officials in executive policy deliberations. By and large they have succeeded, to the point that it has now become very difficult in the United States for senior civil servants to penetrate the inner circles of executive policy-making.

The second trend has been the continuing movement toward debureaucratization in the United States, both by restricting the range of services provided by executive agencies and by deregulatory measures designed to narrow their authority. Bureaucrats have thus been on the defensive for much of recent American history. They have been variously charged with usurping the power of the President and Congress, defeating the aims of reform legislation by administering it apathetically, or — at the opposite extreme — pursuing reform goals with single-minded zeal regardless of their harmful side effects.

[1] Stephen Skowronek, *Building a New American State: The Expansion of National Administrative Capacities, 1877–1920* (New York: Cambridge University Press, 1982).

In the midst of this anti-bureaucratic ferment, the resilience of bureaucracy has been quite extraordinary. The national security establishment has risen from the ashes of Vietnam and regained both its authority and its appropriations. A variety of domestic agencies that were in seeming jeopardy at the beginning of the Reagan administration have survived the austerity measures imposed on them by the White House.

The inevitability of bureaucracy is thus even more evident today than when the earlier editions of this book were published. If bureaucracy is not quite the fourth branch of government that many of its early critics feared, it is still a force to be reckoned with in modern American politics. It continues to operate not only as a power in its own right, but also as a pervasive source of influence on the structure and operation of other political institutions. From the White House to the village pump, no sector of government has been left untouched by the impact of bureaucratic organizations on American political culture.

As in earlier editions, let me record my debt to all those scholars on whose work I have leaned in writing this book. Whatever merit it has comes in large part from their labors.

I am especially indebted to some immediate colleagues who share my interest in some of the topics discussed here: William Ascher and Matthew Crenson at Johns Hopkins and Martha Kumar and Michael Grossman at Towson State University.

All my graduate students have contributed greatly to my understanding of bureaucracy, most recently and most especially Roger Brown, Kenneth Kato and Michael Nelson. While working with me on this project, Kenneth Kato has been of enormous assistance at every stage of the endeavor. I can only envy his prodigious capacity for attending to detail.

Hugh Heclo read the manuscript in its entirety and made many very useful suggestions for improving it. Neither he nor any one else mentioned here bears any responsibility for its defects. That responsibility is, of course, mine alone.

Evelyn Scheulen typed the manuscript. I value her skill in this regard almost as much as I do her friendship.

At Little, Brown I would like to thank Don Palm, Sally Stickney, David Lynch, and Anne Goodrich.

# *Preface to the First Edition*

One approach to public bureaucracy that has won increasing favor in recent years is to look upon government agencies as part of the family of organizations — sharing common problems with churches, factories, trade unions, and a host of other private institutions. The emergence of an organization theory with a scope as wide as society itself has had an enormously stimulating effect upon the study of public administration. It has introduced a whole new range of explanatory concepts as a guide to understanding the behavior of public officials.

At the same time, however, an appreciation of the characteristics that public agencies share with private organizations should not be allowed to obscure the unique function of these agencies as instruments of the state intimately involved in the development and execution of public policy. It is the role of bureaucracy in the policy process that is at the center of concern in this book. For it is in the crucible of administrative politics today that public policy is mainly hammered out, through bargaining, negotiation, and conflict among appointed rather than elected officials. The bureaucratization of the policy process is particularly pronounced in defense and foreign affairs, but it reaches into domestic policy as well. The design and operation of the policy systems in which bureaucracies participate has thus become a primary item on the agenda of contemporary political science.

This study is largely based on materials drawn from the American experience. Consequently, it applies more directly to the interaction between bureaucracy and public policy in the United States than it does to other political systems. Certain features of the policy process that are examined, especially the extensive involvement of executive agencies in the task of creating and nursing a constituency, are almost distinctively American. In the so-called emerging nations, for example — where political institutions are characteristically quite undeveloped — bureaucratic power tends to rest on a monopoly of expertise and command of the formal apparatus of the state. However, the American pattern has many parallels elsewhere, and, as the most advanced industrial system in the world, it may well represent a model toward which other societies will eventually evolve.

Needless to say, I have incurred a great many debts in the course of preparing this manuscript. This debt is obvious in the case of the authors cited in the footnotes and bibliography. Without their assistance, the book could not have been written.

Less obvious is the contribution of those whose assistance has been more personal. Without involving them in any way in mistakes or failures on my part, I would like to express my gratitude to Professors Alan Altshuler, Jerome Gilison, and Robert W. Tucker for reading the manuscript and making many suggestions toward its improvement.

In working on this study, I had the assistance of three very able graduate assistants, Virginia Ermer, Aubrey King, and Paul Lutzker. Mrs. Ermer helped proofread the manuscript, Mr. King did much of the work involved in preparing the bibliography that appears at the end of the book, and Mr. Lutzker's resourcefulness was a constant asset to me.

All the graduate students in my seminar in public administration read the manuscript and gave me the benefit of their sagacious and irreverent comments.

With her customary and still somewhat incredible efficiency, Mrs. Catherine Grover typed the manuscript, correcting my errors as she went along.

Finally, at Little, Brown, I would like to record my appreciation to Donald R. Hammonds, who started me on this project, and David L. Giele, who helped bring it to completion.

# *Contents*

# CHAPTER ONE

# Introduction:
# Bureaucracies
# and Policy Making

The belief that power in the modern state is now centered in the corridors of bureaucracy is more often asserted or assumed than examined. But certainly it is clear that governmental activities have steadily expanded since the New Deal of President Franklin D. Roosevelt in the 1930s, and among the chief beneficiaries of this expansion have been the executive agencies and officials who carry on the day-to-day tasks of government. This book is an inquiry into the role that bureaucracies play in making policy decisions in contemporary political systems. It is focused on both the roots of bureaucratic power — the sources from which administrative agencies derive their influence on the policy process — and the distinctive problems that arise when policy making is carried on within a setting in which executive organizations play such a major role.

In the United States, at least, it is possible to assimilate the study of administrative policy making into the traditional group analysis of political life. Executive agencies provide channels of "access" through which segments of the public can advance or protect their interests in much the same way as they pursue their goals through other governmental institutions — the political parties, the legislature, and even the judiciary.[1] From this bureaucratic politics perspective, an agency's power depends upon its ability to command the support of fervent and substantial clientele groups, or upon its effective use of strategies designed to advance the interests of these groups in the competitive struggle for power among executive organizations that is so prominent a feature of political life in the modern state.

Certainly, there is no disputing that a great deal of administrative influence can be explained within this framework of group theory. It is the agitation of outside groups that commonly leads to the establishment of executive agencies, and agencies and groups are thereafter bound together on a day-to-day basis through a wide variety of mutually rewarding relationships. This relationship applies especially to executive agencies administering domestic programs that serve special clientele groups, where administrative influence often rests entirely on public support, or, as one author puts it, "power is organized around constituency." [2]

This is not, however, a complete picture of the bureaucratic role in the policy process. It is not adequate as a description of bureaucratic power in American administration, even though government agencies in this country have very wide-ranging involvement in the political process, and it is certainly not suitable as a description of bureaucracy in Western European governments, where, by law and tradition, executive agencies are considerably more insulated from the play of external political forces. Political activity such as the negotiation of alliances with outside groups can be a useful source of power for any administrative agency, but it is by no means the sole origin of administrative influence.

The fact of the matter is that bureaucracy is more than a mere conduit through which the values and aspirations of various segments of the community are incorporated into public policy. Within its own ranks, public bureaucracy numbers a great variety of highly organized and technically trained professional personnel, whose knowledge and skills powerfully influence the shape of official decision. Although bureaucratic policy making in many fields has primarily reflected a system of external group pressures, in other areas such as science and national defense the expertise and informational resources of bureaucratic organizations have themselves been controlling factors in the evolution of public policy.

Most policy decisions within bureaucracy thus represent the outcome of an interaction between two sources of power — the needs or aspirations of groups within the community with which executive agencies are allied and the expertise of bureaucrats as it is applied to the issues being resolved. But remember also that bureaucracies themselves have interests to protect — most especially maintenance of their own power and jurisdiction as organizations, not to mention the perquisites of their members, and these bureaucratic interests may also influence the way in which they cope with policy issues. No agency is likely to support a policy that it perceives as diminishing its own standing or effectiveness as an organization. Even though they may be created to achieve some major public good, executive agencies often come to regard preserving their own organizational well-being as the most important of all public goods.

Assessed by its effect on its external environment, the rise of bureaucracy in the American political system has both aggravated and altered inequalities of power within the private sector of society. In some cases, executive agencies have simply echoed the views of major economic interests, in this way augmenting the advantages of those already powerful. The interests of the banking community, for example, are very well represented by a number of government agencies in Washington. In other instances, however, public organizations have been vigorous protagonists of groups at the lower end of the scale in both wealth and power. One of the historic functions of bureaucracy in American society has been to provide a means of effective expression in policy deliberations for community groups that are inarticulate, poorly organized, or for some other reason unable to speak for themselves. With administrative help, these stepchildren of the political system may acquire a measure of equality with other groups that they could never hope to attain through the ordinary processes of politics alone. Bureaucracies may thus alter as well as mirror the patterns of group strength that are so important in the development of public policy in modern democratic societies. They may carry out policies that redistribute both income and power from the haves to the have-nots.

In addition to these cases in which public agencies act essentially as advocates for private groups, there are many issues, especially in foreign policy, on which "decisions are made by high public and private 'officials' in virtually a public opinion and interest-group opinion vacuum." [3] In areas of this sort, bureaucrats are in a commanding position to shape public policy by the weight of their own influence, because they possess not only the professional skills necessary to devise rational courses of action but, because of their control over information, the ability to structure the public attitudes and preferences to which their policy decisions are in theory supposed to respond. In such situations executive agencies may sometimes come close to enjoying monopoly power over the course of public policy.

## Responsiveness and Effectiveness

In evaluating the way in which executive agencies participate in policy making, two criteria have traditionally been emphasized. The first is the responsiveness of the system, the extent to which it promotes correspondence between the decisions of bureaucrats and the preferences of the community or the officeholders who are authorized to speak for the public. The second is the system's effectiveness, the degree to which it leads to decisions that are more likely than alternative choices to bring about the outcomes that are desired — because, however laudable their goals, policies must actually work. Responsiveness and effectiveness are thus the touchstones by which we commonly measure the utility of the system through which bureaucracies participate in policy making in a democratic society.

At all levels of government in the United States, the task of creating acceptable arrangements to achieve these goals has been enormously complicated by the fact that the criteria of responsiveness and effectiveness often point in opposite directions. Organizational arrangements and procedures that appear perfectly designed to enhance the responsiveness of bureaucracies frequently seem less likely to allow them to produce effective decisions.

In national security administration, the effectiveness of policy making has usually seemed to demand great secrecy in bureaucratic deliberations. Apart from the obvious need to prevent disclosure of military or diplomatic information that might be helpful to a foreign adversary, the resort to secrecy in this area of policy has been justified on the grounds that it promotes candor in internal deliberations, and enables the government to gain the advantage of surprise in dealing with other states. The success of American policy in the Cuban missile crisis in 1962 has often been traced to the secrecy that surrounded the discussion within the government preceding the final decision to establish a blockade around Cuba.[4]

At the same time, however, the Cuban missile case highlights the fact that arrangements designed to enhance effectiveness in policy making may clearly preclude the processes of popular consultation that are indispensable if responsiveness is to be secured. Certainly the kind of internal dialogue within bureaucracy that accompanied the Cuban crisis in 1962 could not have taken place in public while officials were considering alternative ways of dealing with the threat to American security that the Soviet missile bases then under construction appeared to represent. Thus decisions jeopardizing the survival of life on the planet were made by a handful of men acting in secret in Moscow and Washington.

There have been situations, of course, in which effectiveness and responsiveness in bureaucratic policy making did not seem as incompatible as they did at the time of the confrontation with the Soviets in 1962. After the invasion of Cuba by a refugee group supported by the United States had failed at the Bay of Pigs in 1961, President Kennedy conceded that the mistake of launching this attack might well have been avoided if there had been full disclosure of the plan to the American public and a broader discussion of it. Thus, in the case of the Bay of Pigs invasion it is possible that both the effectiveness and responsiveness of policy would have been better served by arrangements designed to promote public, rather than secret, decisions within government organizations.

No president more devoutly advocated the necessity of secrecy for effective executive performance than President Richard Nixon. In speaking before American prisoners of war who had returned from Vietnam in 1973, Nixon was quite explicit in linking what he felt to be the great successes of his administration to the use of secrecy. "Had we not had secrecy," Nixon argued, "there would have been no China initiative, there would have been no limitation of arms for the Soviet Union and no summit, and had we not had . . . that kind of secrecy that allowed for the kind of exchange that is essential, you men would still be in Hanoi rather than Washington today."

Yet, it is one of the greater ironies of American history that this passion for secrecy was ultimately to destroy Nixon's own presidency. His establishment of the so-called plumbers unit in the White House was motivated by a desire to maintain secrecy. The principal task of the plumbers was to plug up "leaks" of information that the administration regarded as secret, such as the earlier disclosure of the Pentagon papers, which had revealed much of the planning and discussion that took place in the executive branch in the early stages of the Vietnam War. After the ill-starred burglary of the national headquarters of the Democratic party by the plumbers, the White House made an immediate decision to "cover up" its connection with this covert operation. Thereafter the cover-up required an enormous and continuing investment in secrecy, culminating in the refusal to supply the tape recordings of White House conversations sought by the special prosecutor's office. The suspicion bred by each successive step in this continuing strategy of secrecy brought a precipitous decline in the president's standing in the eyes of both Congress and the public, and led ultimately to Nixon's departure from office under the threat of impeachment.[5]

The Watergate episode and other cases of its kind have led some observers to conclude that — from the point of view of effectiveness alone — the deliberations of executive officials should always be as "open" as possible. Secrecy, it is argued, allows officials to cover up and continue ill-advised policies and to shield their own incompetence or misconduct from discovery. A system of disclosure, on the other hand, has a variety of practical advantages for the government as well as the public. For one thing it enables the president and other responsible executives to obtain better information on what is going on within the agencies they are supposed to supervise. Moreover, by widening the circle of those allowed to participate in executive discussions, an open system enables policy decisions to be informed by the advice and suggestions of many knowledgeable individuals who would otherwise be excluded from the deliberative process altogether.

It is clear that in a good many situations disclosure contributes to the effectiveness as well as the responsiveness of the policy-making process. Help in designing a sensible policy may come from people who would not have been consulted under a system of secrecy. It would greatly simplify the task of designing a bureaucratic policy system if this were the universal situation. Unfortunately, no such convenient correspondence between the requirements of responsiveness and the need for effectiveness can always be anticipated. Although administrative arrangements designed to secure full publicity for all aspects of executive deliberations would help to prevent some mistakes in policy, they would also guarantee fewer successes. Not only in foreign affairs, such as the Cuban missile case, but also in domestic policy making there are many situations in which the ability of executive agencies to carry on discussions in private while policy alternatives are being evaluated contributes to a thorough canvassing and critique of all possibilities. Presidents have long insisted that their ability to make policy in all areas depends upon their ability to receive candid advice from their subordinates and that these officials will be reluctant to speak freely unless their advice is kept confidential.

Consequently, it is not always possible to escape the difficult problem of devising arrangements that will help achieve quite contradictory goals. Gains in the effectiveness of the policy process may have to be paid for by some losses in its responsiveness, and it cannot always be assumed that measures designed to enhance responsiveness will not jeopardize the system's effectiveness.

## DESIGNING A POLICY SYSTEM

Even when there has been agreement on the need to maintain both effectiveness and responsiveness in the design of the bureaucratic policy system, there has not always been a meeting of minds on what each of these criteria requires in the way of institutional arrangements. For some observers, responsiveness may simply entail the right of the public to determine what the ultimate objectives of bureaucratic activity shall be. The agencies themselves are left free to determine how best to attain these goals. Others, however, may extend the idea of responsiveness to include control by the public or its representatives of the day-to-day actions and decisions in which executive agencies engage in order to achieve these fundamental goals. It has long been argued whether legislatures should be confined to spelling out statutory guidelines for agency action, or encouraged in addition to monitor, as they often do, the continuous decisions through which agencies pursue their statutory purposes. Up until the Supreme Court decision disallowing its use, support in Congress was widespread for the "legislative veto," an arrangement under which the legislature could overrule individual agency decisions, especially those made by regulatory bodies.[6]

Similar problems arise on the distribution of authority in the bureaucratic policy system. In studies of national administration, and at lower levels of government as well, responsiveness was long believed to require centralization of authority in the hands of top executives. It was assumed that executives at the commanding heights of an organization had the broadest of all perspectives on policy issues, and that they were most capable of keeping the agency's policies and activities in tune with the public interest. Officials at lower levels of administration, on the other hand, have traditionally been viewed as captive to more parochial concerns — survival of their own unit or the needs of some special clientele, for example.

But a revisionist perspective in organization theory has acquired increasing strength in recent years. The argument is heard more and more often that responsiveness requires organizational arrangements under which a great deal of authority is delegated to lower levels of administration. Such decentralization, it is felt, "humanizes" bureaucracy because officials at the grass roots are more sensitive to the aspirations of the groups in the community immediately affected by the programs executive agencies are carrying out.[7]

Both conservatives and liberals have sung the praises of decentralization in American politics. Conservatives have long cherished the notion of keeping as many governmental functions as possible in the hands of state and local rather than national officials. The "New Federalism" proclaimed by both Presidents Nixon and Reagan reflects this conservative faith in decentralization. It would turn over many activities now being administered by the national government to the states, on the assumption that this shift would bring these programs under greater public scrutiny and control, making them both more responsive and more effective with one bold stroke.

The liberal attachment to decentralization takes a somewhat different turn. It manifests itself in support of proposals for decentralizing decision making by national agencies themselves, rather than turning over national functions to the states. Thus in the 1930s the Tennessee Valley Authority (TVA) was viewed in liberal circles as a dramatic example of the national government's ability to decentralize itself — to run a natural resource program in the Tennessee Valley through a national agency located in the area and primarily responsive to Valley residents. In their initial enthusiasm for TVA, which has since waned, many liberals believed that the example it provided should be followed in administering natural resource programs in other river valley areas.

More recently, liberal support for decentralization was also evident in the design and operation of President Lyndon Johnson's Great Society programs. In seeking to realize the objectives of the War on Poverty, administration planners pinned much of their hope for success on citizen participation, through which ordinary people affected by antipoverty programs would themselves become involved in their development. For some critics of War on Poverty agencies, their emphasis on citizen participation was one of the chief factors that led to their demise.

Be that as it may, both conservatives and liberals see decentralization as an instrument for making bureaucracy more responsive. They differ in that conservatives rely on established state and local authorities as vehicles for achieving decentralized responsiveness, whereas liberals tend to see local elites as captive to powerful interests within their own community. Hence, liberals prefer to decentralize the administration of national programs through national agencies that are grass-roots oriented like TVA, or by encouraging citizen participation in decision making by national agencies.[8]

Effectiveness can be as elusive a goal as responsiveness. Until recent times, most concern over the effectiveness of the bureaucratic apparatus was focused on the need to increase the ability of executives to control and direct the organizational units under their jurisdiction. Implicit in this approach was the assumption that the capacity of executive agencies to choose intelligent courses of action could be taken for granted. The problems of administration were identified as essentially those of mobilizing the energy and resources of executive agencies toward achieving these agreed-upon goals. The efficient delivery of services was what bureaucracy is all about.

Increasingly, however, concern with the effectiveness of the bureaucratic policy system has come to center on developing techniques for arriving at better decisions. Because it is now generally recognized that bureaucrats make, as well as carry out, policies, the quality of their decisions has become as important as the manner of their execution. As this change has taken place, the skills of policy analysis have grown in importance, and there has been less emphasis on the need for purely managerial skills in carrying out programs.[9] To be sure, this shift in perspective may not be permanent. As economy in government has become a more salient issue in contemporary American politics — during the Reagan presidency, for example — interest has been renewed in tightening executive control over agency expenditures.

In any case, the institutional arrangements through which the goals of responsiveness and effectiveness are sought have shifted from one period to another. But the desire to achieve both of these goals has been a constant objective from the first emergence of bureaucracy as an independent factor of major importance in American government late in the nineteenth and early in the twentieth centuries. Very commonly, as we have seen, the relationship between the two goals is zero-sum: gains in one cannot be achieved without simultaneous losses in the other.

## SCOPE OF THIS STUDY

Part one of this book is focused on the factors that account for the extraordinary influence bureaucrats now exert on policy decisions. In chapter two we analyze bureaucratic expertise and the way in which it manifests itself in the policy process. In all societies, whether democratic or undemocratic, modernized or less developed, executive agencies are rich repositories of specialized skills, and they can formulate policy proposals in many areas long before the public is even aware that decisions need to be made. Chapter three deals with a source of bureaucratic influence that is particularly important in democratic societies like the United States — the ability of executive agencies to build political support by mobilizing a constituency. Chapter four concludes this analysis of bureaucratic power with an examination of the factors that enable some agencies to wield so much more influence on policy decisions than others.

In part two, the policy process itself is the main subject. In chapter five we examine the internal politics of bureaucracy. Who are the principal participants in the decision-making process within executive agencies, and what influence does the bureaucratic environment itself have on policy decisions? Chapter six presents an appraisal of current efforts to reform the way in which bureaucratic organizations operate, so as to make them more effective as instruments for achieving policy goals.

In chapter seven, we return to the question that has been implicit throughout this discussion. Does the mounting influence of bureaucracy over all phases of policy in the modern state mean that a new power elite has emerged — controlling all decisions but itself uncontrolled? This is a key problem in every political system today, and it has made attacks on bureaucracy a common feature of political rhetoric in all advanced industrial societies. The fear of bureaucracy is often exaggerated. Bureaucrats commonly share rather than monopolize power in framing public policy. But fear of bureaucracy can itself be a potent force, reshaping the way in which political institutions function in the United States and elsewhere. As we shall see, American presidents have far less to fear from bureaucracy than they sometimes think, but their desire to escape what they regard as undue bureaucratic influence has profoundly affected the structure and operation of the executive branch in this country.

# *Notes*

1. See, in this regard, the analysis of administrative activity as part of the group system of politics in David B. Truman, *The Governmental Process* (New York: Alfred A. Knopf, 1951), pp. 395–478, and Harmon Zeigler, *Interest Groups in American Society* (Englewood Cliffs, N.J.: Prentice-Hall, 1972), pp. 160–183.
2. Matthew Holden, Jr., "'Imperialism' in Bureaucracy," *American Political Science Review* 60 (December 1966): 951.
3. Theodore J. Lowi, "American Business, Public Policy, Case Studies and Political Theory," *World Politics* 16 (July 1964): 680. Of course, there are many foreign policy issues in which domestic groups have an intense interest, such as grain deals with the Soviet Union.
4. For an analysis of the advantages and disadvantages of secrecy in the conduct of foreign affairs, see Thomas M. Franck and Edward Weisband, eds., *Secrecy and Foreign Policy* (New York: Oxford University Press, 1974).
5. For a fuller discussion of Nixon's orientation toward secrecy, see Francis E. Rourke, "Executive Fallibility: Presidential Management Styles," *Administration and Society* 6 (August 1974): 171–177.
6. The Supreme Court decision came in a suit challenging a deportation order by the Immigration and Naturalization Service. See Immigration and Naturalization Service v. Chadha, 51 *United States Law Week* 4907 (1983).
7. For more comprehensive treatments of the contemporary status of organization theory as it affects government agencies, see Peter Szanton, ed., *Federal Reorganization: What Have We Learned?* (Chatham, N.J.: Chatham House, 1981); Herbert Kaufman, "Reflections on Administrative Reorganization," in Joseph A. Pechman, ed., *Setting National Priorities: The 1978 Budget* (Washington, D.C.: Brookings Institution, 1977); and James G. March and Johan P. Olson, "What Administrative Reorganization Tells Us about Governing," *American Political Science Review* 77 (June 1983): 281–296.
8. My colleague at Johns Hopkins, Matthew Crenson, has done much to clarify my understanding of differences between conservative and liberal attitudes toward decentralization.
9. See, in this regard, the burgeoning literature on "cutback management" — the effort at all levels of government to reduce public expenditures. Cf. Charles H. Levine, ed., *Managing Fiscal Stress: The Crisis in the Public Sector* (Chatham, N.J.: Chatham House, 1980). For a very interesting analysis of the changing skills needed in policy making, see Lawrence D. Brown, *New Policies, New Politics: Government's Response to Government's Growth* (Washington, D.C.: Brookings Institution, 1983).

# Part One

## *THE SOURCES OF POWER*

CHAPTER TWO

# The Skills
# of Bureaucracy

In all modern societies, whether democratic or nondemocratic, a first and fundamental source of power for bureaucratic organizations is the expertise they command — the greatly varied skills that administrators bring to the policy process, necessary both for making decisions on policy and for putting these decisions into effect. This is what Max Weber long ago saw as the distinctive attribute that gave bureaucracy its enormous influence in modern government.

> The decisive reason for the advance of bureaucratic organization has always been its purely technical superiority over any other form of organization. The fully developed bureaucratic mechanism compares with other organizations exactly as does the machine with the nonmechanical modes of production. . . .
> Under normal conditions, the power position of a fully developed bureaucracy is always overtowering. The "political master" finds himself in a position of the "dilettante" who stands opposite the "expert," facing the trained official who stands within the management of administration.[1]

Such bureaucratic expertise is indispensable for the effective operation of any modern political system. The presence of bureaucrats in the governmental structure provides assurance that the decisions of political leaders will be guided by competent technical advice and carried out by skilled personnel. Moreover, in some parliamentary political systems in which the upper levels of political decision making are often stymied by partisan strife, it is the experts in bureaucracy who take over and maintain the continuity of the government. No modern state could operate for a day without the performance of myriad tasks by highly trained bureaucracies.

The expertise of bureaucracy is no less important for the industrially underdeveloped nations. In these societies, modernization has required bureaucratization, and where administrative skills have been deficient, social and economic development have inevitably lagged.

But the autonomy that these bureaucratic skills generate is a source of widespread anxiety in all political systems, because of the possibility that administrative agencies will become in effect self-directing organizations — responsive to cues and directions they give themselves rather than to those they receive from the political bodies that are the source of legitimate authority in the state. No fear has been more constant in modern politics — shared by revolutionaries and reactionaries alike — than the apprehension that bureaucrats might become a power elite and dominate the governmental process in which they are meant to play a subordinate role. The basic dilemma, as S. N. Eisenstadt puts it, is "whether bureaucracy is master or servant, an independent body or a tool, and, if a tool, whose interests it can be made to serve." [2]

## Origins of Bureaucratic Expertise

Public bureaucracies acquire in a variety of ways the expertise that is so important an ingredient of their power in the governing process. For one thing, a large organization is itself a mechanism for enhancing human competence. People joined in complex organizational systems can achieve results that individuals alone could never hope to accomplish — constructing an atom bomb, launching a space vehicle into orbit, or establishing an educational system capable of meeting the intellectual needs of all citizens from primary school to postdoctoral training.

Organizations achieve this level of competence by taking complex problems and breaking them down into smaller and hence more manageable tasks. Once problems have been subfactored in this way, each segment can be handled separately, and then by piecing the parts together, an organization can provide solutions to problems that may have originally seemed to be insoluble. This division of labor within large organizations also allows groups of employees to acquire specialized expertise, even though they may not themselves have unusual technical qualifications. It is for these reasons that an organization is itself a source of expertise, quite apart from the skills that its members initially bring to the job.

A second way in which bureaucracies acquire expertise is through the concentrated attention they give to specific problems. Dealing day in and day out with the same tasks gives public agencies invaluable practical knowledge that comes from experience. In time this knowledge becomes part of the memory of a government organization and is transmitted to new employees by training and indoctrination programs. The task an agency performs may not on the surface appear terribly complex — cleaning streets or removing snow, for example — but the agency is the institution in society that by experience has come to know the most about it.

The sustained attention that bureaucrats can devote to specific problems gives them a decided advantage over political officials who deal with many kinds of problems and confront each issue of public policy at infrequent intervals. This advantage is characteristic of both democratic and nondemocratic societies. It is perhaps particularly important in the United States because American bureaucrats tend to specialize early and to remain in the service of one agency throughout their government career. But in European as well as American bureaucracies, expertise reflects continuity in office as well as concentration of energy. Not only do bureaucrats focus on specific problems but they usually remain in office longer than is customary for politicians.

The knowledge that agencies acquire by continuous attention to particular functions puts them in an especially advantageous position to influence policy when the facts they gather cannot be subjected to independent verification or disproof. Intelligence units are especially well situated, because they have privileged access to secret information. Though it is not the only intelligence agency in the government, the CIA gathers and communicates data to the president that can heavily influence his decisions on foreign policy issues without his having any assurance that the data on which he is acting belong in the realm of fact or fancy. Suppose, for instance, that "central intelligence were to report to the President that there was positive intelligence that the Soviet Union would attack the United States in forty-eight hours, how could he challenge the information? And the dilemma he would face would be particularly cruel because an enemy decision to attack can always be reversed, while a defensive action might, in some circumstances, itself provoke an attack." [3]

A monopolistic or nearly monopolistic control of the "facts" thus provides tremendous reinforcement to the power that bureaucrats possess from specialized and continuous attention to particular responsibilities.

But though organizations have inherent assets that contribute greatly to their decision-making skills, it is not these organizational characteristics alone that account for the expertise that is the hallmark of modern bureaucracy. In the modern state this expertise comes preeminently from the variety of highly trained elites who practice their trade in public organizations — physicists, economists, and engineers, for example. In the roster of professions in American society there is not a single skill that does not find extensive employment in one or more executive agencies. And several professions such as the military are employed only in the public service. Moreover, the tendency for professionals to seek employment in public as well as in private organizations is on the increase. Amitai Etzioni argues that as "the need for costly resources and auxiliary staff has grown, even the traditional professions face mounting pressures to transfer their work to organizational structures such as the hospital and the law firm." [4]

Of course, not all public organizations exhibit the same degree of professionalism in their employment pattern. Some administrative units like the U.S. Postal Service still hire mainly clerical employees. In other agencies, however, such as the National Institutes of Health (NIH), the level of professionalism is very high. Agencies like NIH are in fact often described as "professional organizations," because they are dominated by individuals whose primary commitment is to the skill they practice rather than to the institution by which they are employed. Moreover, recent studies in comparative politics have shown wide differences among societies in the opportunities afforded various skill groups to influence the development of public policy.[5]

Agencies that are highly professional in their orientation and employment patterns often occupy a preferred position within the structure of public bureaucracy. State universities are commonly conceded — by law or custom — a degree of administrative independence not allowed to other public agencies. The same tradition of autonomy ordinarily protects a research agency like the Bureau of Standards from political pressures. When a professional agency enjoys such independence, the influence it exerts in all bargaining with other governmental units is greatly enhanced. In parts of the country where the standing of public higher education is at its peak, the state university has far more leverage than other agencies with the governor's office, the budget bureau, and legislative committees.

In the early history of American bureaucracy, such claims to expertise as administration could make were based largely on the factor of continuity. The expertise of the clerical employees who then staffed government agencies came from the sustained attention they gave to particular problems. And it exacted little deference from politicians. President Andrew Jackson's statement is often taken as the classic expression of widespread disdain for the skills of bureaucracy in early nineteenth-century America: "The duties of all public officers are, or at least admit of being made, so plain and simple that men of intelligence may readily qualify themselves for their performance; and I can not but believe that more is lost by the long continuance of men in office than is generally gained by their experience." [6]

Since Jackson's days, however, the skills required to run the modern state have been sharply upgraded. As the innovations wrought by science and technology have increasingly complicated both the responsibilities of government and the environment in which it operates, the duties of the public service are no longer so "plain and simple" as Jackson regarded them. Moreover, with the abolition of spoils and the increasing acceptance of merit as the essential qualification necessary for public employment, there has been a growing effort to recruit experts to the public service, to provide in-service training programs designed to improve the skills of public employees once they are hired, and in a variety of other ways to encourage and enhance bureaucratic expertise. Such expertise has thus evolved from its earlier dependence on experience to its contemporary reliance on professional training.

Perhaps the one accomplishment in modern times that best exemplifies the success that expertise in bureaucracy can bring is the record of the United States space program under the administration of NASA. In this area at least, bureaucratic expertise has been widely visible and has won broad popular acclaim.

In summary, it can be said that bureaucratic expertise is rooted both in the characteristics of public organizations and, increasingly, in the skills of their members. In modern times the operation of executive agencies at all levels of government demands employment of an increasingly diverse and complex range of specialized personnel. In sharp contrast to President Jackson's belief in the simplicity of the administrator's task stands a statement by President John F. Kennedy, delivered in support of an increase in pay for government employees: "The success of this Government, and thus the success of our Nation, depend in the last analysis on the quality of our career services. The legislation enacted by the Congress, as well as the decisions made by me and the Department and Agency heads, must all be implemented by the career men and women in the federal service. In foreign affairs, national defense, science and technology, and a host of other fields, they face unprecedented problems of unprecedented importance. We are all dependent on their sense of loyalty and responsibility as well as their competence and energy." [7]

## EXPERTISE: CHANNELS OF INFLUENCE

Whether it stems from the characteristics of organizations or the skills of their members, bureaucratic expertise exercises influence over the development of public policy through three primary channels: (1) the ability of bureaucrats to gather information and to give advice that often shapes the decisions of political officials; (2) the capacity of bureaucratic organizations to carry on the tasks that must be performed once policy goals are decided upon — the power of implementation; and (3) as a critical dimension of this power to implement policies, the discretion with which bureaucracies are commonly vested as they carry on the work of government.

In supplying advice, the power of bureaucrats is indirect, resting as it does upon their ability to persuade political officials that a course of action should be taken. Bureaucrats have influence only if politicians are willing to take their advice. Once policies have been turned over to bureaucrats to implement, however, their power is direct. It is especially direct when, as is common practice in all political systems, bureaucrats are granted the right to exercise discretion in the execution of policy. The actual content of policy may become predominantly a matter for bureaucratic determination.

## ADVICE AS INFLUENCE

Nothing contributes more to bureaucratic power than the ability of career officials to mold the views of other participants in the policy process. Bureaucracies are highly organized information and advisory systems, and the data they analyze and transmit cannot help but influence the way in which elected officials perceive political issues and events. Herbert Simon emphasizes the importance of being able to shape the value or factual premises of decision makers as a means of ensuring control over decisions themselves, and it is precisely in this way that bureaucratic information and advice commonly function in the policy process.[8]

A notable illustration of this bureaucratic role was the influence exerted by George Kennan from his vantage point in the State Department in the years immediately following World War II. During this period, Kennan's arguments on the need to contain Soviet power and the methods by which this goal might be achieved did much to shape the assumptions on which American foreign policy was based in dealing with the Communist powers around the world. The views he expressed in a widely read article on foreign policy, which he wrote under the pseudonym "X," became the basic American text of the Cold War both for government officials and for attentive publics outside the government.[9]

The influence that bureaucrats exert on the policy process through this power to give advice should not be exaggerated. The American experience during the Cold War suggests that it is easiest for bureaucrats to appear powerful when their advice matches and reinforces the preexisting views of the political officials responsible for policy. As we saw, Kennan's advice seemed highly influential in the early days of the Cold War, when the doctrine of containment was eminently congenial to the goals of leading political elites in the country. Later on, however, when Kennan attempted to restrain policy makers from putting undue emphasis upon military force in applying the principle of containment, his advice was largely ignored, and he found himself increasingly isolated from power.[10]

Hence, the best way for a bureaucrat to acquire a reputation as the power behind the throne may be to confine himself to advice that fits in with the views of his political superiors, or to give advice only in areas in which he knows his superior has no very strong opinions. When Henry Kissinger served as special assistant for national security affairs during President Nixon's tenure in the White House, he enjoyed a wide reputation as a highly influential presidential adviser. But it is a fair assumption that Nixon initially chose Kissinger for this position precisely because his views generally coincided with Nixon's own orientation toward foreign policy.

Kissinger's role may often have been that of reinforcing Nixon's capacity to pursue policies of his own choice, serving as advocate or defender of the president's program with the National Security Council and the other executive agencies charged with the conduct of foreign affairs.

But though the appearance and reality of bureaucratic power may not always coincide, it is clear that the ability to channel information into policy deliberations provides substantial leverage with which bureaucrats can affect the shape of decisions. If administrators sometimes appear only to be telling political officials what they want to hear, staff members of executive agencies can substantially reshape the attitudes of political leaders in both Congress and the executive.

A notable example is the shift in the views of Clark Clifford on the Vietnam War following his appointment as secretary of defense in 1968. Clifford's transformation from a supporter to an opponent of American involvement in the war came about mostly as a result of briefings he received from his civilian staff after he took over at the Pentagon. From these briefings, Clifford became more and more critical of the war in his advice to President Johnson, and helped push the president toward accepting the idea of a negotiated settlement.[11]

Another illustration of this phenomenon is the shift in President Eisenhower's views on a nuclear test-ban treaty after a change in his scientific advisers. When James Killian replaced Edward Teller and Ernest Lawrence as Eisenhower's chief source of scientific advice, the president became progressively more sympathetic to the idea of negotiating such a treaty. "James Killian brought in a wider range of technical opinion, and by exposing the President and Secretary of State to the views of experts such as Rabi and Bethe, he opened up alternatives that had not been considered before at the top levels of government." [12]

*Advising the President.* A group of agencies in which the power of advice can be seen in its most prominent form in American administration are the staff agencies that surround the presidency, administrative units like the Council of Economic Advisers or a scientific advisory committee like the Office of Science and Technology. These agencies have little operational authority of their own. They influence policy primarily by influencing the president.

The economists who serve with the Council of Economic Advisers can shape the president's perspective on fiscal policy, and hence his recommendations to Congress on tax and expenditure measures. Natural scientists who give advice to the president are equally influential with the chief executive in the areas of their scientific and technical competence.

The relationship between the president and his advisers at this level of administration involves reciprocal benefits: through their role as bureaucratic advisers, professionally trained economists and natural scientists obtain influence in the policy process that they would never otherwise enjoy. Most of the members of professional groups do not have the time, inclination, or capacity to win political office, and involvement in bureaucracy is, therefore, the only avenue to political power open to them.

At the same time, however, the president also derives tangible political benefits from his use of experts. The wisdom of his policy decisions is greatly enhanced in the eyes of the electorate when it appears that these decisions rest on the best professional advice the White House has been able to obtain. It has been said of the Council of Economic Advisers: "The acceptance of the Council's expertise as the President's economists increases the acceptance of his authority in matters of economic policy, and where applicable it adds economic persuasion to his strategies of influence. In return, the President provides the principal market for the Council's expertise." [13] The same point has been made on the role of natural scientists in government: "The scientist may find himself on the political firing line, placed there by a politician interested in using the scientist's prestige as an 'expert' to disarm the critics of his (the politician's) choices." [14]

There are risks as well as benefits for any political executive in his relationship with his advisers. It is, for example, highly important to a president that no one adviser be allowed to exercise monopolistic influence over his decisions. "An executive relying on a single information system became inevitably the prisoner of that system." So wrote Arthur Schlesinger, Jr., in describing the elaborate system of checks and balances that Franklin D. Roosevelt maintained to prevent any adviser from becoming the Rasputin of his administration. "Roosevelt's persistent effort ... was to check and balance information acquired through a myriad of private, informal, and unorthodox channels and espionage networks." [15]

The danger to which Schlesinger was pointing became abundantly clear during World War II when the Joint Chiefs of Staff began to exercise substantial influence over Roosevelt's decisions in military affairs: "The mere fact of direct access to the President did not account for the authority of the Joint Chiefs in the conduct of the war. Their power was rather a product of their direct access combined with the exclusion of civilian advice. . . . Ironic as it was, Roosevelt, who normally skillfully played subordinates off against each other in order to maximize his own authority, allowed one set of advisers to preempt the field with respect to his most important decisions." [16]

One of the chief reasons why Roosevelt was not able to maintain the same balance with respect to military advice that he had earlier established in the domestic area was that military decisions had to be surrounded with so much more secrecy than domestic policy discussions. This requirement prevented use of an open system in which the president could draw advice from as many quarters as he chose: "Wartime . . . imposed secrecy and censorship. No longer could the President look anywhere and everywhere for scraps of information and advice on his preeminent concerns, his most compelling choices. No longer could he pick up any aide or friend he chose to spy out the terrain of his official advisers. His instinct for alternative sources, his avid curiosity, his reach for information and ideas, now had to be confined to men with a 'need to know.'" [17]

In domestic as well as military affairs, a president can overcome some of the disadvantages of dependence upon a closed circle of advisers by relying for advice upon committee structures that permit broader canvassing of alternatives and even for the emergence of majority and minority points of view between which the president may choose. With a committee, a president has some assurance that the advice he is getting reflects pure expertise rather than — as it might be with a single adviser — professional prejudice or personal idiosyncrasy. C. P. Snow's account of the excessive influence exercised over British Prime Minister Winston Churchill during World War II by his scientific adviser Lord Cherwell points up this problem. According to Snow, Churchill was led into serious mistakes in judgment by his dependence on Cherwell as his sole adviser on scientific matters.[18]

In American government each of the major advisory institutions in the executive branch — such as the Joint Chiefs of Staff, the Na-

tional Security Council, and the Council of Economic Advisers —
is in fact a committee. In the literature of public administration,
committees are usually held in low regard as instruments of management because they disperse rather than focus executive leadership and control. But as an advisory institution, a plural body has
a great deal of utility, and with administrative agencies moving increasingly into the development as well as the execution of policy,
committees have become as indispensable for deliberative purposes
in the administrative process as they have long been in legislative
decision making.

In recent years some presidents faced with the necessity of making
critical decisions have set up high-level ad hoc committees to serve
as advisory groups. Thus, in 1962 President Kennedy created the
so-called Executive Committee of the National Security Council to
weigh alternative strategies that the United States might pursue in
countering emplacement of Soviet missiles in Cuba. In 1968 President Johnson established a Senior Advisory Group to reevaluate
American policy in Vietnam after the so-called Tet offensive by the
Vietcong and North Vietnamese troops. In each case these advisory
committees included members drawn from outside the government,
and their recommendations strongly influenced ultimate presidential decisions.

From the perspective of the president or any agency head who
uses an advisory body, such a group is most valuable if it is under
his jurisdiction and owes its primary administrative loyalty to him.
With this arrangement the executive has some assurance that advisers will look at problems from his perspective rather than from
the vantage point of some institutional interest of their own. A
model is the office of special assistant for national security affairs
in the White House. This office has no constituency other than
the president himself. It has no responsibility to Congress because,
under the doctrine of executive privilege, the special assistant does
not have to testify before Congress. Of course, recent history suggests that national security advisers can use their office to pursue
their own administrative interests and ambitions, as when Henry
Kissinger and Zbigniew Brzezinski served Presidents Nixon and
Carter respectively.

When creation of a Council of Economic Advisers was first being
considered in 1946, some congressmen tried to have it established
as an independent agency responsible as much to Congress and the

public as it was to the president. Their hope was that with independent status the agency would become a conservative influence upon President Truman, offsetting the influence exerted by liberal economists in his political entourage. This effort to create an independent council was not successful, however, and the agency was set up as a staff arm of the presidency. To be sure, the first chairman of the council, Edwin Nourse, tried to maintain a position independent of the president, but council members since that time have defined their role as requiring close identification with the president. Their influence on policy has been chiefly a function of the president's willingness to call on them for advice.

Much the same evolution was traced by the National Security Council (NSC), which was originally set up after World War II because Congress hoped to involve Cabinet officers in the conduct of foreign affairs. In the view of many legislators, Roosevelt's conduct of negotiations during World War II had been far too personalized, and they hoped that the NSC would become an inner cabinet that the president would be obliged to consult before making major national security decisions. However, President Truman, in whose term of office the NSC was established, made it clear very quickly that the NSC would meet and give him advice when and if he chose. Worth recalling is the principle enunciated long ago by Machiavelli: "A wise prince, then, seeks advice continually, but when it suits him and not when it suits somebody else." [19]

Of course, the mere presence of an advisory unit in the White House entourage generates public and congressional expectations that the president will call upon it for advice. When President Johnson failed to solicit any advice from his Office of Telecommunications Management, he came under sharp criticism in the legislature.[20] Thus, the creation of an advisory unit by the White House may narrow rather than expand the president's options.

When an advisory group is totally dependent upon the chief executive for its own survival, it may be highly reluctant to tell him unpleasant truths he ought to hear. In time, the advice a president gets from these experts may do little more than mirror his own opinions, if advisers refrain from giving advice they perceive as going against the presidential grain. It may contribute to candor in the advisory process if advisers are drawn from universities or other outside institutions to which they can return if they fall out of favor at the White House.

George Reedy argues, however, that even members of the president's own staff, who generally come to the White House from outside the government, experience great difficulty in telling a president things that they believe he does not want to hear. Reedy writes: "White House Councils are not debating matches in which ideas emerge from the heated exchanges of participants. . . . The first strong observations to attract the favor of the president become subconsciously the thoughts of everyone in the room." [21] Recognizing this tendency of advisory groups to defer to the chief executive, President Kennedy absented himself from the meetings of the NSC group charged with advising him during the Cuban missile crisis. But the strongest recommendations to come out of the NSC committee seemed to parallel closely proposals that Kennedy himself had initially favored.

To increase the likelihood that all alternatives will be canvassed before presidential decisions on foreign policy are made, Alexander George proposes a system of "multiple advocacy" within the executive branch.[22] Under this arrangement the president would be obliged to intervene in the advisory process to make certain that important points of view are not being suppressed or ignored. In practice this has proved very difficult to do. Irving Janis contends that committees charged with making decisions have a seemingly irrepressible tendency toward "groupthink." According to Janis, there is a strain toward premature and erroneous consensus in committee decision making — the members tend, whatever the diversity of their original views, to come together and reach agreement. The committee is not, therefore, a foolproof device for enabling a chief executive to escape the peril of the advisory process.[23] Of course, presidents are at liberty to ignore the advice they receive from committees or from any other source.

*Administrative Legislation.* The influence of bureaucratic advice upon policy decisions stands out very clearly not only in the internal activities of the executive branch, but also in the deliberations of Congress on "agency bills" — legislation originally drafted in the office of executive agencies. This administrative initiative in drawing up new legislation has not received as much attention in recent years as it had earlier.[24] Analysis of the origins of legislation has mainly been focused on the increasing role of presidential leadership in the legislative process. Yet, this apparent presidential

hegemony over Congress masks the fact that much of what ultimately comes to be regarded as the president's legislative program
stems from the advice of bureaucrats in the executive establishment.
Located as they are in intimate contact with the everyday processes
of government, bureaucrats have an unexcelled vantage point from
which to see the need for new legislation. As Lawrence Chamberlain
long ago pointed out in tracing the influence of bureaucracy on
legislation: "The administrative officer lives with his job. In his
daily concern with the raw material of administration, at the point
where the government and the public meet, he becomes keenly conscious of the inadequacies, ambiguities, and lacunae of the law he
administers." [25]

Of course, the role of executive agencies in actually originating
legislation should not be exaggerated. Many bills drafted by bureaucrats have their inspiration outside of the executive branch
altogether. These bills may be drawn up by executive agencies at
the request of congressmen, or constituency groups may seek an
agency's sponsorship of legislative proposals designed to protect or
advance their interests. Moreover, outside experts may be consulted
or involved in the deliberations of executive agencies before new
legislation is developed — as they were in the "task forces" employed by President Johnson to come up with new ideas for his
administration.[26] But even when these factors are taken into account, the role of executive agencies in formulating legislation is
still critical. Robert S. Gilmour cites the Department of Housing
and Urban Development, which proposed "approximately 300 separate bills in the space of a single legislative year," and most of these
were "initiated by the HUD bureaucracy." [27]

Modern presidents have sometimes regarded this bill-drafting activity of executive agencies as a threat to their own position of legislative leadership. This concern gave rise to the requirement that each
agency clear its recommendations with the Bureau of the Budget
(now Office of Management and Budget — OMB) before submitting
them to Congress, a procedure designed to ensure that these plans
are in accord with the program of the president.[28] Since the 1960s,
however, the White House staff no longer relies on OMB to protect
the president's interests on major legislative proposals. Members of
the staff have themselves begun to work jointly with departments
that are developing legislation they regard as crucial. In the Nixon
administration, this staff function was institutionalized in the Do-

mestic Council, which was established to initiate and coordinate legislative proposals within the executive branch.[29] During the Carter administration this function was performed by a Domestic Policy Staff. Thus, the task of monitoring legislative proposals to make certain they are in accord with the president's program continues, but that function is increasingly performed by the White House staff rather than OMB. Structures change, but the function remains constant. Of course, from the point of view of OMB, the function is no longer performed as well when it is managed by the White House staff, because the staff is a highly politicized, transient group, whereas OMB is run by a permanent bureaucracy that prides itself on serving the presidency rather than any one president.

The power that accrues to executive agencies through their control over information and the advisory process is thus reflected first by their ability to influence the policies carried on or the laws enacted by elected officials. It is also evident in their ability to influence the attitudes of the general public — to generate information that structures public opinion on major policy issues. Thus, NASA has enjoyed extraordinary success in winning public support for the nation's space programs, and the ability of the Pentagon to shape public perceptions of defense needs is legendary.

When agencies are thus successful in manipulating public opinion in their own favor, they automatically enhance the strength of their position as advisory bodies to elected officials, because politicians are much more attentive to the advice of agencies they perceive as respected by the public. Agencies may thus use their control over information to their own advantage in essentially two ways: first, by directly influencing the attitudes of elected officials, and second, more indirectly, by creating public demands to which politicians must respond. These demands may be for new laws that will strengthen an agency's powers, or for an increase in appropriations that an agency believes will enable it to carry out its responsibilities more effectively. If the Navy convinces the public of the need to expand the number of ships in the nation's fleet, then it will have little trouble persuading Congress to take the same view.

## POWER OF IMPLEMENTATION

The expertise of bureaucratic organizations also manifests itself through control over the techniques by which policy is carried out and upon which its success eventually depends. Elected officials may have far-reaching ambitions for new programs or policies, but the actual policy alternatives open to them in many situations are restricted to the courses of action their organizational machinery can carry out. Bureaucratic resistance or incapacity may spell the doom of even their most modest policy proposals. What a political leader can do in government mainly turns on what the bureaucratic organizations under his jurisdiction have the capacity to do. Presidents have sometimes felt that executive agencies lacked not the capacity but the will to help them achieve their policy objectives.

Consider an American president. In many ways the enormous organizational apparatus over which he presides in the executive branch is an annoying burden to the chief executive. It often drags its feet in carrying out his proposals or generates jurisdictional disputes that he must settle, in this way consuming his time and exhausting his energy. But in the end the president depends heavily upon the ability of bureaucratic organizations for his own success. Indeed, as President Johnson discovered with Vietnam, a president's orders may be disastrous for him if their execution is beyond the capabilities of his bureaucracy.

Graham Allison gives us an illuminating description of the degree to which the options open to political leaders are limited by the talents of the bureaucratic organizations under their jurisdiction:

> existing organizational routines for employing present physical capabilities constitute the range of effective choice open to government leaders confronted with any problem.... The fact that fixed programs (equipment, men and routines that exist at the particular time) exhaust the range of buttons that leaders can push is not always perceived by these leaders. But in every case it is critical for an understanding of what is actually done.[30]

A telling illustration of Allison's argument was the role played by the development of a counterinsurgency capability in the American military apparatus. During the 1950s, one of the chief complaints leveled against the Eisenhower administration was that it lacked the organizational capacity to conduct small-scale, limited wars. Because of this deficiency, it was argued, policy makers were forced to threaten nuclear war in situations in which it was not realistic to expect other countries to believe that this threat would ever be carried out. In the view of critics, this weakness in its military arsenal deprived American foreign policy of much of its capacity to deter undesired behavior on the part of adversaries in international politics.

When John Kennedy was elected president in 1960, one of the primary items on his agenda was creating a limited war capability that would end the nation's exclusive and ineffective reliance upon the nuclear deterrent and enable it to cope with guerilla movements that were believed to be Communist-led in the underdeveloped nations. The creation of this capability under Kennedy made it possible for President Johnson to choose in 1965 to have American forces become directly and massively involved in ground combat in South Vietnam.[31] In 1954, at an earlier stage of the war in Indo-China, when the United States had not yet developed such counterinsurgency techniques, President Eisenhower refused to permit direct American participation in the war.

This is not to say that there is any iron law dictating that a bureaucratic capability once established will inevitably be used. But certain consequences do usually follow when an administrative organization is created to provide policy makers with a desired capability. For one thing, such an organization inevitably has a vested interest in its own survival. It will thus tend to search for missions through which its value to society can be demonstrated and the flow of resources into the organization encouraged. It thus stands to benefit from policies that enable it to display its skills, and these policies acquire a weight in executive deliberations they would never otherwise possess.

Hence, a policy option that is strongly supported by an executive agency is much more likely to be adopted than one that lacks such sponsorship. Predicting which of several possible alternatives will be followed as public policy develops can in no small measure be based on assessment of the relative strength of the agencies responsible for carrying out each option under consideration. Policy makers will always be under pressure to follow courses of action that have support from strong bureaucratic organizations and to ignore those which do not. This pressure especially applies in national security affairs, where executive organizations play a large role in developing national policy.[32]

Moreover, because bureaucratic organizations provide the capabilities through which policy decisions are executed, the shape of policy as it emerges from the machinery of bureaucracy reflects not only the intentions of decision makers at the head of government, but also the characteristics of the organizations through which decisions are carried out. Policy outputs thus generate many surprises among political officials responsible for decisions, often referred to as "unanticipated consequences." In extreme cases the original intention of policy makers may hardly be visible in the outputs of the organization charged with putting decisions into effect.

Several characteristics of organizations help account for this tendency of organizational outcomes to diverge from original policy decisions. It is common for executive agencies to execute decisions through what organization manuals describe as standard operating procedures — predetermined ways of handling specific problems as they arise. These routines are the set procedures through which an organization has carried out its responsibilities in the past, and they have been sanctified by tradition and usually by successful experience. Employees have been programmed to perform these procedures and they are often subject to severe penalties if they deviate from them.

The ironic fact about such bureaucratic routines is that they are developed essentially to curb the ability of individual bureaucrats to influence policy by exercising personal discretion. Routines are designed to make employees' behavior conform to organizational goals rather than to their own personal inclinations. Organizations without routines make policy subject to the whims of individual bureaucrats. But, though intended to limit the power of individual executive officials, such routines may also enormously increase the overall influence of bureaucratic organizations in the governmental process.

These bureaucratic routines derive much of their influence on policy from the fact that they are very difficult to start and, once begun, no less difficult to stop. Thus, the celebrated law of bureaucratic inertia: "bureaucracies at rest tend to stay at rest, and bureaucracies in motion tend to stay in motion." The slowness with which bureaucratic organizations respond to presidential desires for action is legendary and a constant source of exasperation for chief executives. It was not until six weeks after President Kennedy's Vienna meeting with Soviet Premier Nikita Khrushchev that the State Department finally prepared a response to the Russian leader's *aide-mémoire* on Berlin, in which he had threatened that the Soviet Union would once again close off Western access to Berlin.[33] Similarly, at the time of the Cuban missile crisis in October 1962, Kennedy discovered that the American missiles he thought he had ordered removed from Turkey several months earlier were still there — a highly vulnerable target for Soviet efforts to win American concessions in exchange for removing Russian missiles from Cuba. Subsequent historical research suggests, however, that Kennedy never clearly ordered the missiles out of Turkey.[34]

Exasperating as this inertia of bureaucratic organizations often is for American presidents, it is not altogether without value to them. The cumbersome routines through which bureaucratic organizations operate often save political officials from making an overly rapid or rash response in an emerging crisis. In 1969 an American reconnaissance plane was shot down by North Korea, and it was President Nixon's first inclination to launch a retaliatory air strike against North Korean airfields. He could not do so immediately, however, because it took considerable time for the American military apparatus to deploy the forces necessary to conduct such a mission. As it turned out, this delay provided Nixon with an opportunity to change his mind. "As the military slowly moved air and sea reinforcements toward Korea, his anger cooled and he decided against retaliatory raids." [35]

If the slowness with which executive agencies act in emergencies can be described as a function of the inertia that characterizes large organizations, the difficulty of stopping bureaucratic organizations once they are launched upon a course of action reflects the momentum that bureaucratic routines acquire after being initiated. This momentum may take the form of carrying on procedures no longer needed simply because they have been built into an organization's repertoire, and their discontinuance would reduce the scope of an agency's activities or perhaps require release of personnel. It may also reflect the fact that bureaucratic services generate constituencies that oppose their liquidation.

In 1970, for example, it was discovered that the army was still carrying on surveillance over civilian political activities that had been started during the period of civil disorders some years earlier to help the military cope with riots in several American cities. Once they were begun, these procedures proved very difficult to stop, mainly because other agencies of the government came to depend upon military intelligence for information on suspected subversives. "The intelligence operation generated a demand for its product from the Justice Department, the FBI, police departments and other government agencies. A source close to the operation said, 'We created addicts for this stuff all over the Government.' " [36]

In the cases just cited, bureaucratic momentum manifests itself in the continuing performance of routines that are no longer required because the problem to which they were addressed no longer exists. Such momentum may also take the form of a series of logically progressive short-term decisions that escalate into consequences far beyond those originally intended. Some observers have interpreted the American involvement in Vietnam in precisely this way, as the product of a series of continuing steps by bureaucratic organizations that were never intended to lead, as they ultimately did, into a major conflict. The commitment of the air force to Vietnam to assist the South Vietnamese army led inescapably to assignment of ground combat forces to protect the air bases that then became necessary, and the activities of such ground forces inevitably escalated from a simple protective role to "search and destroy" missions designed to forestall enemy attacks. [37]

This tendency of bureaucratic momentum to transform small commitments into large ones is highly visible in weapons development. Warner Schilling shows that the original decision to develop the hydrogen bomb was intended to leave open the possibility of discontinuing the project. Once the H-bomb project was started, however, it required such formidable investment of resources over long periods that policymakers found themselves committed to the eventual production of the bomb as soon as they had decided to launch a preliminary inquiry to see if it was feasible to construct such a weapon. [38]

This kind of bureaucratic momentum tends to invalidate the argument of David Braybrooke and Charles E. Lindblom that policy making in democratic societies is protected from irrationality when it moves incrementally in one sequential step after another from initial decision to final outcome, thus permitting discontinuance of effort or reversal of direction any time either is considered desirable. [39] In fact the momentum of the organizations charged with putting a decision into effect may make it very difficult to stop or reverse gears once the bureaucratic machinery has been set in motion. Irreversibility may thus become a major hazard of policy decisions carried out through large organizations.

A chief factor contributing to such irreversibility is that large bureaucracies arrive at policy positions only after elaborate consultation and accommodation among diverse organizational interests. Agreements negotiated with such painstaking effort resist change, because such change would require reopening the whole bargaining process with no guarantee that the trade-offs required will yield a more effective policy outcome.[40]

Recent years have seen increasing attention to these various problems of implementation — the difficulties that beset efforts to attain policy goals once they have been placed in the hands of bureaucracies. It has become much clearer than it once was that no policy decision should be finalized before the ease or difficulty of carrying it out has been taken into account, at least where large-scale organizational processes are essential for achieving program objectives. In the past, the appraisal of policy alternatives has not always included the feasibility of implementation within the framework of analysis. This is what Graham Allison calls the "analysis gap," the failure to study the area lying "between preferred solutions and the actual behavior of the government." [41]

This new interest in implementation contrasts sharply with the concern of many management experts with improving techniques for deciding on courses of action — systems analysis, cost-effectiveness ratios, and the other instruments of managerial science. It is now recognized that the most advanced techniques for making decisions are of little avail when no effective organizational procedures exist for translating these decisions into results. Jeffrey L. Pressman and Aaron Wildavsky wrote a revealing study on the failure of a manpower training program in one American city, which they trace to the inadequate attention Washington gave to the obstacles that implementation of this program would confront once it was established.[42]

## EXERCISE OF DISCRETION

Control over implementation of policy becomes especially important as a source of bureaucratic power when it includes the authority to exercise discretion in achieving policy goals. As used here, "discretion" means the ability of an administrator to choose among alternatives — to decide how the policies of the government should be implemented in specific cases. The range of situations in which bureaucrats exercise discretion is virtually boundless. It includes the policeman deciding whether to make an arrest, a regulatory agency choosing either to issue or refuse a license or permit, or a public housing official evicting a tenant family on grounds of "undesirability." These decisions may vitally affect the fortunes or even the fate of the individual. Whether or not discretion is, as it has been asserted, the lifeblood of administration, its exercise may certainly affect the individual citizen. The capacity of administrators to use discretion in this way justifies Martin Shapiro's description of administrative agencies as "supplementary law-makers," functioning like courts to expand the meaning of congressional legislation through their own decisions and interpretation of statutes.[43]

In the traditional theory of public administration in the United States, it was assumed that the administrator's discretion extended only to decisions on means, while the actual goals of administrative action were fixed by statute or by the directives of a responsible political official. This was the celebrated distinction between politics and administration presented by such pioneers as Woodrow Wilson and Frank J. Goodnow. This distinction was designed among other things to provide a rationale for insulating administrative agencies from exploitation by politicians bent on using administrative offices and powers as the spoils of victory at the polls. If bureaucrats did not shape policy, then there was no reason why administrative agencies could not be left in splendid isolation, free to make decisions on personnel, or on administrative organization and procedure, to attain maximum efficiency in carrying on the business of government. As Wilson puts it "The broad plans of governmental action are not administrative; the detailed execution of such plans is administrative." [44]

This was a highly useful doctrine late in the nineteenth century and early in the twentieth in the United States, when public bureaucracy was an infant industry that needed a protective ideology behind which it could develop. It made the expansion of bureaucracy much less threatening to American democracy than it might otherwise have appeared to be. The doctrine cannot, however, be regarded as valid today when the center of power in policy making has shifted from the legislative to the executive branch and when a great many bureaucratic decisions are recognized as having very large implications for policy.

The scope of this administrative discretion is vast in all societies both in the everyday routine decisions of government agencies and the major innovative or trend-setting decisions of public policy. These two broad types of administrative decision are categorized by Herbert Simon as programmed and nonprogrammed decisions: "Decisions are programmed to the extent that they are repetitive and routine, to the extent that a definite procedure has been worked out for handling them so that they don't have to be treated *de novo* each time they occur. . . . Decisions are non-programmed to the extent that they are novel, unstructured, and consequential." [45] Philip Selznick draws a parallel distinction between "routine" and "critical" decisions.[46]

The policy influence of administrative discretion when it is exercised with respect to nonprogrammed decisions is clear and unmistakable. If the Federal Reserve Board abruptly changes the discount rate, or alters the reserve requirements for member banks to control inflationary pressures in a booming economy, or to stimulate investment in the face of an impending economic recession, these are major policy decisions obviously important to the society at large. When the Federal Communications Commission sets forth criteria for determining how many television stations are to be allowed in each section of the country it is obviously taking the lead in designing a national communications policy by exercising its discretionary authority. The independent regulatory agencies as a group have been assigned major responsibilities by Congress for making nonprogrammed decisions that require "a high degree of expertness, a mastery of technical detail, and continuity and stability of policy." [47]

Perhaps not quite so clearly apparent is the power inherent in the capacity of bureaucrats to exercise discretion in programmed or routine decision. In fact, however, decisions that may seem merely routine from the point of view of an administrative agency are often critical to the parties affected by these administrative determinations. An individual denied the right to practice a profession as a result of a negative judgment on his or her qualifications by a licensing board has been grievously affected by the routine exercise of discretion where the state controls entry into a profession. This penalty has been described as "professional decapitation."

Moreover, a government agency responsible for awarding defense contracts makes vital decisions for industries dependent upon these contracts for their survival, although the decisions may seem quite routine from the point of view of the agency. The exercise of discretion in an area of this kind has side effects that reach far beyond the business firms immediately affected. The economy of an entire region may depend heavily upon the prosperity of one industry, and denial of a defense contract or closing of a military installation may be an economic disaster for many communities.

Routine administrative decisions can have such wide-ranging effects for individuals, private organizations, and local communities that a variety of governmental arrangements designed to prevent anyone from being unfairly injured by these decisions have been established. Individuals subject to the jurisdiction of regulatory agencies are commonly given an opportunity to appeal a decision adversely affecting their interests to a higher administrative authority. If this review does not lead to satisfactory results, aggrieved parties have an additional opportunity to obtain a judicial review of the administrative decision. Much of this review procedure rests upon statutory safeguards, such as the Administrative Procedure Act of 1946, or upon the due process requirements of state and national constitutions.

The judiciary is by no means the only outside institution that reviews administrative decisions. In some areas of national administration Congress has a more and more important role in overseeing the use of routine administrative discretion, although agencies often have this discretion in the first place because legislative mandates have been deliberately vague, passing on to the bureaucracy the responsibility for making policy decisions. Congressional intervention in administrative discretion is mainly focused on areas where large sums of money are involved, the temptation to administrative corruption is great, and the political side effects may be intense. Since 1964, the secretary of defense has been obliged to give Congress thirty days' notice before closing any military installation.[48] And pressure is growing in Congress today to develop better methods for reviewing the innumerable decisions by national regulatory agencies that affect private citizens and organizations as well as state and local units of government.

The president himself may find it expedient to monitor the exercise of bureaucratic discretion very closely when it is used in an area of critical national importance. In the 1950s President Eisenhower went over the planned routes for U-2 spy flights over the Soviet Union, examining each in great detail. During the war in Vietnam President Johnson personally participated in the selection of targets for American planes bombing in the North, a range of decision that in other wars was left to subordinate military officials. These illustrations suggest that decisions that may in one set of circumstances be regarded as routine may in another context become crucial.

In the Watergate affair, President Nixon demonstrated that it may be equally advantageous for a president to maintain distance between himself and the exercise of discretion by his underlings, if these subordinates are engaged in activities that are illegal or would embarrass the White House if they were disclosed. Watergate introduced the concept of "deniability" into the national political vocabulary: an executive may find it useful not to know about some kinds of activities that he has given his subordinates discretion to carry out. In the conventional wisdom at least such deniability is considered acceptable if it applies to the discretionary acts of American espionage agencies like the CIA abroad.[49] But one of the many revealing aspects of Watergate was that it demonstrated how easily "dirty tricks" exported for use in the international arena could be imported back into domestic politics.

An administrative agency can itself go a long way toward controlling the decisions of its own employees with an effective program of internal training. In a study of the Forest Service, Herbert Kaufman showed how subordinate officials can be so thoroughly indoctrinated with policy goals that the exercise of their discretion can be relied upon to mirror faithfully the organization's objectives. The premises on which their decisions rest have been firmly implanted by a uniform educational background, an effective program of in-service training, and an agency manual that clearly spells out the choices appropriate in particular situations.[50] When such indoctrination is not feasible, agency heads have to rely on good monitoring devices to know whether their subordinates are using their discretion correctly.

But even though there are many ways in which the use of discretion can be circumscribed and influenced by other participants in the policy process — political officials, judges, and nongovernmental groups — the power that accrues to administrative agencies because of their discretionary authority is still vast. Regulatory agencies exercise a great deal of power merely because they have the authority to give or withhold benefits, and to inflict or refrain from imposing sanctions. When these agencies have such discretion, groups subject to their jurisdiction must defer to them even if their legal authority is not altogether clear. One of the most powerful sanctions a regulatory agency can impose upon a business firm is to publicize allegations detrimental to the product the firm is selling, even though subsequent investigation may show that these charges are not supported by the evidence.[51] Although judicial review of administrative discretion may theoretically be available, its use in practice may be discouraged by many citizens' fear of unpleasant publicity, or of incurring legal expenses, or simply of the distraction and delay of litigation.

The history of the Central Intelligence Agency presents countless situations in which administrators have exercised discretion with far-reaching effects on the national welfare. The decisions involved in launching the abortive Bay of Pigs invasion in 1961, the unlawful intervention in the domestic political process through subsidies given to student and other nongovernmental groups in the United States during the 1960s, and the domestic spying activities of the agency revealed in the 1970s are cogent examples of the ways in which discretionary authority vested in bureaucrats may come back to haunt responsible officeholders.

These illustrations should not, however, lead us to conclude that delegation of decision-making power to administrative agencies always has disadvantageous consequences. If it did, no such delegation would ever occur. But the exercise of discretionary authority by administrators has a vital role in protecting and advancing human welfare. Illustrations of these beneficial effects of discretion abound in the daily life of every American community, as public health officials inspect restaurants, fire departments enforce theater safety regulations, and the police attempt to control and prevent traffic accidents. Without administrative discretion, effective government would be impossible in the infinitely varied and rapidly changing environment of twentieth-century society. To be effective, social control must be flexible, and such flexibility inevitably requires that administrators be given discretion. But the exercise of judgment involves choice, and choice means formulating policy. Hence, the high development of administrative discretion in modern society necessarily projects bureaucrats into the center of the policy process.

As many of these illustrations suggest, the use or misuse of administrative discretion has its greatest influence over what Kenneth C. Davis has called "discretionary justice" — the use of discretion in ways that affect individual parties.[52] Discretionary justice is distinct from the general discretion administrators exercise in developing public policy affecting classes of people or society as a whole. It arises in connection with innumerable programs where administrative agencies determine whether or not an individual is entitled to a benefit, or should be subject to a penalty. "Street-corner" bureaucrats, particularly the police, have an especially big part in carrying out this function. As Davis puts it:

> Among the most important administrators in America are the police — all 420,000 of them. They make some of our most crucial policies and a large portion of their function is the administration of justice to individual parties. . . . The police are constantly confronted with problems of fairness to individuals, and such problems are often intertwined with problems of policy. When should they not make an arrest that can be properly made? When should they stop and frisk? When should they say "break it up"? When should they make deals with known criminals, as with the addict-informer? What minor disputes should they mediate or even adjudicate? . . . These mixed problems of justice and policy are seldom decided by heads of departments but are left largely to the discretion of individual policemen.[53]

Studies have shown that police officials use the discretion thus placed in their hands in many ways, depending on such factors as the nature of the official, the identity of the alleged offender, and the part of the country in which the law is being enforced.[54] Other parts of the law enforcement process are also characterized by a great deal of administrative discretion. Prosecutors have extensive latitude to determine what charges, if any, to bring against a defendant, and a parole board is equally free to determine when, if ever, to release prisoners prior to expiration of their term.

Discretion can involve a great deal of anxiety for the person who exercises it as well as the private party subject to it. Administrators control access to resources other people prize very highly — freedom, for a parole board dealing with a prisoner — and not all bureaucrats enjoy using the power thus thrust upon them. Some retreat from the exercise of discretion whenever possible. William K. Muir cites the local police officers who are "avoiders." They shun situations in which they might have to make troublesome decisions.[55] In police administration as in other areas, an administrator with a sensitive conscience may be haunted by the possibility that an error in using discretion may have disastrous consequences for the persons subject to his or her authority.

Air traffic controllers have constantly complained to the Federal Aviation Administration (FAA) about the physical and emotional stress to which they are subject when they make decisions affecting the lives of thousands of people flying in aircraft under their guidance. This stress was one of the principal factors contributing to the ill-fated strike of controllers in 1981, when the controllers charged the FAA with being insensitive to the tensions associated with their job.

As we have seen, concern has been growing in recent years about the breadth of administrative discretion, and efforts have been made in Congress and elsewhere to curtail its exercise. Such efforts have been focused most often on the powers of regulatory agencies, which, from the very beginning of their establishment in the latter part of the nineteenth century, have been vested with a great deal of discretionary authority over the conduct of economic activities. In fact, until the establishment of these agencies, administrators were not thought of as having much discretionary power.[56]

And yet, giving administrative agencies so much discretion very much reflects basic forces in American political life. For one thing, the belief in individualized justice runs deep in this country's political tradition. There has long been a conviction that, rather than relying on generalized legal codes, justice is more likely to be served when we follow the common law practice of considering the unique features that each case presents. When administrators enjoy discretionary authority, they can tailor their decisions to the circumstances of individual cases.

Otherwise, executive agencies would be much more "bureaucratic" in the style of their decision making than they are commonly alleged to be. They would have to enforce general rules in all cases in a rigid and inflexible way, even though the rules often need to be bent in particular situations in order to provide justice or to secure results.

The discretion administrators enjoy also grows out of the fact that much of policy making in the modern state is experimental. Legislators often have to cope with social and economic problems before they know how to solve them, or they anticipate that agencies may eventually have to deal with issues that cannot now be foreseen. Hence, statutes as enacted often shift the burden of finding solutions to administrators, by granting them broad discretionary authority. There is the expectation that an appropriate policy can best be devised by leaving administrators free to seek solutions by trial and error and day by day decision making.

Political factors also contribute to expansion of administrative discretion. Congress has turned over a great deal of authority to the executive branch in order to shift the onus of making unpopular decisions from itself to an executive official. The growth in the president's power over the tariff in this century primarily reflects willingness by members of Congress to sacrifice their power in the interest of decreasing their political vulnerability. Congress has followed the same practice in delegating power to administrative agencies in, among other fields, civil rights.[57]

In placing broad discretionary powers in the hands of administrative agencies, Congress produced one result that it almost certainly did not intend. The legislature made it much easier for a new president to shift the direction of policy when he takes office without having to ask Congress to amend the law before doing so. This can make the government more responsive to shifts in voter preferences in presidential elections, at least as perceived by the president. It may also, however, enable a president to turn public policy in directions that Congress does not want to take, or to introduce volatility in economic policies where Congress was trying to achieve stability.

In any case, reform groups working for the enactment of regulatory legislation have long favored delegation of discretionary power to administrators. Their ostensible justification for doing so has been that administrators are more likely to be professional and nonpolitical in their decisions and less inclined than Congress to bow to political pressures. But a major influence on the thinking of both reformers and groups opposed to regulation has been the expectation that these groups will be able to influence the way in which administrators use their discretion once it is given to them.

In this country there has been persistent criticism of administrative discretion because it seems to flout the basic commitment of American democracy to government by the people when it shifts control over decision making from elected to nonelected officials.

But, as we have tried to show, there are valid grounds for believing that administrative discretion, if not as American as apple pie, is certainly compatible with our political culture and very convenient for many of the groups interested in or affected by the exercise of such discretion.

# *Notes*

1. H. H. Gerth and C. Wright Mills, eds., *From Max Weber: Essays in Sociology* (New York: Oxford University Press, 1946), pp. 214, 232.
2. Samuel N. Eisenstadt, "Bureaucracy and Bureaucratization," in *Essays on Comparative Institutions* (New York: John Wiley, 1965), p. 179.
3. Harry Howe Ransom, *Can American Democracy Survive Cold War?* (Garden City, N.Y.: Doubleday Anchor Books, 1964), pp. 163–164.
4. Amitai Etzioni, *Modern Organizations* (Englewood Cliffs, N.J.: Prentice-Hall, 1964), p. 77. For an analysis of the role of the professions in executive agencies, see Frederick C. Mosher, *Democracy and the Public Service*, 2nd ed. (New York: Oxford University Press, 1982).
5. Joel D. Aberbach, Robert D. Putnam, and Bert A. Rockman, *Bureaucrats and Politicians in Western Democracies* (Cambridge: Harvard University Press, 1981), and B. Guy Peters, *The Politics of Bureaucracy: A Comparative Perspective* (New York: Longman, 1978).
6. James D. Richardson, comp., *Messages and Papers of the Presidents* (New York: Bureau of National Literature, 1897), 3: 1012. For a full account of the origins of the Jacksonian attitude toward bureaucracy, see Matthew A. Crenson, *The Federal Machine: Beginnings of Bureaucracy in Jacksonian America* (Baltimore: Johns Hopkins Press, 1975).
7. *Congressional Quarterly Almanac, 1962*, p. 907.
8. Herbert Simon, *Administrative Behavior*, 3rd ed. (New York: Free Press, 1976).
9. George F. Kennan, "The Sources of Soviet Conduct," *Foreign Affairs* 25 (July 1947): 566–582.
10. George F. Kennan, *Memoirs 1925–1950* (Boston: Little, Brown, 1967), esp. pp. 354–367.
11. See Townsend Hoopes, *The Limits of Intervention* (New York: David McKay, 1969), pp. 151–224, and Patrick Anderson, *The Presidents' Men* (New York: Doubleday, 1969), pp. 156–158. Cf. Clark M. Clifford, "A Vietnam Reappraisal," *Foreign Affairs* 47 (July 1969): 601–622, and Herbert Y. Schandler, *The Unmaking of a President: Lyndon Johnson and Vietnam* (Princeton: Princeton University Press, 1977).
12. Robert A. Divine, *Blowing on the Wind: The Nuclear Test Ban Debate, 1954–1960* (New York: Oxford University Press, 1978), p. 211.
13. Edward S. Flash, Jr., *Economic Advice and Presidential Leadership* (New York: Columbia University Press, 1965), pp. 309–310.

14. Warner R. Schilling, "Scientists, Foreign Policy, and Politics," in Robert Gilpin and Christopher Wright, eds., *Scientists and National Policy-Making* (New York: Columbia University Press, 1964), p. 169.
15. Arthur M. Schlesinger, Jr., *The Coming of the New Deal* (Boston: Houghton Mifflin, 1959), p. 523. Roosevelt, however, took a number of major steps in domestic politics, including the decision to establish TVA and the court-packing scheme, without using the method of extensive prior consultation that Schlesinger attributes to him as a decision-making style.
16. Samuel P. Huntington, *The Soldier and the State* (Cambridge: Harvard University Press, 1957), p. 320.
17. Richard E. Neustadt, "Approaches to Staffing the Presidency: Notes on FDR and JFK," *American Political Science Review* 57 (December 1963): 859.
18. C. P. Snow, *Science and Government* (Cambridge: Harvard University Press, 1961). The Mentor edition, published in 1962 by the New American Library, has an excellent appendix on the Cherwell affair.
19. See *The Prince*, in *Machiavelli, The Chief Works and Others*, vol. I, trans. Allan Gilbert (Durham, N.C.: Duke University Press, 1965), p. 92.
20. Francis E. Rourke, "The Presidency and the Bureaucracy: Strategic Alternatives," in Michael Nelson, ed., *The Presidency and the Political System* (Washington, D.C.: Congressional Quarterly Press, 1984), p. 353.
21. George Reedy, *The Twilight of the Presidency* (New York: World, 1970), p. 12.
22. Alexander M. George, "The Case for Multiple Advocacy in Making Foreign Policy," *American Political Science Review* 66 (September 1972): 751–785.
23. Irving L. Janis, *Groupthink*, 2nd ed. (Boston: Houghton Mifflin, 1982).
24. See, for example, *General Interim Report of the House Select Committee on Lobbying Activities*, 81st Cong., 2nd Sess., House Report No. 3138, Oct. 20, 1950, pp. 51–62.
25. Lawrence H. Chamberlain, *The President, Congress and Legislation* (New York: Columbia University Press, 1946), p. 24. For an early analysis of the administrator's role in framing legislation, see Edwin E. Witte, "The Preparation of Proposed Legislative Measures by Administrative Departments," in U.S. President's Committee on Administrative Management, *Report with Special Studies* (Washington, D.C.: U.S. Government Printing Office, 1937). A more recent review may be found in Louis Fisher, *President and Congress* (New York: Free Press, 1972), pp. 42–54.
26. See Norman C. Thomas and Harold L. Wolman, "The Presidency and Policy Formulation: The Task Force Device," *Public Administration Review* 29 (September/October 1969): 459–471. Cf. also, Lester M. Salamon, "The Presidency and Domestic Policy Formulation," in Hugh Heclo and Lester M. Salamon, eds., *The Illusion of Presidential Government* (Boulder, Colo.: Westview Press, 1981). For a more general view of policy innovation, see Nelson W. Polsby, *Political Innovation in America: The Politics of Policy Innovation* (New Haven: Yale University Press, 1984).
27. Robert S. Gilmour, "Central Legislative Clearance: A Revised Perspective," *Public Administration Review* 31 (March/April 1971): 152.
28. See Richard E. Neustadt, "Presidency and Legislation: The Growth of Central Clearance," *American Political Science Review* 48 (September 1954): 641–671, and "Presidency and Legislation: Planning the President's Program," *American Political Science Review* 49 (December 1955): 980–1021.
29. See Gilmour, "Central Legislative Clearance," pp. 156–158, and John H. Kessel, *The Domestic Presidency* (North Scituate, Mass.: Duxbury Press,

1975). Kessel's analysis is the best account we have of what the staff members of a White House organization actually do.

30. Graham T. Allison, *Essence of Decision: Explaining the Cuban Missile Crisis* (Boston: Little, Brown, 1971), p. 79.

31. Cf. in this regard, Larry Berman, *Planning a Tragedy: The Americanization of the War in Vietnam* (New York: W. W. Norton, 1982).

32. See discussion of this point in chapter three, pp. 81–83.

33. Arthur M. Schlesinger, Jr., *A Thousand Days: John F. Kennedy in the White House* (Boston: Houghton Mifflin, 1965), pp. 383–384.

34. See Barton J. Bernstein, "The Cuban Missile Crisis: Trading the Jupiters in Turkey?" *Political Science Quarterly* 95 (Spring 1980): 97–125.

35. *The New York Times*, January 21, 1971, p. 12.

36. Ibid., January 18, 1971, p. 22.

37. See, however, Leslie H. Gelb with Richard K. Betts, *The Irony of Vietnam: The System Worked* (Washington, D.C.: Brookings Institution, 1979). Gelb argues that Vietnam policy as it developed was the product of administrative planning rather than a case of an administration being carried along by irresistible momentum.

38. Warner Schilling, "The H-Bomb Decision: How to Decide without Actually Choosing," *Political Science Quarterly* 76 (March 1961): 241–246.

39. David Braybrooke and Charles E. Lindblom, *A Strategy of Decision* (New York: Free Press, 1963).

40. See in this connection, Henry A. Kissinger, *American Foreign Policy*, expanded ed. (New York: W. W. Norton, 1974).

41. Allison, *Essence of Decision*, p. 267. For a thorough analysis of this implementation problem, see Erwin C. Hargrove, *The Missing Link: The Study of the Implementation of Social Policy* (Washington, D.C.: Urban Institute, 1975).

42. Jeffrey L. Pressman and Aaron Wildavsky, *Implementation*, 2nd ed. (Berkeley: University of California Press, 1979). For a searching analysis of the factors that give rise to failures in implementation, see George C. Edwards, III, *Implementing Public Policy* (Washington, D.C.: Congressional Quarterly Press, 1980).

43. Martin Shapiro, *The Supreme Court and Administrative Agencies* (New York: Free Press, 1968).

44. Woodrow Wilson, "The Study of Administration," *Political Science Quarterly* 2 (June 1887): 212. The origins and development of this essay are traced in Richard J. Stillman, II, "Woodrow Wilson and the Study of Administration: A New Look at an Old Essay," *American Political Science Review* 67 (June 1973): 582–588.

45. Herbert A. Simon, *The New Science of Management Decision* (New York: Harper & Row, 1960), pp. 5–6.

46. Philip Selznick, *Leadership in Administration* (Evanston, Ill.: Row, Peterson, 1957), pp. 29–64.

47. Marver H. Bernstein, *Regulating Business by Independent Commission* (Princeton: Princeton University Press, 1955), p. 4. See also Louis M. Kohlmeier, *The Regulators* (New York: Harper and Row, 1969).

48. For an analysis of the legislative veto, see Louis Fisher, "A Political Context for Legislative Vetoes," *Political Science Quarterly* 93 (Summer 1978): 241–254, and U.S. House of Representatives, *Studies on the Legislative Veto*, submitted to the Committee on Rules by the Congressional Research Service, 96th Cong., 2nd Sess. (1980).

49. President Dwight D. Eisenhower was widely criticized in 1960 when he revealed personal knowledge of and assumed responsibility for an unsuccessful U-2 spy flight over the Soviet Union. High officials are considered to have the discretion to lie in dealing with foreign adversaries. See David Wise, *The Politics of Lying* (New York: Random House, 1973). As Wise shows, however, these officials can use this discretion by pretending to lie to enemies abroad in order to lie to their own people.

50. Herbert Kaufman, *The Forest Ranger* (Baltimore: Johns Hopkins Press, 1960).

51. For some graphic illustrations of this unwarranted use of publicity as a punishment see Ernest Gellhorn, "Adverse Publicity by Administrative Agencies," *Harvard Law Review* 86 (June 1973): 1380–1441.

52. Kenneth C. Davis, *Discretionary Justice* (Baton Rouge: Louisiana State University Press, 1969).

53. Ibid., p. 8.

54. Among the best of these studies are Jerome Skolnick, *Justice Without Trial* (New York: John Wiley, 1966), and James Q. Wilson, *Varieties of Police Behavior* (Cambridge: Harvard University Press, 1968).

55. William K. Muir, Jr., *Police: Streetcorner Politicians* (Chicago: University of Chicago Press, 1977), esp. pp. 292–293.

56. See James Q. Wilson, "The Rise of the Bureaucratic State," *The Public Interest*, 41 (Fall 1975), pp. 94–95.

57. Gary Bryner, "Congress, Courts and Agencies: Equal Employment and the Limits of Policy Implementation," *Political Science Quarterly* 96 (Fall 1981): 411–430.

# CHAPTER THREE

# *Mobilizing Political Support*

Although, as we saw in chapter two, expertise is a vital source of power for all bureaucracies, it is equally important, especially in democratic societies, for an administrative agency to command strong political support. In the United States, it is fair to say, strength in a constituency is no less an asset for an administrator than it is for a politician, and some agencies have succeeded in building outside support as formidable as that of any political organization. The lack of such support severely circumscribes the ability of an agency to achieve its goals, and may even threaten its survival as an organization. Norton Long writes: "The bureaucracy under the American political system has a large share of responsibility for the public promotion of policy and even more in organizing the political basis for its survival and growth." [1]

This entanglement with politics has been a prominent characteristic of American administration since the days of President Andrew Jackson, though it certainly existed before that time. The intrusions of politics came first from the political parties, eager to use administrative jobs as building blocks in constructing party organizations. After the Pendleton Act in 1883 established the Civil Service Commission, however, the ability of political parties to exploit administrative agencies in this way was increasingly subject to legal restriction. Slowly but surely the principle came to be accepted that appointments to career positions in the public service should go to those who are technically qualified without regard to their party affiliation.[2] The parties were reluctant to accept this change, because they viewed access to the positions and preferments of bureaucracy as indispensable incentives for party workers and as necessary for the health of party organizations.

But even with this development, politics was by no means banished from American administration. American political parties did not always function effectively as organizations for developing and supporting policy objectives, so that administrative agencies were forced to develop their own basis of political support, negotiating alliances in and out of government with a variety of groups that could be used to advance bureaucratic objectives or to assist an agency in fending off attack. The political neutralization of bureaucracy is impossible in a country in which the political parties are incapable of performing the functions expected of them in the governmental structure of which they are a part. When the parties do not provide for program development and mobilization of political support, executive agencies must perform these tasks for themselves, seeking support from outside groups that will help advance their policy objectives. It is noteworthy that legislation like the Pendleton Act excluded political parties from intervening in the affairs of executive agencies but left other political organizations such as interest groups free to become involved in agency decision making.

From the point of view of an administrative agency, political support may be drawn from three vital centers: the outside community, the legislature, and the executive branch itself. All these sources of political strength may be cultivated simultaneously, and usually are; or one may be nursed virtually to the exclusion of the others. The possibility of choice often calls for exercise of administrative statecraft of a high order to balance one source of strength against another, in this way building an enclave of political independence. Sometimes, however, no choice is possible. A state treasurer directly elected by the legislature cannot easily look elsewhere for political support. An executive budget office is, in most circumstances, politically captive to the chief executive it serves. If the executive does not choose to give it political standing, then it has none. These and other possibilities are examined in the pages that follow, as each of the various ways in which administrative agencies build political support is examined in turn.

## BUREAUCRACY AND ITS PUBLICS

Basic to any agency's political standing in the American system of government is the support of public opinion. If it has that, an agency can ordinarily expect to be strong in the legislative and the executive branch as well. Because public opinion is ultimately the only legitimate sovereign in a democratic society, an agency that seeks first a high standing with the public can reasonably expect to have all other things added to it in the way of legislative and executive support. Power gives power, in administration as elsewhere, and once an agency has established a secure base with the public, it cannot easily be trifled with by political officials in either the legislative or the executive branch.

*Attentive and Mass Publics.* Public support may be cultivated essentially in two ways. The first is by creating a favorable attitude toward the agency in the public at large. The second is by building strength with "attentive" publics — groups that have a salient interest in the agency — usually because it has either the capacity to provide them with some significant benefit, or the power to exercise regulatory authority in ways that may have a critical effect on the groups.

These methods are not mutually exclusive. An agency can seek to create general public support while assiduously building alliances with interest groups that have a special stake in its work. This is in fact the strategy most agencies follow, to the extent that is available to them. Actually, comparatively few agencies carry on functions that have high visibility for the general public. An agency like the FBI, which has been performing a dramatic role in American life for several decades, does command a broad pattern of public support that stretches through all strata of society. Part of this public standing may be said to spring from skillful use of publicity — agencies like the FBI exploit every opportunity to catch the public eye with their achievements. But the power of publicity is not boundless, even in America where good public relations are an obsession with every large organization, and an agency whose activities do not match the FBI's in intrinsic dramatic appeal will not equal it in public esteem no matter how assiduously it carries on public relations activity.[3]

There may be occasions, of course, when any agency may find itself basking temporarily in the limelight. The Food and Drug Administration may languish out of sight of the general public until suddenly the injurious effects of a new drug arouse public concern, as in the 1960s with thalidomide, a tranquilizer whose use by pregnant women brought about delivery of a large number of infants with birth deformities. Immediately, the agency and its pronouncements became a matter of front-page interest. For a brief period at least, it was an organization with a very extensive public indeed. Or a state air pollution commission, conducting its affairs in almost total obscurity, may suddenly find itself projected to the forefront of public attention by severe atmospheric smog. Or consider the Nuclear Regulatory Commission — on the front pages of every newspaper in the country after a nuclear accident at Three Mile Island in Pennsylvania in 1979. In the Reagan administration the EPA suddenly found itself the object of unwelcome publicity as the dangers posed by toxic waste became a critical problem in various parts of the country. An administration that had sought to downplay the importance of environmental issues quickly found that those issues were high priority concerns for large segments of the public. In situations of this kind agency heads may find that they have become celebrities overnight, with television reporters camped on their doorstep, and their every word recorded for posterity.

These illustrations suggest that many agencies have a potential public that far exceeds the size of their normal clientele. That it has such a potential public means that an agency carries on activities that affect the interests of a far larger group than the public that consistently identifies itself with its program. Both the food and drug and air pollution agencies are in the public health field, where agencies perform functions that are vital to a general public that may not even be aware of their existence. If events arouse the attention of a latent public, however, as the environmental and energy crises have done in recent years, an agency's image in the community and the legislature may suddenly swell in importance. To the extent that it is affected by shifts in the general climate of public opinion, administrative power may thus be extremely volatile, shifting, like a politician's, with changing tides of public sentiment, which Anthony Downs calls the "issue-attention cycle." [4]

Any sudden expansion in the public that takes an interest in its activities may be a threat rather than an opportunity for an executive agency. Its new following may include groups of organizations that are extremely suspicious of the way in which the agency has been carrying on its activities. The agency may thus come under a critical scrutiny it had never experienced, and it may soon find itself under strong pressure to change the thrust of its decisions. E. E. Schattschneider emphasizes that the outcome of the policy deliberations in which governmental actors engage can be altered by shifts in the size and character of the audience before which these deliberations take place.[5] A forestry agency may find that decisions on the use of public lands in harvesting timber that were quite acceptable to the lumber industry with which it has long worked are highly repugnant to environmentalists who move into the agency's constituency.

A study by Charles Jones of the national air pollution agency shows the kind of danger that a sudden and substantial expansion in its constituency can represent for an agency.[6] Between 1965 and 1970 the number of people who cared about air pollution jumped markedly, and these new constituents expected the national agency to do much more to solve the problem of pollution than it was capable of doing. Great expectations can thus be as threatening to an agency as public indifference. If these expectations are disappointed, they can quickly be converted into hostility.

Hence, it is essential to every agency's power position to have the support of attentive groups whose attachment is built on an enduring tie. The groups to which an agency provides tangible benefits are the most natural basis of such political support, and it is with these interest groups that agencies ordinarily establish the firmest alliances. Such groups have often been responsible for establishment of the agency in the first place. Thereafter, the agency and the group are bound by deeply rooted ties that may be economic, political, or social. From an economic perspective, the agency usually carries on activities that advance the material welfare of members of the group. The group in turn may supply private employment opportunities for employees of the agency.

Moreover, in return for the political representation with which the agency provides the group in the executive apparatus, the group ordinarily supports the agency's efforts to achieve a variety of its own political objectives, including its requests for financial support, its attempts to secure passage of legislation expanding its powers, or its need to defend itself against legislative proposals that threaten its administrative status. Finally, frequent social contact between the agency and the group breeds familiarity and friendship that help seal the alliance. The Smithsonian Institution through its Associates program and in other ways has been very adept at using social ties to build support for the agency. In its most highly developed form the relationship between an interest group and an administrative agency is so close that it is difficult to know where the group leaves off and the agency begins.

This identity between an interest group and an executive agency is strongly reinforced by the practice, especially common at the state level, of having occupational or professional qualifications as a requirement for appointment to administrative office. Under law, the members of a state real estate commission may have to be licensed real estate brokers, and similar requirements often prevail with other administrative boards having the power of occupational licensing in the states. In fields such as law or medicine, the state may virtually turn over a licensing agency to its professional constituency — to be used at the group's discretion for its own purposes.

Such arrangements merely give formal legal blessing to the common political practice of allowing interest groups to have a major voice in, if not veto power over, appointments to agencies that administer functions in which they have a vital stake. Legal support for interest group involvement in the affairs of administrative agencies may also come from statutes requiring group representation on agency advisory committees, or stipulating, as is common in agricultural administration, that the agency secure the consent of interest group members before exercising certain regulatory powers. There are also cases — administration of grazing on public lands in the West, for example — where individuals representing interest groups are given the power to enforce administration regulations at their point of application.[7]

*Organizing a Clientele.* Agencies that are not in a position to dispense important benefits or favors of substantial value to any segment of the community are in a disadvantageous position with respect to their ability to attract organized group support. The State Department is commonly regarded as having no "natural constituency" in the sense of clientele groups for which the department is able to do tangible and significant favors. Even though the fate of the entire population may depend on the effective conduct of foreign affairs, no strongly organized group structure in the outside community regards the department as "its department," and stands ready to defend and assist it in attaining its goals.

Even the State Department, however, has been able to identify a large number of groups with which it maintains close liaison on foreign policy matters.[8] And some of these groups can play a significant role in the conduct of foreign affairs. The International Longshoreman's Association has periodically refused to load commodities like wheat on ships destined for the Soviet Union and other Communist countries. For many of these outside organizations, however, the work of the department is of secondary rather than primary importance. Except for ethnic groups that have an intense attachment to their homeland, their interest in foreign affairs is something less than a persistent preoccupation.

Hence, in order to secure public backing on matters of major interest to it, the department itself has often had to resort to organizing outside group support. If the mountain will not come to Mahomet, Mahomet will go to the mountain. The organization by the department of a blue-ribbon committee of distinguished citizens to lead a campaign in behalf of the Marshall Plan in 1947 illustrates the department's success in establishing its own public support,[9] and this kind of stratagem has since been used by the State Department to accomplish a variety of other foreign policy objectives. A committee of prominent citizens was organized to support President Johnson's policies during the Vietnam War and was given the resounding title of Citizens Committee for Peace with Freedom in Vietnam.

The truth of the matter is that agencies in the field of national security affairs give a good deal of lip service to the idea of consulting with the public, but in practice this consultation commonly consists of getting groups of citizens together so that they can be indoctrinated with the official point of view. These national security agencies are much better at transmitting than they are at receiving messages from the public. Viewing themselves as having the best information available on the issues with which they deal, they communicate with the public not to obtain feedback that will be useful in shaping policy, but to structure public opinion so as to make it more supportive of their policies, or to prevent opposition from developing.

Executive agencies like the State Department can also be extremely adroit in organizing pressures upon themselves to which they seem to be responding, but which they are in fact initiating. The organization of such apparent pressure group activity thus provides a means by which these agencies can conceal their own central role in the policy process. The initiative appears to be with outside organizations, but the activities of these external groups are actually instigated by the agency itself. Of course, one risk an agency runs in following this strategy is that the mass opinion it is helping to create may eventually be a constraint upon it if it decides to change the policies for which it is currently seeking public support.

Critics of the State Department would argue that although the agency has been weak in traditional kinds of interest group support, it has been locked into or even captured by a peculiar community of its own — sometimes referred to as the "Eastern establishment" — an amorphous title that seems to embrace Ivy League schools, Wall Street lawyers, and international bankers. The members of this group have a journal, *Foreign Affairs,* through which their views are reflected, and an organization, the Council on Foreign Relations, that brings them together at meetings that generate solidarity in outlook. From this perspective the State Department is linked not so much to one set of interest groups as to a social class, whose consensus on foreign policy issues is mirrored in the department's decisions.[10]

Whatever may happen in foreign affairs, domestic agencies have always been quite adept at organizing an infrastructure of interest group support. The Department of Agriculture played a principal role in the organization and development of the American Farm Bureau Federation, the largest and most powerful of the agricultural interest group organizations.[11] And very early in its history the Department of Labor became convinced that the only way in which it could reach the wage-earning clientele it was obligated to serve was by encouraging the development of trade unions. Labor organizations provided an avenue for disseminating the informational material that was, in the beginning, the department's chief contribution to improving the welfare of its wage-earner clientele. The department had to communicate with its constituency, and, as it was to point out itself: "Freely as conferences with unorganized wage earners are welcome, official intercourse with individuals as such has practical limits which organization alone can remove."

Not only did the department thus defend its close liaison with trade union organizations; it also came, not illogically in view of the need to facilitate communication with its clientele, to support extension of trade union organization among wage earners. The reason the department gave for this support was that the growth of labor union membership would facilitate collective bargaining and promote industrial peace. "The absence of organization," the department stated, "means the absence of a medium through which the workers en masse can discuss their problems with employers. The denial of this organization  is the denial of the only means of peaceable settlement they have." Of course, pragmatic considerations were also involved in the department's support of expanded trade unionism, including the fact that the strengthening of wage-earner organizations would increase the department's effective clientele and the weight of its political support.[12]

Perhaps the worst hazard an agency faces, when it deliberately sets out to establish an infrastructure of interest group support, is the possibility that, once established, these groups may break away from agency control, or even become a focus of opposition to it. The parent-teacher associations set up in conjunction with school systems at the local level generally are useful in providing citizen support for the education officials. But if these PTA organizations are captured by opponents of the educational system, as they have been in some areas in the United States, they provide a formidable vehicle for mobilizing opposition to school administrators — more effective, because of their organizational capability and the legitimacy that flows from their semi-official status, than any other resource at the disposal of critics of the educational establishment.

One major advantage that the support of interest groups has for an executive department is that such groups can often do for a department things that it cannot easily do for itself. In national politics, interest groups can take a position on policy questions that department officials secretly hold but cannot publicly advocate because it may put them in disfavor with the president. The outside groups that support each of the various branches of the armed forces in the Department of Defense have often given military officials assistance in precisely this way. Samuel P. Huntington writes:

> The allies and supporters of a service are at times more royalist than the king. They do not necessarily identify more intensely with service interests than do the members of the service, but they do have a greater freedom to articulate those interests and to promote them through a wider variety of political means.[13]

Although deference to their commander in chief may not permit military officials to disagree openly with the president when he cuts their appropriation or gives another service jurisdiction over a weapons system they believe to be rightfully theirs, no such restrictions prevent defense industries with which they have contractual relations from springing to their defense, or keep a backstop association, such as the Navy League and the Air Force Association, from vociferous protest against efforts to trim the appropriations or the jurisdiction of a military agency.

Outside organizations thus have a valuable role in enabling administrative agencies to oppose directives from the chief executive. They are also useful in helping these agencies evade legislative controls. Congress has enacted statutes designed to prevent administrative agencies from propagandizing the public in their own behalf, or lobbying in the legislature to secure passage of bills they favor. These laws are difficult to enforce, because administrative agencies are also charged with keeping the public informed of what they are doing, and the line between unlawful propaganda and legitimate public information activity is as fine as any distinction in the American political system. But agencies can always escape these restrictions by having outside organizations carry on such public relations or lobbying activity for them. Senator Barry Goldwater of Arizona observed that "the aircraft industry has probably done more to promote the Air Force than the Air Force has done itself." [14] This kind of claim could be made for a great variety of interest groups that identify and associate themselves with the fortunes of an executive agency.

There are other intermediaries that bureaucratic organizations can use in their efforts to shape public opinion. Agencies will often give information they want disclosed to sympathetic members of Congress and rely on them to perform the task of disseminating it to the public at large. Transmitting information in this way is a profitable exchange for both parties. Members of Congress attract public attention to themselves and enhance their own careers by generating news. The executive organization gets its message across to the public and in doing so ties congressional supporters even more firmly to its own cause, because they have benefited from their role as intermediary for the organization. Members of the Armed Services Committee in both the House and the Senate have often served their own and the Pentagon's purposes in precisely this fashion.

A friendly representative of the news media can perform the same function. An agency can "leak" information to reporters or allow them to identify it as coming from "anonymous" or "highly placed" sources in the agency. Again the transaction serves the interests of both the giver and the receiver of information. The agency succeeds in getting information disseminated to the public and the reporter or columnist obtains a highly prized exclusive story. Such relationships between secretive agencies like the CIA and friendly newspaper columnists are not uncommon in the United States.[15] An agency with secrecy as a distinguishing characteristic is in an advantageous position to give a reporter preferred access to a story.

*The Captive Agency.* The help an administrative agency receives from interest groups is not without its perils, however. The agency may come to lean so heavily on the political support of an outside group that the group in time acquires veto power over many of the agency's major decisions. In extreme cases, the agency becomes in effect a "captive" organization, unable to move in any direction except those permitted it by the group upon which it is politically dependent.

Administrative units that are especially vulnerable to domination of this sort are clientele agencies — public organizations established to provide comprehensive services to a special segment of the population. On the national scene such clientele agencies include the Veterans Administration, the Department of Agriculture, and the Department of Labor. Each has a long history of close association with and subordination to outside organizations representing its clientele.

We have seen that the Department of Labor was from its very beginning closely identified with the trade union movement. When it was first set up in 1913, the department was, as Samuel Gompers put it, intended to be "Labor's Voice in the Cabinet." Although this relationship was helpful in many ways, it also tended to narrow the scope of the department's authority. For one thing, the trade unions were allowed to exercise a great deal of influence over major department decisions, including selection of assistant secretaries of labor. This association with the union movement also made the department suspect in the eyes of other groups — employers, for example — and for a long time its jurisdiction over labor activities was limited by the reluctance of business and agricultural groups to allow the department to administer functions where its bias in favor of the trade unions might be disadvantageous to their interests. An agency makes enemies as well as friends when it identifies itself with a population group, because it inherits hostilities directed at the group with which it has entered into an alliance.

The submissive posture of a clientele agency toward its constituency is not, of course, a permanent genuflection. During the Eisenhower administration the assistant secretaries of labor were not chosen by the trade unions. Compared with other periods in its history, the Veterans Administration displayed a great deal of independence from the veterans' groups with which it is allied when it was headed by General Omar Bradley, a career officer with a distinguished record in World War II. Leadership by a vigorous personality may thus uncover latitude for independent action by an executive agency that previously had not been thought possible.

The tendency of clientele agencies to fall under the control of the groups they serve has often been used as an argument against organizing the executive branch upon the clientele principle. The contention is that executive agencies can be prevented from becoming the tools of political groups only if administrative tasks are divided on some other principle of organizational design. But in fact it is difficult to identify a principle of organization that will not engender a very close relationship between an administrative agency and the groups that benefit from the activities it carries on. In classical organization theory, the principal alternatives to clientele as a basis for allocating tasks among administrative agencies are the criteria of function to be performed, process or skill to be carried on by agency personnel, or geographical area to be served. Agencies organized by function, however, such as highway, welfare, or education departments, are also susceptible to domination by outside groups, as are agencies organized on the process or skill criterion — the Corps of Engineers, for example.

On organization by area, Philip Selznick's classic study of the interaction between a public agency and its environment — *TVA and the Grass Roots*[16] — clearly revealed a pervasive pattern of outside control over the foremost agency of the national government organized on the basis of geographical area, the Tennessee Valley Authority. In return for the support it received from important groups in the Valley area, the TVA proceeded to modify many of the original objectives of its agricultural program that were offensive to this constituency.

Of course, in its own defense, the agency could point out that the goals it modified were not vital to it, that its real concern was with its public power program in the Tennessee Valley, and if support for this activity could be obtained only by "selling out," so to speak, on agricultural goals, then this was an exchange well worth making. Selznick himself later conceded the validity of such a strategy:

> ... the TVA purchased a considerable advantage with these concessions. It gained the support of important local interests and of a powerful national lobby. These defended not only the agricultural program but TVA as a whole. In this way, by modifying its agricultural program and certain broad social policies, the Authority was able to ward off threatened dismemberment and to gain time for the successful development of its key activity — the expansion of electric power facilities.[17]

Any public agency may thus find it necessary to yield control over a segment of its program to a significant interest group in order to buy the support of that group for more important policy goals. A state university may tailor its program of agricultural education to the needs of important farm groups, so as to obtain the support, or at least neutralize the opposition of rural groups to other educational activities in which the university may wish to engage. Some of an agency's activities may thus serve as "loss leaders" — activities which represent a loss or at least small profit from the point of view of an agency's major goals, but which simultaneously widen the basis of political support for objectives that are more significant to it. For a state university, its intercollegiate football program may represent just such a "loss leader." The support engendered by the achievements of its football team may quicken the allegiance of alumni and other citizen groups to the university in areas of science and culture far from the gridiron.

There is always the possibility that this kind of support will be purchased at the price of great damage to major institutional goals. Activities that are initially designed to be merely supportive may in time grow so large as to have wide-ranging and debilitating effects upon an institution's capacity to achieve its major goals. For the state university an agricultural school may dominate the image a university radiates to the outside world, and this reputation as a "cow college" may badly handicap its ability to attract faculty and students for nonagricultural programs. Or a football program established to win support for academic activities may eventually lead to some dilution in educational quality as standards are lowered in order to recruit athletic talent.

Goal distortion of a serious kind is thus always a possible price of constituency support. The worst instances have occurred in regulatory administration. At both the state and national level of government, agencies established to regulate particular kinds of economic activity have exhibited an extraordinary penchant for falling under the control of the groups placed under their jurisdiction. The regulatory agency thus becomes in effect the pawn of the regulated industry. This kind of relationship is a radical inversion of organizational goals, for the agency enters into collusion with the very group whose behavior it is supposed to control.[18] However, recent studies have tended to question whether regulatory agencies are really captured by the groups they regulate. In many cases, such as the FCC, regulatory agencies were set up at the behest of such groups.[19]

Although it is easy to censure this kind of collusion, a close relationship between a regulatory agency and the groups under its jurisdiction is often essential to an agency's achievement of its goals. The effectiveness of an air pollution commission may be enormously enhanced by including in its membership representatives of some of the principal industries responsible for discharging waste materials into the atmosphere. These representatives can help secure compliance by their firms with air pollution regulations — a consideration that is especially important when an agency has very little coercive authority and must rely mostly on voluntary compliance to achieve its regulatory goals. In its inception, at least, cooperation with the groups it is trying to control may thus be functional for a regulatory agency. It becomes dysfunctional only when, further along in the relationship, an agency modifies or even abandons its goals in order to retain group support.

Generally speaking, in clientele, regulatory, and other administrative agencies, the tendency for capture by an outside group is greatest when an agency deals with a single-interest constituency. Here an agency has nowhere else to turn if the group upon which it depends threatens to withdraw its support. Diversification of support is as desirable for a government agency as product diversification is for a private business firm eager to minimize the impact that shifts in consumer taste will have if it sells only a single product. Consider the case of grazing administration:

> The Grazing Service suffered because of its rather complete dependence on stockmen and those who spoke for them in Congress. By merging the Service into an expanded Bureau of Land Management, an act accomplished with the aid of interests adversely affected under the previous arrangement, the new organization has reduced its dependence by being able to appeal to a broader constituency.[20]

Of course, if diversification brings into an agency's constituency groups that are weak or unpopular, then its net effect may be harmful. The Social Security Administration was certainly not strengthened when it was given jurisdiction over the Supplemental Security Insurance program and impoverished groups were added to its clientele.

In any case, the heterogeneity of an administrative agency's group support thus seems to be more important in determining its freedom of action than the question of whether it is organized on the basis of clientele, purpose, process, or area to be served. The design of its political system, rather than its organizational structure, is the critical consideration.

For all agencies it is highly important to keep abreast of changes in the structure of interests affected by the activities they carry on. Huntington traces the administrative decline of the Interstate Commerce Commission to the failure of the agency to develop support among the new transportation interests that grew in the twentieth century out of technological change — the truckers, the water carriers, and the airlines. Instead, the agency tied itself to the railroads — a declining industry whose excesses it had been originally created to curb in the nineteenth century but which it now spent more and more of its time trying to resuscitate. "The ICC," Huntington says, "has not responded to the demands of the new forces in transportation. . . . Consequently, it is losing its leadership to those agencies that are more responsive to the needs and demands of the times." [21] The establishment of the Department of Transportation in the 1960s as the major transportation agency of the national government provided striking confirmation of this argument.[22]

*Public Interest Groups.* The relationships described here between executive agencies and their constituencies have long presented American democracy with some of its most perplexing problems. At its best this interaction enhances the representative character of government. Agencies serve as advocates for major community groups and in this way ensure that the interests of these groups are not neglected when governmental decisions are being made. Although legislators represent citizens grouped in geographic localities, administrative agencies usually represent them in their productive role in society — in a variety of professions and occupations and in innumerable subcategories of activity in the broad fields of business, agriculture, and labor.

Viewed in this way, the executive branch provides a system of representation based on economic and social role, supplementing the territorial representation furnished by Congress and other legislative bodies.[23] This system might be criticized as redundant on the grounds that the executive is performing a task that the legislature already carries on. But it is doing so in a different way — representing people by what they do rather than where they live. At the least, this is a useful sort of redundancy, because it sensitizes and more finely tunes the governmental apparatus to the intensity and variety of citizen concerns and needs.[24] Matthew Holden argues that it is in the interest of agencies to seek out groups that are not presently part of any executive constituency, because these new groups can add to an agency's administrative strength and security.[25] In this way the selfish interest of agencies in expanding their constituency coincides with the public interest in having the government be as inclusive as possible in performing its representational role.

But there is a dark side also to the intimacy between agencies and their publics, and it has been starkly drawn.[26] At its worst — in the captive-agency phenomenon already discussed — the relationship degenerates into the transfer of public authority to private groups that use it to advance their own interests at the expense of the general public. An executive agency then becomes simply the governmental outpost of an enclave of private power — able to exercise its public authority only at the sufferance of private groups. A result may be total neglect of the public interest in administrative decision making, and underrepresentation of groups in society that are too weak to compel an executive agency to heed their complaints.

One of the most important developments in American politics has been the rise to power in recent years of public interest organizations — groups like Common Cause and the cluster of reform organizations sponsored if not actually managed by Ralph Nader. Although much of their activity has been directed at the legislature, they have also been extremely important in monitoring the activities of executive agencies. Spokesmen for public interest groups have criticized the preferential treatment agencies often give to powerful private groups, and pressured them to expand their conception of their clientele to include the public at large and disadvantaged groups whose needs have been previously neglected in administrative decision making.

One major development in modern American society to which the rise of public interest groups testifies is the increasing ability of citizens affected by the exercise of administrative power to mobilize in their own defense. Recent decades have seen the multiplication of citizen groups designed to offset the power of bureaucratic organizations. Most of the new citizen associations aim to speak for interests not previously represented or grossly underrepresented in political decision making. A variety of new environmental groups have sprung up, older citizens are now represented by their own lobbying organizations, and the women's movement has acquired a new power and effectiveness. The roster of new citizen organizations and of established citizen groups "reborn" in some sense is a long one. A study of public interest groups in modern American society shows that 63 percent have been established since 1960.[27]

The influence such citizen or public interest organizations have been able to exert over executive agencies stems in no small measure from their ability to arouse the indignation and rally the support of their followers through the media of mass communication. The news media have been tremendously important in the ascending power of public interest organizations.[28] They provide an avenue through which an alleged misuse of administrative power can be quickly and widely publicized. Moreover, investigative reporters often work together with public interest organizations to expose misconduct in office, whether by an agency like the FTC that is felt to be insufficiently vigilant in enforcing consumer protection legislation,[29] or a water resource agency like the Corps of Engineers that is charged by conservationists with neglecting environmental interests in constructing dams, dredging harbors, and other activities.[30]

In assessing these efforts to push executive agencies toward responsiveness to a broader public we must realize that the administration of a good many governmental functions demands a narrowness in perspective on the part of an executive agency. A public agency charged with administering a program of assistance for the handicapped will be expected to give priority and preference to the needs of its special clientele. Such specialization in viewpoint would not ordinarily be regarded as inconsistent with the pursuit of the public interest. Moreover, it can be argued that competition within the executive branch from a variety of agencies advocating support for special groups is a necessary part of the entire process through which the public interest can ultimately be determined.

Perhaps the most important function that public interest groups perform is to provide the reform impulse with a continuing presence in the governmental process. In a celebrated analysis of political "quiescence," Murray Edelman argues that reformers have traditionally tended to be satisfied with merely symbolic rewards for their political efforts.[31] They tend to lose interest in politics once they have succeeded in establishing a regulatory agency, because this achievement gives them a false sense that the public is now being protected against exploitation. A typical result of this dissipation of reform energy is that the agency's decisions become more and more sympathetic to the regulated groups with which it is dealing continuously. With the rise of public interest groups, however, the reform spirit may be said to have become permanently institutionalized. Under the watchful eye of these groups, the day-to-day decisions of regulatory agencies can be made to correspond much more closely with the public interest, and reformers may begin to obtain more than a merely symbolic return on their investment in political activity.

In at least one important respect the perspective of many public interest organizations differs sharply from that of traditional interest groups. In their attitudes toward the work of administrative agencies, many public interest groups like Common Cause tend to be "process-oriented" — to have a high-minded interest in the procedures agencies follow rather than the policies they carry out. Thus, these public interest groups lobbied strongly and successfully for freedom of information laws designed to open up the proceedings of administrative agencies to public scrutiny. Traditional interest groups are much less interested in the character of the procedures agencies follow than they are in whether agency decisions, however arrived at, benefit or contribute to their own needs and welfare. Hence, they may work harder at influencing an agency's day-to-day decisions on policy, while the attention of public interest groups is focused on the agency's procedures.

## LEGISLATIVE SUPPORT

The legislature is a source of political strength for administration in essentially two ways. In the first place, it is from laws enacted by the legislature that agencies derive their basic legal powers — to give advice to policy makers, to exercise regulatory authority, or to provide services to the public. Such laws often determine as well the organizational structure of an agency and its ability to hire personnel, or to engage in a host of other housekeeping activities. Law is a fundamental basis of administrative authority, and it is the legislature that, initially at least, writes the law.

A second reason for administrative dependence upon legislative support is that the money administrative agencies need to fuel their activities must come through appropriation bills passed by the legislature. No matter how broad an agency's formal authority, its real power turns ultimately upon its fiscal resources. A regulatory agency left with inadequate funds to enforce the law that it administers has the shadow but not the substance of power. Similarly, the range of services any agency can provide is determined ultimately by the money it is authorized to spend. Money talks, in administration as elsewhere.

The power of Congress in money matters was greatly strengthened when the Supreme Court held in 1975 that the president had no power to impound funds that were clearly authorized for expenditure by Congress. This case, as well as many others, grew out of the Nixon administration's strategy of refusing to expend funds for agencies and programs it disliked, or felt were funded at too high a level, even though appropriations had been voted by Congress. If the court had upheld the broad view of impoundment taken by the Nixon regime, the importance of congressional appropriations for executive agencies would have been greatly reduced. The White

House would then have had discretion to determine whether or not an agency would actually get the money Congress had voted, and executive organizations would have to look primarily to it rather than to Congress for financial support.

As indicated in the previous section, high standing with the public gives any agency substantial leverage in dealing with the legislature. Legislative support is not simply a function of public favor, however. As the work of Richard Fenno on the appropriation process in Congress clearly reveals, an agency can have a great deal of outside support without enjoying corresponding esteem with influential elites in the legislature. Conversely, a number of agencies are held in very high regard in Congress but are virtually unknown by the general public.[32]

Fenno used two yardsticks for measuring agency success in dealing with the House Appropriations Committee and ultimately with Congress itself. The first was the percentage of its request for appropriations that an administrative agency succeeded in obtaining from the House committee. A number of agencies that scored very high in this regard are little known in the outside community. The Bureau of Customs is one, and the Bureau of the Public Debt is another. Both agencies are in the Treasury Department, which has intimate ties with Congress while not having a great deal of visibility with the public generally.

A second index used by Fenno for measuring administrative success in the legislature was the rate of growth in the financial support that an agency received from the House Appropriations Committee. Here he discovered that several agencies with a high growth rate nevertheless were subjected to deep budget cuts annually by the House Committee, so that their appropriations as a percentage of their requests were not as high as those of other agencies with a lower growth rate. Among the agencies in this category were the Bureau of Land Management, the Fish and Wildlife Service, and the Bureau of Labor Standards. Conversely, a number of the agencies that had been very successful in avoiding budget cuts showed very little increase in their appropriations over the years.

Success in avoiding cuts from appropriations requests is not, therefore, the same as ability to obtain continuously expanding support from the House Committee responsible for appropriations. The difference between these two criteria of success is explained by Fenno: *"High growth rates can be accounted for primarily by factors external to the Committee, whereas the ability to keep budget cuts to a minimum can be accounted for primarily by factors internal to the Committee-agency relationship."* [33] An agency's success in fending off budget cuts in the House is a measure of its rapport with legislators. Its ability to maintain a continuing increase in appropriations reflects expanding demand for its services by significant segments of the public. Alternatively, high standing in the legislature may coincide with strength in the outside community, so that an agency avoids budget cuts while maintaining a high growth rate in its appropriations; or an agency may have the misfortune of being weak in both legislative and public support, in which event it is subject to both budget cuts and a low appropriations growth rate.

In all these cases, the legislature reveals itself as an independent force of substantial importance in the life of administrative agencies. Good relations with legislators are especially useful when an agency does not enjoy strong support from outside groups, because this rapport provides assurance that an agency's appropriations, though not expanding, will remain reasonably stable. Even agencies with powerful constituencies can help themselves a great deal by cultivating the goodwill of legislators. Congressmen may not be able to prevent the growth of an agency's appropriations as the public demand for its services expands, but they can substantially retard this rate of growth by cutting back the agency's budget requests each year.

When an agency does have strong external support, it may use this constituency to bring pressure to bear upon lawmakers to reverse legislative decisions on appropriations that it considers disadvantageous. Not uncommon is the practice of cutting back on services provided outside groups following a legislative cut in appropriations. This reduction in services is designed to provoke protests from the agency's clientele to the legislature, bringing about restoration of at least part of the sum cut from the budget. This tactic often succeeds. Thus, though the cuts imposed by Congress will commonly be aimed at what the legislature regards as the least essential of an agency's activities, those the agency makes in consequence of such outside decisions are often directed at services that would generally be viewed as among its most essential.

As a variety of studies of the legislative process make clear, the administrative relationship with the legislature is, in the United States at least, mainly with legislative committees, and increasingly subcommittees.[34] The legislators who must be cultivated are the key men who sit on the committees that have significant power over the agency. The chief aim of administrators here is to win these legislators over to a favorable attitude toward the agency and an appreciation of the skill and dedication with which it carries on its work. If these committee members, particularly a committee or subcommittee chairman, can be socialized to the agency's point of view, they may become spokesmen for the organization in Congress.

There is, in fact, no better lobbyist for any administrative agency than a legislator, because members of Congress are more likely to listen to advice from their colleagues than from outsiders.[35] Thus, the most fortunately situated of all agencies number legislators as members of their own organization. Each of the Armed Services has had the good fortune to have a number of legislators within its reserve units, and though it is difficult to determine how captive a congressman actually became as a result of his reserve status, this relationship certainly assures an agency some capital in the form of legislative support both from the members of Congress who are reservists, and other legislators who look to them for advice. In state administration, a highway department may derive a similar advantage because some state legislators who are attorneys earn fees by conducting title searches for the department, and other state agencies use devices such as the consultantship to bring legislators within their own organizational network.

The relationship between an administrative agency and legislative committees may vary a great deal from one committee to another. During the Vietnam War military officials testifying before Congress could expect to receive far more favorable treatment from the Senate Armed Services Committee than from the Senate Foreign Relations Committee, a large number of whose members were highly critical of American involvement in Southeast Asia. Relations with any committee may also change with the passage of time, as the agency or the committee alters its personnel, or as public attitudes toward the agency and its program shift. The arrival of a number of freshman congressmen on a committee may bring about a much more critical perspective toward the agencies under its jurisdiction.

One of the most consistent differences in the reception an agency may encounter in Congress is between the committee that considers legislation in the area of its responsibilities and the appropriations subcommittee that actually decides how much money the agency can spend to achieve its objectives. Usually the legislative committee is program-oriented and eager to see that an agency obtains adequate resources with which to achieve its goals, whereas the appropriations subcommittee is economy-minded and more inclined to trim back appropriations that the legislative committee may have authorized. Harold Seidman describes the great difference in the treatment that agency executives receive in these two legislative settings:

> Lords of the executive establishment generally enjoy the cozy atmosphere of legislative committee hearings where they are received with courtesy and the deference due their office. They shun, wherever possible, meetings with appropriations subcommittees whose chairman upon occasion may accord them about the same amount of deference as shown by a hard-boiled district attorney to a prisoner in the dock.[36]

An agency may also experience substantial variation in the treatment it receives from the House and Senate. One significant difference between the two branches of the legislature is that the Senate appropriations committee is usually more generous in handling agency requests for financial support than its counterpart unit in the House. Nelson Polsby provides an explanation for this difference: "in the House, money bills are seen primarily in the context of assaults on the Treasury; in the Senate, they are seen as financial extensions of programs, as expressions of legitimate social and political demands."[37] One reason is that members of the House committee specialize in appropriations, but senators also sit on substantive committees and thus deal with programs to which they become attached.

One official important for a growing number of executive agencies in their efforts to cultivate legislative support is the congressional liaison officer. The task of this administrative official is essentially that of keeping in touch with legislators, answering their requests for information, providing help to their constituents, or even writing a speech for a congressman. In an increasingly complex bureaucratic apparatus, liaison officials have become almost indispensable in enabling legislators to find their way around the labyrinthine corridors of bureaucracy.[38] It is, however, questionable if liaison officers can relieve departmental executives of any save the routine chores of legislative-executive relations. On matters critical to an agency, such as passage of legislation affecting its power, the task of winning legislative support must inevitably be assumed by officials at a high level of responsibility.

Moreover, some departmental executives even complain that liaison officials are a burden as well as a help. Spending, as they do, a great deal of time in congressional offices, liaison personnel may generate a good many requests for assistance that, as one irate executive put it, "might never come to us if our liaison man did not spend a lot of time on Capitol Hill, running into administrative assistants to congressmen." [39]

Our analysis of efforts by administrative agencies to secure legislative support has centered on the essential resources that the legislature controls and agencies seek to obtain — legal authority and appropriations. In its relations with the legislature, however, an agency is motivated by a desire not only to obtain these positive assets but also to escape punitive sanctions that the legislature has the power to inflict. These sanctions include exposure of the agency to unpleasant publicity through a highly publicized investigation of its shortcomings, refusal to approve the appointment of agency executives when (as is true of the United States Senate) a legislative body possesses this power of confirmation, and veto of financial transactions an agency is contemplating. The dependence of administrative agencies upon legislative goodwill thus springs from negative as well as positive considerations — the desire to escape penalties as well as to obtain rewards.

Of course, in providing executive agencies with appropriations and the other resources they seek, legislators receive in exchange benefits that are of substantial value to them. No aspect of their role is of greater importance to members of Congress than their relations with their constituency, and there are innumerable ways in which agencies can be of practical assistance — ranging from help in establishing or retaining a government facility that may be a major economic asset in a congressman's district to assisting a legislator in answering an inquiry or resolving a vexing problem that one of his or her constituents has with the government.

Morris Fiorina links the ability of so many incumbent members of Congress to get reelected every two years to their being able to get so much credit in their own districts for the help they give their constituents in dealing with executive agencies.[40] It can therefore be argued that Congress itself has a vested interest in the continued growth of bureaucracy. The more agencies there are for constituents to deal with, the more important becomes the congressional role as intermediary between the citizen and bureaucracy. From this perspective Congress becomes the protagonist rather than the antagonist of bureaucracy in government.

In the formal theory of American government, the posture of the legislature with respect to the bureaucracy is one of oversight. Congress is supposed to monitor the behavior of bureaucrats to see that they carry out the tasks assigned to them and do not exceed their authority while doing so. For many legislators, however, the oversight role has never been a high-priority task, because it does not contribute to their reelection nearly as much as nursing a constituency — being an effective "errand-boy" congressman.[41] Madison's expectation in the *Federalist Papers* was that all government officials would seek always to maximize their own share of power in the political system, but the behavior of modern legislators often seems to belie this assumption.[42] As we saw in chapter two, members of Congress often seek not so much power as safety — tenure in office rather than vigorous use of the powers of office. Hence, the attitude of many congressmen toward the executive agencies under their jurisdiction is that they are assets they must protect rather than organizations they must oversee.

But however lightly some congressmen may regard their role as overseers, executive agencies themselves tend to look toward the Hill with anxiety — as a place where one can find powerful friends, or encounter dangerous enemies. An invitation to testify before Congress is an event for which careful preparation is made. A call from a congressman's office requesting information is given very special attention and treatment. Congressional oversight may not look potent to an outsider, but it is taken very seriously in the corridors of bureaucracy.

## POWER IN THE EXECUTIVE BRANCH

By assiduous cultivation of legislative and public support, it is possible for an administrative agency to establish a position of virtually complete autonomy within the executive branch. When agencies like the FBI and the Corps of Engineers succeeded in doing this in the past, they became virtually immune from the hierarchic controls exercised by either the president or officials in their own executive department. Historically, therefore, the quest for outside support has often been a divisive force within the structure of American national bureaucracy, weakening the identification of departments with the president or of bureaus with their department. Agencies that use outside support to acquire independence within the executive branch may ultimately come to regard themselves as congressional rather than presidential agencies, or indeed as being a law unto themselves.

There are, of course, administrative units at the other extreme that possess almost no independent standing with the public or the legislature. Performing functions that are primarily useful within the executive branch itself, they remain almost entirely presidential in their orientation. The purest cases of this type are the staff agencies of the presidency, such as the Office of Management and Budget. If the president does not choose to give a staff unit like this any power, then it has little or no influence. Of these staff agencies it can truly be said that the president is their principal if not their only constituent, and their power can therefore fluctuate a great deal between one chief executive and another, as it has with OMB.

Most agencies, however, do not fall squarely into either of these categorical extremes. They have not formed such strong alliances with outside groups as to become entirely independent of presidential control, nor are they wholly dependent upon their standing as executive agencies for their vitality. Occupying a middle position, they seek to draw strength from sources inside as well as outside the executive branch. While not doing anything to jeopardize their ties with the legislature, they nevertheless seek to maintain strong lines of support with the White House.

Having good relations with the president is in fact a major asset for any administrative agency or official. Morton Halperin emphasizes how important such presidential favor can be in the national security field:

> ... there is nothing that Washington officials watch more closely than the relationship of particular individuals to the President. When a participant's standing is going up, the sense that one should defer to that individual, rather than taking issues

to the President, will increase. When the reverse occurs, when
an individual or an organization is seen to go down in presidential standing, then the sinking party will begin to find it
necessary to compromise and yield to other groups whose status
has, at least by comparison, risen.[43]

According to Halperin, the CIA fell from grace at the White House
after the Bay of Pigs fiasco in 1961, and as a result it lost standing
as an organization not only in the United States but in other countries as well.

One of the best measures of an agency's strength in dealing with
the president is the extent to which the White House has to bargain
with it in order to secure its cooperation. During the withdrawal of
American troops from Vietnam, President Nixon was obliged to
make many concessions to the armed services in order to maintain
their support for his troop-withdrawal program. Moreover, in order
to secure Department of Defense acceptance of disarmament agreements being negotiated with the Soviet Union, the White House
has often had to give strong support to the department's demand
for the continued development of strategic weapons. One secretary
of defense insisted in testimony before Congress that the department
would oppose an arms-control agreement if the increased appropriations necessary to continue a weapons development program were
not forthcoming. Recent administrations have thus been put in the
paradoxical position of supplementing presentation of a disarmament treaty to Congress with a proposal for increased military
appropriations.

Agencies also seek support from housekeeping units within the
executive branch that have partial control over resources upon
which they depend for their operational effectiveness. The Office
of Management and Budget exercises powers that are vital to every
other executive agency. The annual hearings it conducts in framing
the executive budget provide a basis for determining how much
money each agency needs during the ensuing fiscal year, and this
determination by OMB often becomes a ceiling on the appropriations that an agency can expect to receive from Congress. As we
have seen, all agencies must also clear their communications with
the legislature through OMB so that consistency of these communications with the president's policy goals can be checked. The
budget agency also has the power to recommend to the president
whether he should veto legislation enacted by Congress — legisla-

tion that will inevitably affect the fortunes of executive agencies. Finally, OMB conducts studies of efficiency in executive operations that may well lead to proposals for reorganization that will greatly alter the power and status of the agencies affected by these plans.[44]

Hence, good relations with the Office of Management and Budget are an invaluable asset for any executive agency. To be sure OMB is not as powerfully situated today in the network of presidential staff agencies as it once was. We have seen that White House staff members now take the lead in giving the president advice on policy issues, a task that the budget agency used to perform. But as the costs of running the federal government continue to mount, and as agencies increasingly compete for scarce fiscal resources, budget officials can certainly be expected to play a prominent role in shaping presidential decisions on fiscal issues in the years to come.

One thing that has happened to OMB in recent years is that the agency has become increasingly politicized. Dominant power in the agency is now held by a cadre of presidential appointees instead of by the highly professional civil servants who ran the agency in the period immediately following World War II. In this earlier period agency professionals regarded themselves as serving the presidency rather than any particular president. Nowadays, however, the agency is much more closely tied in attitude and interests to the White House incumbent.[45]

Other staff units that also control resources of value to executive agencies include the Office of Personnel Management, which administers personnel regulations that affect an agency's ability to recruit and retain employees, and the General Services Administration, which constructs and operates most government buildings. Of course, in dealing with all these housekeeping units an agency may have bargaining power of its own. Aaron Wildavsky's study of the budgetary process showed that the Bureau of the Budget (now OMB) tended to be generous with those agencies with which it felt Congress would itself be generous: "The Bureau finds itself treating agencies it dislikes much better than those it may like better but who cannot help themselves nearly as much in Congress." [46] An agency's high standing in the legislature may thus be reflected in the treatment it receives at the hands of a staff agency that presumably is responsive to the interests of the president alone, a striking illustration of the extent of legislative influence upon executive behavior and decisions.

For individual bureaus, maintaining good relations with the hierarchy of the department in which they are located is also of strategic value. Even though the phenomenon of "bureau autonomy" has not vanished from American bureaucracy, there has certainly been a secular trend toward increasing the power and capacity of departmental officials to control the activities of bureaus under their jurisdiction. Through successive reorganization measures, bureaus have been clustered in more homogeneous department groupings where they can be subjected to more effective supervision; the size and authority of departmental staffs have been strengthened; and legal powers that once resided in the bureaus have been moved upward into the hands of the department.

Moreover, since World War II a new science of management has been growing steadily in the public service. The total effect of these new quantified styles of decision making will be considered later (chapter six). These advanced management techniques have greatly strengthened the capacity of departments for overhead control, and have generally had a centralizing effect upon the operations of American bureaucracy.

But these changes have not affected the power of all bureaus to the same degree, and they have certainly not been uniform for all departments. Moreover, some current trends are highly decentralizing. The growth in professionalism in government employment has tended to make many bureaus more specialized, and hence more difficult for generalists in the department hierarchy to control. The activities of natural scientists working at the bureau level are not easily monitored by lay administrators in departmental headquarters units. Witness a department like Health and Human Services, where the high degree of professionalism at the bureau level — in medicine, science, welfare, and educational specialties — has long frustrated efforts to establish departmental authority.

We have looked at the structure of power within the executive branch from the perspective of the vertical distribution of authority, focusing upon either the ability of a president and his staff agencies to influence the decisions and behavior of bureaucrats at lower echelons, or the extent of control that department officials can exert over their own bureaus. Looked at in this way, the executive branch presents a picture today of bureaus possessing a great deal of independent authority, based among other things on the fact that bureau chiefs generally have much longer tenure than departmental officials, but with a constantly expanding overlay of centralized controls.

But it is also possible to look at power in the executive branch by assessing the lateral distribution of influence — between agencies at approximately the same hierarchic rank but with responsibility for different programs. From this perspective, there are many possibilities for conflict or cooperation among administrative units, and an agency's success in turning these situations to its advantage will go far to determine its real power or status within the executive branch.

Conflicts between administrative units often arise because two agencies are pursuing goals that are diametrically opposed. The Anti-Trust Division of the Department of Justice has frequently been in conflict with one or another of the regulatory agencies that administer statutes covering a major industry within the economy. The division has opposed the merger of business firms when this would seem to affect economic competition negatively, whereas agencies like the Interstate Commerce Commission or the Federal Power Commission have been quite sympathetic to such mergers when they appear to promise a stronger and more stable industry. Here administrative conflict is a function of a lasting ambivalence in public policy, because some executive agencies have been charged with promoting economic competition, but others have been allowed to protect selected industries from the hazards and uncertainties of the competitive life. In the years to come the movement toward deregulation may reduce such conflict by stripping some industries of the protection that paternalistic administrative regulation once gave them from economic competition.

Interagency conflicts are also likely to arise when two agencies pursue goals that are not opposing but closely related. Here conflict occurs for the same reason that it prevails in the private economy — agencies are competitors in the same market. This competition may take place in a variety of areas — over questions of jurisdiction, for the support of outside groups, or in the quest for presidential or congressional favor. Competition of this sort has given rise to some of the most celebrated interagency conflicts in American administrative history. The ancient struggle between the Corps of Engineers and the Bureau of Reclamation is perhaps the classic, as these two agencies fought for jurisdiction over water resource projects.[47] Similar conflicts have broken out between the

Forest Service and the Bureau of Land Management over adminis-
tration of public lands in the West,[48] and between the Extension
Division and the Soil Conservation Service in the Department of
Agriculture over agricultural policy.[49]

In some areas of policy, agencies administering closely related
functions develop a "separate spheres of interest" doctrine as a
means of avoiding jurisdictional conflict. Two state universities may
emphasize different educational programs as their chief responsibility, as they have traditionally in Indiana, or, as in California,
the university and state college systems may be set up to serve
students with different levels of academic achievement. Of course,
the equilibrium produced by this arrangement does not always
remain stable. In modern times, state agricultural colleges have
commonly become full-fledged universities, which has frequently
triggered conflict with the existing state university. Have-not organizations, like have-not nations, are particularly likely to violate
any spheres-of-interest agreement when an opportunity presents itself to improve their position in relation to a stronger competitor.

Cooperation as well as conflict may characterize relations among
executive agencies. Because many agencies share common or complementary interests, they may establish an informal alliance to
achieve their objectives. Sometimes agencies, like nations, may negotiate such alliances despite a long history of hostility between
them. As in international relations, this occurs most frequently
when a common danger threatens both of them more than each
endangers the other.

In 1944 those lifelong antagonists, the Corps of Engineers and
the Bureau of Reclamation, were able to arrive at a mutually
agreeable arrangement for developing water resources in the Missouri Valley area. The treaty they signed for this purpose was called
the Pick-Sloan plan, and it was forced upon them by, among other
developments, the threat that an agency like TVA might soon be
established to take over all water resource activities in the Missouri
River area. Labeled by one of its critics "a shameless, loveless shot-
gun wedding," this treaty between the Bureau and the Corps helped
to dissipate any real possibility that a valley authority might be
given comprehensive jurisdiction over administering water resources
in the Missouri basin.[50] Bilateral and multilateral alliances of this
sort may often be as essential to an organization's survival as they
are to the defense of a nation's security.

A cooperative relationship among executive agencies may also reflect linkages among levels of government in a federal system. National agencies that dispense grants to state or local units look upon these organizations as perhaps their most important allies. And increasingly, all domestic programs in the United States have been "intergovernmentalized" — carried on, that is, by a network of national, state, and local agencies. Charles Jones describes the situation facing state and local air pollution agencies: "Part of an emerging national network of control, they receive funds, technical aid, training, and support from the federal agency. Further, they are potential sources of support as well as potential organizers of support among the public." [51] The same mutually beneficial relationship prevails with other national agencies administering grant-in-aid programs. Moreover, as state and local agencies receiving federal grants have established lobbying organizations to protect their interests in Washington, they have acquired great influence over policy development at the national level. Very commonly, they have as much power over the national agency as it has over them. The national agency may supply the fiscal resources on which state and local agencies depend, but these lesser units of government have a large voice in determining how this money is allocated and spent.

Interagency cooperation may also be initiated by legislative or executive action requiring two or more agencies to work together to handle a program. At the national level the system of regulating private pension funds (ERISA) is jointly administered by the Department of Labor and the Internal Revenue Service. In state government some programs are still carried on through administrative boards or commissions on which several departments are represented. In metropolitan areas, public organizations in individual localities commonly belong to areawide councils through which a great deal of interorganizational cooperation can take place in, for example, health care.

Moreover, at all levels of government problems arise that require joint consideration by several agencies for their solution. In such cases interdepartmental committees are commonly established to handle the situation either temporarily or permanently. Though created as instruments of cooperation, such committees may also become theaters of conflict. In describing national security affairs, where the State, Defense, Treasury, and other executive depart-

ments have been yoked together on many interdepartmental committees by the president or Congress, the Senate Subcommittee on
National Policy Machinery wrote:

> Inter-agency committees are the gray and bloodless ground
> of bureaucratic warfare — a warfare of position, not of decisive
> battles. State commonly sees them as devices for bringing "out-
> siders" into matters it regards as its own, and resists encroach-
> ment. The other departments and agencies use them as instru-
> ments for "getting into the act." [52]

When formal interdepartmental cooperation is thus enforced upon
executive agencies by either legislative or executive order, it may
mask bitter and protracted warfare between them.

But these cases of friction should not obscure the fact that in a
variety of bureaucratic settings agencies have found it possible to
establish very cooperative and mutually profitable relations based
on systems of exchange. Very commonly agencies exchange one
commodity that is useful to both of them, such as information.
Law enforcement agencies need to trade a great deal of data in
order to carry out the task of apprehending criminals, and public
health officials may find it similarly useful in developing plans for
the best use of hospitals in a metropolitan area.[53]

Sometimes the commodities that agencies exchange are quite dis-
similar. A study of interorganizational exchanges in which the State
Department was involved showed a number of such transactions,
including an agreement under which the department assisted the
National Aeronautics and Space Administration in locating suitable
sites for space tracking stations around the world, in return for
NASA lending the department the services of its astronauts for
goodwill missions abroad.[54]

Of course, in some areas of administration exchange is very difficult. In the intelligence community an agency may regard the information it possesses as the core of its power and be unwilling
to share this data with what organizations it regards as rivals. This
has long been a problem in relations among the CIA, the FBI, and
the Secret Service. The CIA justified its excursion into domestic
intelligence — an activity barred to it by the statute under which
it was established — on the grounds that the FBI would not pass

on information in its files on alleged espionage activity in the United States. The Secret Service has long complained about the FBI's unwillingness to convey information that might be useful to it in warding off presidential assassinations. The establishment of such "information screens" to conceal data is most likely to occur when agencies regard information not only as an element of power but as synonymous with it. They are much less reluctant to trade a commodity like information when it is not the principal source of their power.

## EXPERTISE, POLITICS, AND POWER

In this and the preceding chapter we have distinguished between the influence administrative agencies exercise as a result of their professional skills and the power they acquire by developing political support. These two sources of bureaucratic power, expertise and politics, though easy to distinguish in analysis, are not as readily separated in the actual practice of executive agencies. More often than not, they are so linked as sources of influence that it is difficult to tell how much of an agency's influence upon policy stems from its expertise and how much rests on the size and strength of its political constituency.

Military officers are, Morris Janowitz wrote, "professionals in violence." [55] They have a great deal of influence over the framing of national security policy purely because of their mastery of the art and science of warfare, and of the use of force to accomplish national objectives. Hence, their role in the policy process would be strategic even if they had no constituency at all. But in modern American society at least, the power of the professional soldier has been enormously enhanced by the formidable network of outside support each military service has managed to cultivate. This network includes congressmen and congressional committees with responsibilities in national security matters, industrial firms that depend upon defense contracts, and the so-called backstop associations of the military — the Navy League and the Army and Air Force Associations. These and other groups collectively represent the military-industrial complex that has received so much attention and been the source of so much alarm in contemporary American politics.

The power of this military-industrial complex can easily be exaggerated, because on many issues of national security policy the military point of view has not prevailed, and on specific issues the military often generates a variety of policy perspectives. But certainly military officers as a group do have substantial influence over the framing of national security policy. It is perhaps impossible to know how much of this influence simply reflects the pressures of the military lobby behind the Pentagon and how much springs from deference accorded military expertise itself.

Whatever the relative weight of expertise and politics as sources of bureaucratic power, all executive agencies in the United States recognize the value of political support, and devote a great deal of energy to seeking out and nursing a constituency. The extent to which American bureaucracy is thus politicized reflects the fact that a democratic political system was already well established in this country when a substantial bureaucracy first began to appear later in the nineteenth century. The development of political skills was part of the process by which executive agencies adapted to their environment in order to survive in the egalitarian democratic society in which they found themselves.[56]

This American experience stands in stark contrast to the historical development of bureaucracy in European democratic states. There a highly developed bureaucratic apparatus commonly existed and played a large role in governing the state long before democratic political institutions formed. In Europe it was democracy that had to accommodate itself to the presence of a strongly entrenched bureaucratic system. Partly because they enjoyed a security of position that American bureaucracies lacked, and partly because of conventions in the parliamentary system, executive agencies in European states have historically had less reason and less opportunity to engage in direct political activity of the sort that is so common in the United States.

But if a politicized bureaucracy is deeply rooted in the American political tradition, so too is much deference to expertise in the governing process. The creation of varied political institutions in the United States — including the council-manager form of government in urban communities, the special-authority device in both state and local government, and the independent regulatory commissions at the national level — testifies that it is very much in the American grain to attempt to defuse political controversy by transforming political issues into technical problems. Both city and county managers are expected to furnish their local area with professional gov ernment based on nonpolitical criteria, and the special authority and the independent regulatory commissions have both been set up to take government away from the politicians and put it in the hands of the experts. School systems are commonly run by administrators who piously maintain that all educational policy decisions are made on a nonpolitical basis, thus paradoxically enhancing their political power by denying their involvement in politics. The appointment by presidents of special commissions to study and report on major issues of public policy also reflects this national faith in expertise. The Reagan administration used such a commission to break a political deadlock that had stymied reform of the Social Security system.

Since World War II at least, expertise has certainly had a dominant role in foreign or national security policy, where the involvement of domestic political groups often takes place only after a decision has been made. Many decisions are reached in secret, and public opinion is acquainted with what has transpired only through "leaks" — which may come from executive officials who disapprove of what has been decided and are trying to reverse the decision by arousing public opinion against it.

Bureaucratic experts of various kinds thus exercise pervasive influence over national security decisions. These professional groups include diplomats, military officers, scientists, and what Bernard Brodie calls "scientific strategists." [57] Samuel P. Huntington describes the development of national defense strategy: "The relative absence of nongovernmental groups concerned with strategy enhances the extent and the importance of the bargaining roles of governmental officials and agencies." [58] In this case public participation in actual policy decisions tends to be indirect. The public participates as the officials making decisions take potential public reactions into account in reaching their own conclusions. Although the public is not likely to question the competence of government officials to define the national interest, it is quite capable of eventual resentment against the sacrifices and burdens any international involvement may entail.

In many areas of domestic policy making, on the other hand, varied nongovernmental groups have long taken an interest in the policy-making processes of administrative agencies. As we saw earlier, this relationship is initiated in many instances by the agencies themselves. The views of an agency's public can thus be incorporated into the initial design of policy. In fact, bureaucratic policy

making in such areas commonly represents reconciliation of con
flicting group interests as much as it does the application of expertise
toward solving particular problems.

This distinction between policy making in the administration o
foreign and domestic affairs should not be exaggerated. Bureaucrat
in the national security area enjoy somewhat more freedom from
outside political pressures in at least the early stages of their delib
erations. But these pressures are never entirely absent from any
area of bureaucratic decisions in the United States, so wide and
well traveled are the channels of access between administrative
agencies on the one hand and the community on the other.

Moreover, since Vietnam the public has been far less deferential
to the foreign policy elite in government than it once was. An
increasing number of citizens have even become involved in the
activities of groups like the nuclear freeze movement that question
some of the principal tenets of American foreign policy. In any
case, it seems clear that there are important variations in the rela
tive weight of expertise and political activity as sources of bureau
cratic power at different levels of government in the American
federal system. By and large, administrative agencies in the state
and localities are much more intimately involved in the politica
process than are similar units at the national level. It is still com
mon in state and local government for the heads of administrative
agencies to be elected rather than appointed, and this practice
inevitably politicizes the atmosphere in which administration is
carried on. Moreover, in some of the more backward jurisdictions
patronage is still rife, and agencies serve mainly as auxiliaries for
the party organizations.

It should be noted also that the employees of administrative
agencies represent a sizable group in state and local politics, and
the votes of employee organizations of policemen, firemen, or teach
ers can easily be decisive in local elections. In New York City, public
employee votes dominate the Democratic primary contests, and in
New York as in many other cities, political victory in a Democratic
primary is virtually equivalent to election.

It is also standard practice for issues as well as offices to be voted
upon in state and local elections, and many of these issues are of
salient importance to one or more administrative agencies. A school
system will lend every effort to secure the passage of a school bond
issue on a local ballot, and all agencies face at every election the
possibility of becoming involved in a struggle over a public ex

penditure issue, a referendum, or a constitutional amendment affecting their power or the scope of their activity. However politicized national agencies may be in other ways, they are nevertheless insulated from such election contests. The FBI, though adept at many aspects of political activity, does not, like a local police department, have to concern itself with the success or failure of items on the ballot, such as establishment of a civilian review board, that critically affect the interests of the organization and its members.

There are marked differences in the sources of bureaucratic power, not only between national administration and agencies at lower echelons of government but also among agencies at the state and local level. In many rural states administrative agencies are highly politicized and still have little tendency to develop or defer to bureaucratic expertise. In urban, industrialized states, on the other hand, the professionalization of bureaucracy is often quite advanced, and the operations of administrative agencies have been sealed off from the cruder kinds of political pressure.[59] A great deal of this professionalization at the state level has resulted from the pressure or example of national agencies interacting with the states through intergovernmental programs. The TVA has done a great deal to raise levels of professionalism in state natural resource agencies in the southern region that it serves.

Substantial variations in bureaucratic power are also found among units of local government. From their study of New York City, Wallace Sayre and Herbert Kaufman concluded that the city's bureaucracies have a large role in its political life.

> Extending the merit system of employment for city employees has had ... a history of steady and eventually almost complete acceptance in the city's government. ... The consequences have included not merely the anticipated increase in competence and conventional rationality in the conduct of the city government, but also, and equally significant, the rise of a new form of political power in the city: the career bureaucracies, and especially the organized bureaucracies. Once closely allied to, and greatly dependent upon, the party leaders, the bureaucracies now have the status and the capacity of autonomous participants in the city's political process.[60]

Studies of other cities do not show bureaucracies exerting comparable influence in the policy process. From Robert Dahl's study of New Haven, it is almost impossible to tell if the city has a bureaucracy, so invisible is it in his account of the community's governing process.[61] Both Edward Banfield's analysis of Chicago and M. Kent Jennings's examination of Atlanta assign a more important role to the bureaucratic component in the policy process, but it is still far less significant than that which Sayre and Kaufman depict in New York.[62]

Assuming that these findings are correct in all cases, the strong position of the bureaucracy in New York's government may be traced to the extraordinary size of the city, and the necessity this imposes for the devolution of authority by the mayor's office to administrative agencies. Or the critical factor may be the sharp cleavage between reform and Tammany machine politics in New York's governmental tradition which led, first, to the practice of giving public agencies strong guarantees in law and custom against political interference, and, second, to the bureaucracies' conversion of this protection into a mandate for virtually complete autonomy for themselves in the governing process. However, this autonomy was sharply curtailed in the aftermath of the fiscal crisis that beset New York in the 1970s, when a state fiscal board was given power over the city's budget and spending decisions.[63]

In any case, cities differ across the country in the power that administrative agencies enjoy and in the sources of this power. Parallel differences are found among the states, and between state and national administration. Differences in expertise between national and state agencies have narrowed in recent years, and, as we found earlier, the national government can claim some credit for the development, because it results at least in part from the efforts national agencies have made to strengthen state administration.

Generally speaking, it seems safe to say that in the United States bureaucratic expertise varies directly with the size of the population and the complexity of the environment being governed. The national bureaucracy is more technically proficient, as a group, than are state administrative agencies, and the states at the same time are more expert at administration than their own rural units of local government. (Of course, some states like California have administrative systems that are at least equal in competence to the national apparatus.) Cities on the other hand are more likely to have highly skilled bureaucracies than rural states because of the environmental complexity and expansion of population that urbanization both reflects and engenders. Hence, as governmental jurisdictions become more urbanized, the need for bureaucratic expertise grows apace,

and there is an increasing tendency for the power of administrative
agencies to rest upon deference to their expertise as well as upon the
ability of these agencies to cultivate political support.

# *Notes*

1. Norton Long, *The Polity* (Chicago: Rand McNally, 1962), p. 53. The best
   study of the origins, structure, and operation of the outside groups with
   which executive agencies deal is James Q. Wilson, *Political Organizations*
   (New York: Basic Books, 1973).
2. For a careful analysis of this development over the course of American history, see Herbert Kaufman, "The Growth of the Federal Personnel System,"
   in Wallace Sayre, ed., *The Federal Government Service* (Englewood Cliffs,
   N.J.: Prentice-Hall, 1965), pp. 7–69. For a more recent view, see Michael
   Nelson, "A Short, Ironic History of American National Bureaucracy," *Jour-
   nal of Politics* 44 (August 1982), especially pp. 764–767.
3. For analysis of the power of government publicity, see Francis E. Rourke,
   *Secrecy and Publicity: Dilemmas of Democracy* (Baltimore: Johns Hopkins
   Press, 1961); Delmer D. Dunn, *Public Officials and the Press* (Reading,
   Mass.: Addison-Wesley, 1969); Leon V. Sigal, *Reporters and Officials: The
   Organization and Politics of Newsmaking* (Lexington, Mass.: Lexington
   Books, 1973).
4. Anthony Downs, "Up and Down with Ecology — the 'Issue Attention Cycle,' "
   *The Public Interest* 28 (Summer 1972): 38–50.
5. E. E. Schattschneider, *The Semisovereign People* (New York: Holt, Rinehart
   and Winston, 1960).
6. Charles O. Jones, "The Limits of Public Support: Air Pollution Agency Development," *Public Administration Review* 32 (September/October 1972):
   502–508. Cf. also his *Clean Air: The Policies and Politics of Pollution* (Pittsburgh, Penn.: University of Pittsburgh Press, 1975).
7. See Phillip O. Foss, *Politics and Grass* (Seattle: University of Washington
   Press, 1960).
8. See William O. Chittick, *State Department, Press, and Pressure Groups* (New
   York: John Wiley, 1970), esp. chap. 8.
9. See Richard E. Neustadt, *Presidential Power: The Politics of Leadership
   from FDR to Carter* (New York: John Wiley 1980), pp. 38–39.
10. Compare also the description of the American Establishment in Arthur M.
    Schlesinger, *A Thousand Days: John F. Kennedy in the White House* (Bos-
    ton: Houghton Mifflin, 1965), p. 128.
11. See David B. Truman, *The Governmental Process* (New York: Alfred A.
    Knopf, 1951), pp. 90–92.
12. Francis E. Rourke, "The Department of Labor and the Trade Unions,"
    *Western Political Quarterly* 7 (December 1954): 661–662.
13. Samuel P. Huntington, *The Common Defense: Strategic Programs in Na-
    tional Politics* (New York: Columbia University Press, 1961), p. 397.
14. Ibid., p. 400.
15. For an analysis of the role of leaks in the relationship between executive
    agencies and the media see Sigal, *Reporters and Officials*, pp. 143–148, and

Morton B. Halperin, *Bureaucratic Politics and Foreign Policy* (Washington, D.C.: Brookings Institution, 1974), pp. 173–195.

16. Philip Selznick, *TVA and the Grass Roots* (Berkeley: University of California Press, 1949). For more recent studies of the TVA, see Martha Derthick, *Between State and Nation: Regional Organizations of the United States* (Washington, D.C.: Brookings Institution, 1974); pp. 18–45, Marguerite Owen, *The Tennessee Valley Authority* (New York: Praeger, 1973); and North Callahan, *TVA: Bridge over Troubled Waters* (South Brunswick, N.J.: A. S. Barnes, 1980).

17. Philip Selznick, *Leadership in Administration* (Evanston, Ill.: Row, Peterson, 1957), p. 44.

18. For an analysis of this tendency in regulatory agencies, see Marver H. Bernstein, *Regulating Business by Independent Commission* (Princeton: Princeton University Press, 1955), pp. 74–102. Bernstein argues that all regulatory agencies go through a "life cycle" in which capture by the regulated groups is a culminating phase.

19. See Erwin G. Krasnow, Lawrence D. Longley, and Herbert A. Terry, *The Politics of Broadcast Regulation*, 3rd ed. (New York: St. Martin's Press, 1982). For a more general critique of the "capture" model, see Paul Sabatier, "Social Movements and Regulatory Agencies: Toward a More Adequate — and Less Pessimistic — Theory of Clientele Capture," *Policy Sciences* 6 (September 1975): 301–342.

20. Aaron Wildavsky, *The Politics of the Budgetary Process*, 3rd ed. (Boston: Little, Brown, 1979), p. 172.

21. Samuel P. Huntington, "The Marasmus of the I.C.C.: The Commission, the Railroads, and the Public Interest," *Yale Law Journal* 61 (April 1952): 472–473.

22. For an analysis of this development, see Emmette S. Redford and Marlan Blissett, *Organizing the Executive Branch: The Johnson Presidency* (Chicago: University of Chicago Press, 1981), pp. 46–76.

23. For an interesting discussion of the executive role in representation see Roger H. Davidson, "Congress and the Executive: The Race for Representation," in Alfred DeGrazia, coord., *Twelve Studies of the Organization of Congress* (Washington, D.C.: American Enterprise Institute, 1966).

24. For a compelling argument on behalf of redundancy in the design and operation of governmental institutions, see Martin Landau, "Redundancy, Rationality, and the Problem of Duplication and Overlap," *Public Administration Review* 29 (July/August 1969): 346–358.

25. Matthew Holden, "'Imperialism' in Bureaucracy," *American Political Science Review* 60 (December 1966): 943–951.

26. The disadvantageous aspects of this relationship are clearly spelled out in Grant McConnell, *Private Power and American Democracy* (New York: Alfred A. Knopf, 1966), and Theodore J. Lowi, *The End of Liberalism*, rev. ed. (New York: W. W. Norton, 1979).

27. Jeffrey M. Berry, *Lobbying for the People: The Political Behavior of Public Interest Groups* (Princeton: Princeton University Press, 1977), p. 34. Jack L. Walker presents a comprehensive survey of the birth of interest groups in the United States in "The Origins and Maintenance of Interest Groups in America," *American Political Science Review* 77 (June 1983): 390–406.

28. However, these groups seemed much less influential in the early years of the Reagan administration than had earlier been the case. See, in this regard, Hugh Heclo, "One Executive Branch or Many?" in Anthony King, ed., *Both Ends of the Avenue: The Presidency, the Executive Branch, and Congress in*

*the 1980s* (Washington, D.C.: American Enterprise Institute, 1983), pp. 26–58.

29. Edward Cox, Robert Fellmeth, and John Schulz, *The Nader Report on the Federal Trade Commission* (New York: Grove Press, 1970). There are a great many task force reports by Nader study groups on other executive agencies, including the National Institute of Mental Health, the U.S. Forest Service, and the Interstate Commerce Commission.

30. See Walter A. Rosenbaum, *The Politics of Environmental Concern* (New York: Praeger, 1973), esp. pp. 172–189.

31. Murray Edelman, *The Symbolic Uses of Politics* (Urbana: University of Illinois Press, 1964).

32. Richard F. Fenno, *The Power of the Purse* (Boston: Little, Brown, 1966). For some interesting illustrations of agency efforts to cultivate congressional goodwill, see R. Douglas Arnold, *Congress and the Bureaucracy* (New Haven: Yale University Press, 1979).

33. Fenno, *The Power of the Purse,* p. 404.

34. Ibid., p. xvi. "No generalizations about Congress are voiced more frequently or held more firmly than those which proclaim the dominance of committee influence in congressional decision making."

35. John W. Kingdon, *Congressmen's Voting Decisions* (New York: Harper and Row, 1981).

36. See Harold Seidman, *Politics, Position, and Power: The Dynamics of Federal Organization,* 3rd ed. (New York: Oxford University Press, 1980), p. 57.

37. Nelson W. Polsby, *Congress and the Presidency,* 3rd ed. (Englewood Cliffs, N.J.: Prenctice-Hall, 1976), p. 172.

38. G. Russell Pipe, "Congressional Liaison: The Executive Branch Consolidates Its Relations with Congress," *Public Administration Review* 26 (March 1966): 17, and Abraham H. Holtzman, *Legislative Liaison* (Chicago: Rand McNally, 1970).

39. Marver H. Bernstein, *The Job of the Federal Executive* (Washington, D.C.: Brookings Institution, 1958), p. 115.

40. Morris P. Fiorina, *Congress: Keystone of the Washington Establishment* (New Haven: Yale University Press, 1977).

41. For an argument to this effect, see David Mayhew, *Congress: The Electoral Connection* (New Haven: Yale University Press, 1974). There is some evidence, however, of increasing congressional interest in the oversight function.

42. See Roy P. Fairfield, ed., *The Federalist Papers* (Garden City, N.Y.: Doubleday Anchor edition, 1961), esp. Federalist No. 51.

43. Halperin, *Bureaucratic Politics and Foreign Policy,* p. 221.

44. For a review of the origins and historical development of OMB, see Larry Berman, *The Office of Management and Budget and the Presidency, 1921–1979* (Princeton: Princeton University Press, 1979).

45. The evolution of the budget bureau from its professionalized past to its politicized present is traced by Margaret J. Wyszomirski, "The De-Institutionalization of Presidential Staff Agencies," *Public Administration Review* 42 (September/October 1982): 448–458.

46. Wildavsky, *The Politics of the Budgetary Process,* p. 42.

47. See Arthur Maass, *Muddy Waters* (Cambridge: Harvard University Press, 1951).

48. See Norman Wengert, *Natural Resources and the Political Struggle* (Garden City, N.Y.: Doubleday, 1955), p. 52.

49. See Charles M. Hardin, *The Politics of Agriculture* (Glencoe, Ill.: Free Press, 1952). For a recent analysis of the USDA's role in agricultural politics, see Graham K. Wilson, *Special Interests and Policymaking: Agricultural Policies*

    *and Politics in Britain and the United States of America, 1956–70* (New York: John Wiley, 1977).

50. For an account of the development of the Pick-Sloan plan, see Henry C. Hart, *The Dark Missouri* (Madison: University of Wisconsin Press, 1957), pp. 120–135.

51. Jones, "The Limits of Public Support," p. 503.

52. U.S. Senate, 87th Cong., 1st Sess. *Organizing for National Security.* Study submitted to the Committee on Government Operations, United States Senate, by its subcommittee on National Policy Machinery, Jan. 28, 1961 (Washington, D.C.: U.S. Government Printing Office, 1961).

53. See Sol Levine and Paul E. White, "Exchange as a Conceptual Framework for the Study of Interorganizational Relationships," *Administrative Science Quarterly* 5 (March 1961): 583–601.

54. David Davis, *How the Bureaucracy Makes Foreign Policy: An Exchange Analysis* (Lexington, Mass.: Lexington Books, 1972).

55. Morris Janowitz, *The Professional Soldier* (New York: Free Press, 1960), pp. 3–16.

56. The modern development of the national administrative apparatus in the United States is closely examined in Stephen Skowronek, *Building a New American State: The Expansion of National Administrative Capacities, 1877–1920* (Cambridge: Cambridge University Press, 1982). Cf. also William E. Nelson, *The Roots of American Bureaucracy, 1830–1900* (Cambridge: Harvard University Press, 1982).

57. Bernard Brodie, "The Scientific Strategists," in Robert Gilpin and Christopher Wright, eds., *Scientists and National Policy-Making* (New York: Columbia University Press, 1964), pp. 240–256.

58. Huntington, *The Common Defense,* p. 147.

59. For a discussion of these differences between rural and urban states, see Robert B. Highsaw, "The Southern Governor — Challenge to the Strong Executive Theme," *Public Administration Review* 19 (Winter 1959): 7–11. For descriptions of the role of state administrators, see Joseph A. Schlesinger, "The Politics of the Executive," and Ira Sharkansky, "State Administrators in the Political Process," in Herbert Jacob and Kenneth N. Vines, eds., *Politics in the American States* (Boston: Little, Brown, 1971), pp. 210–237, 238–271.

60. Wallace S. Sayre and Herbert Kaufman, *Governing New York City* (New York: Russell Sage Foundation, 1960), p. 732.

61. Robert A. Dahl, *Who Governs?* (New Haven: Yale University Press, 1961).

62. Edward C. Banfield, *Political Influence* (New York: Free Press, 1961), and M. Kent Jennings, *Community Influentials* (New York: Free Press, 1964). For a comprehensive survey of the role of state and local bureaucracies, see Douglas M. Fox, *The Politics of City and State Bureaucracy* (Pacific Palisades, Calif.: Goodyear, 1974). See also the analysis of urban bureaucracy and the ways in which it differs from bureaucracy in other sectors of government by Matthew A. Crenson, "Urban Bureaucracy in Urban Politics" in J. David Greenstone, ed., *Public Values and Private Power in American Politics* (Chicago: University of Chicago Press, 1982), pp. 209–245. Crenson argues that urban bureaucracies are "relatively immune to the direct pressures of clientele groups and organizations" (p. 218).

63. For an excellent discussion of recent developments in New York, see Martin Shefter, "New York City's Fiscal Crisis" in Charles H. Levine, ed., *Managing Fiscal Stress* (Chatham, N.J.: Chatham House, 1980), pp. 71–94. Shefter presents an intriguing analysis of the way in which fiscal crisis in New York shifts power from elected to nonelected officials.

# CHAPTER FOUR

# Differentials in Agency Power

Though all administrative agencies have at least some of the professional and political assets upon which bureaucratic power depends, these agencies vary a great deal in their capacity to influence policy decisions. Some agencies are extraordinarily gifted in their ability to achieve their goals, but others often seem to be stepchildren of the executive branch. At the lowest ebb of its power, an agency may come to be "an object of contempt to its enemies and of despair to its friends." [1]

Several factors help to shape these variations in agency power. The nature of an agency's expertise is of strategic importance, for not all bureaucratic skills command equal respect in the community. Moreover, agencies differ greatly in their constituencies. Some organizations enjoy the support of more influential groups or have fewer powerful enemies. They may be equal under law, but agencies are not equally blessed with either expertise or strong cohorts of political support.

Along with these basic resources of expertise and clientele support, two factors are highly instrumental in determining the political effectiveness of an administrative agency. One is its organizational vitality. Because of their mission or the dedication of their personnel, some agencies generate more energy than others. The second of these instrumental factors is the quality of leadership with which an agency is blessed. However well endowed it may be in other respects, an agency that is not effectively led will fall far short of its potential influence. Obviously, these elements are related. One quality of good leadership, for example, is the ability to arouse enthusiasm in an agency's rank-and-file members, and their zeal in pursuing its purposes.

The factors that help to shape differentials in agency power can thus be sorted out, yet there is no easy way in which the effectiveness of one source of power can be weighed against another. No common unit of measurement makes such comparisons possible. This problem arises in all efforts to measure power or influence.[2] It is not, for example, very feasible to use the outcomes of disputes between agencies having apparently different sources of power as a test of the relative value of two kinds of power. In the United States at least, abundant resources make it possible to have power contests in which all participants gain at least some of their original objectives. In any case, an agency may draw power from several sources, and no one can tell how much of an agency's success should be attributed to bureaucratic expertise, strength of constituency, organizational vitality, or skillful leadership.

## Varieties of Bureaucratic Expertise

All administrative agencies have some expertise in the functions they perform, but not all bureaucratic skills exact equal deference from the community. In some areas the notion of expertise is lightly regarded. Fields like education and diplomacy have many self-styled "experts" but very little of what an outsider would necessarily accept as expertise. Or the amount of expertise available in the private sector of society may equal or outweigh that which a government organization commands. In cases of this sort, a public agency is not in a strong position to use its special skills as a source of influence over public policy.

Where there is a lack of respect for the intrinsic function that an agency performs, the search for clientele support can be particularly intense, because a strong constituency is imperative for a public agency whose technical proficiency is not held in high esteem. In such a situation an agency may easily become, in Burton Clark's words, a "precarious organization" — constantly obliged to curry public favor in order to survive.[3] In the California adult education program that Clark studied, the administrators found it very difficult to adhere to professional standards in the educational field, because of the constant need they faced to satisfy their clientele. Because adult education lacked legitimacy as part of the regular educational program, survival depended upon ability to attract a noncaptive student body. Decisions on curriculum and personnel came to be based on student demands rather than professional criteria. As Clark explains it: "The adult schools are torn between being a service facility and a school enterprise ... acceptance is sought on the basis of service rather than on intrinsic educational worth and professional competence." [4]

As a source of power, expertise reaches its fullest development in organizations that have skills on which society is critically dependent. Scientists and military officers are in a highly advantageous position today to command respect for their talents. Professionals in each of these groups exercise powers that may have life-or-death consequences for the citizen. For the military professional, the deference that the public accords may be the product of fear as well as respect, because military organizations alone among public agencies have the capacity to take over physical control of the apparatus of the state. Feit calls them "armed bureaucrats." [5]

The ascendancy of military professionals within the bureaucracy seems, however, to be a more pronounced characteristic of underdeveloped than of advanced societies. In the so-called emerging nations, the military bureaucracy is in a commanding position in the state because it is the only well-trained elite and is the most efficiently organized institution in the country.[6] In this context, the military bureaucracy is not subject to effective restraint by either a system of political parties or the countervailing power of civilian agencies. The temptation to seize control of the state is strong, and military coups have, therefore, been prominent in the politics of underdeveloped nations.

In a highly industrialized society like the United States, however, with an extremely well organized and highly literate population, the influence of the military is offset by that of various other groups and organizations. The military is only one of many skilled professions, and its dominance even in national security policy cannot be ensured. The standing of any bureaucratic role is thus shaped in part by the stage of political development a society has reached.

It also varies a good deal from one period to another in society. Prior to World War II, American foreign policy was very much the exclusive preserve of the professional diplomat. Following the outbreak of hostilities, however, the military began to exert increasing influence on foreign policy decisions, and since the war other professions have also come to exercise influence over such decisions. As a result, the Department of State has been hard put in recent years to maintain its hegemony in foreign policy. The skills of a diplomat may be much less relevant to negotiation of a nuclear test ban treaty than those of a nuclear physicist. The department has also had to confront the fact that, with the growing importance of the president's National Security Adviser and his highly professional staff, the White House itself has become a major center of diplomatic skills.

Changes in the state of knowledge play an important part in bringing about these alterations in the status of a professional group. The emergence of a new managerial science in recent years — operations research, systems analysis, and other associated techniques — has brought a group of management specialists to the fore in public as well as private organizations. During the Kennedy administration these specialists helped civilian strategists impose their will on military professionals in decisions involving arms development. Against such software weaponry as cost-effectiveness ratios, traditional military tactics as taught at the service academies proved virtually helpless. In the Nixon years a similar group of management experts had a large part in the administration's effort to cut back welfare expenditures.[7]

Two characteristics are especially valuable in enhancing the influence of any body of experts within a bureaucracy. The first is possession of a highly technical body of knowledge that the layman cannot readily master, and the second is capacity to produce tangible achievements that the average citizen can easily recognize. This combination of obscurity in means and clarity of results seems an irresistible formula for success for any professional group.

Since World War II, the natural scientists have been the group most strongly exhibiting these two characteristics in bureaucracy. Although these scientists may not be quite the "new priesthood" some writers claim, still there is no doubt about the prestige and public respect in which the so-called hard sciences are today held.[8] This standing rests in part upon the awe with which scientific wizardry is regarded by the general public, and in part upon the fact that the natural sciences have been — in their primary areas — extraordinarily successful in obtaining results, whether in developing nuclear weapons, exploring space, or conquering disease.

Scientific or engineering agencies whose power rests upon their esoteric knowledge include NASA, the National Science Foundation (NSF), and NIH. The professional employees of these agencies are masters of arcane bodies of knowledge that the public cannot readily fathom. Such agencies trade on an air of magic and mystery associated with what they do, and the public tends to accept that their activities are mostly beyond its comprehension. Though not altogether immune to outside influence, such agencies are more resistant to it than other bureaucracies. The forms of control to which they are primarily subject come from within the organization — the norms of scientific investigation, for example, as enforced by the professional community to which their most skilled employees belong.

Among social scientists, only economists have achieved comparable standing in recent years in the prestige and influence of their expertise in the framing of public policy.[9] Their role is most visible in the work of the Council of Economic Advisers, an agency charged with chief responsibility for making recommendations to the president on the larger economic issues of the day, such as controlling inflation or reducing unemployment. But it is also apparent in the increasing use of economic skills in other areas of administration, especially the cost-benefit analysis and program evaluation used in making decisions on allocating budgetary resources among administrative agencies.

The field of administrative regulation, long dominated by lawyers, is another area in which economists have been very influential. Recent efforts to improve the performance of regulatory agencies have shifted from concern over the process through which regulation is carried on, especially its fairness, to emphasis upon results — the influence regulation is having on the health of the economy. This change has put economists as well as lawyers at the center of regulatory decision making. (Other groups such as environmental experts have also moved to the fore in the regulatory process.)

As with natural scientists, the power of economists results from their specialized discipline and their demonstrated capacity to help elected officials make the hard choices that the development of public policy entails. To be sure, these hard choices have not always achieved successful results. But managing the economy is an inescapable necessity for every modern government, and this elevates economists, whatever the limitations of their craft, into prominent administrative roles.

Of expertise generally as a source of bureaucratic power, it must be said that recent years have seen considerable erosion in its authority, as the confidence of the public in many kinds of experts has diminished. People have become more aware that a great many environmental hazards to which they are now exposed flow from advances in chemistry and other scientific fields. Military professionals failed to deliver the results expected in Vietnam or the Iranian rescue mission in 1980, and economists have been unable to come up with solutions for the simultaneous onslaught of inflation and unemployment in Western economies. Cities have continued to decay in spite of the best efforts of urban planners, and social workers have been baffled by the phenomenon of "permanently poor" inner-city residents. In the private sector as well, people are now prepared to challenge through malpractice suits the competence of professionals to whom they would once have automatically deferred.

Hugh Heclo traces the extent to which government policy making is now dominated by "policy elites," but he suggests that these experts disagree so much that they undermine each other's professional credibility. The public thus becomes increasingly skeptical of the competence of its seers. As a result, Heclo writes:

> the non-specialist becomes inclined to concede everything and believe nothing that he hears. The ongoing debate on energy policy, health crises, or arms limitation are rich in examples of public skepticism about what "they," the abstruse policy experts, are doing and saying. While the highly knowledgeable have been playing a larger role in government, the proportion of the general public concluding that those running the government don't seem to know what they're doing has risen rather steadily.[10]

There is perhaps no better illustration of the "high-tech" character of many policy debates than the discussion today in this country and abroad of nuclear arms control. For the most part participation by experts in this debate has seemed to confuse more than enlighten the public. A cynic might suggest that it is sometimes designed to have this effect — the less the public understands a problem, the more likely it is to turn it over to experts for a solution.

But however skeptical people may recently have become about expertise, their dependence on it has certainly not diminished. None of the social, economic, and political pathologies with which public agencies must grapple, such as crime, environmental deterioration, or international conflict are going to disappear in the years ahead. Bureaucratic expertise, however limited its value may now seem in a great many areas, will remain one of society's chief means of coping with problems it can never altogether solve.

## ADMINISTRATIVE CONSTITUENCIES

The most obviously important characteristic of any agency's constituency is the effective size of its political following. Differentials in agency power are often alleged to rest more than anything else on the number of people an agency serves as well as upon the strategic dispersion of this clientele around the country. Comparing the relative influence of the Corps of Engineers and the Bureau of Reclamation upon water resource policy, Arthur Maass traces the superior influence of the corps precisely to its providing significant services to a larger and more strategically dispersed clientele.[11] Although the bureau's irrigation orientation has confined its activities mainly to the western part of the United States, where rainfall is often sparse, the corps performs not only irrigation but also navigation, flood control, harbor dredging, and other water resource functions, which give it a substantial following in every section of the country.

The number of congressional districts or states in which an agency's activities are significant often provides a convenient measure of an agency's clientele, where this yardstick is appropriate. The power of the Department of Defense in American politics in recent years has often been calculated in just this way. Observers have linked the department's influence to the number of congressional districts in which defense contracts are significant in the local economy. A measure of the department's potential influence in the Senate rather than in the House can be derived by identifying the number of states in which domestic industries depend heavily upon defense contracts.

Among federal agencies that distribute grants to states and localities, it is common to allocate this federal largesse as broadly as possible across the country as a means of building political support. This is the practice even with project grants, where federal administrators are empowered to decide which states or localities will have their applications for financial assistance approved. Instead of targeting grants where the need is greatest, or the merit of the application most compelling, these administrators commonly adopt a formula designed to ensure that every section of the country gets its "fair share" of federal aid. Hale and Palley point out that "administrators place a premium on building geographically broad support for programs to avoid criticism during congressional oversight and appropriations hearings." [12]

For any agency, whether it distributes grants-in-aid or not, the size and dispersion of its clientele has a very significant bearing upon its influence, and every agency is understandably interested in increasing the geographical spread of its support. The Department of the Interior has traditionally been regarded in American politics as devoted primarily to the interests of the West. The department's program heavily emphasizes water resource and public land management activities that are chiefly of concern in the western states, and in deference to this geographical identification the secretary of the interior has customarily been selected from the West. When the Bureau of Outdoor Recreation was placed under its jurisdiction, however, the department for the first time gained an administrative foothold in the metropolitan areas in the Northeast, where both the population and the demand for outdoor recreation have enormously expanded. This added clientele gave the department an opportunity to serve substantial population groups in a part of the country in which it had not previously had a significant role.

The breadth of an agency's following is not, however, the sole determinant of its ability to provide an agency with political support. To measure the scope of an agency's power, it is necessary to do more than determine how many followers the agency can muster in its own behalf. However large it may be, a clientele that is weak in other salient respects will not be in a position to give effective political assistance. A small clientele that is highly self-conscious and dedicated to the pursuit of tangible objectives that it shares with the agency can be much more helpful than a large clientele that has neither of these characteristics. Consumers as a group represent as large a following as any agency could reasonably hope to command, and yet agencies representing consumers have traditionally been in a weak political position, primarily because consumers lacked self-consciousness as a group, were poorly organized, and usually did not have strong identification with agencies set up to serve their interests.

This situation changed dramatically when public interest organizations began to make their weight felt in the political system.

Consumer advocates like Ralph Nader and public interest lawyers have now given the needs of consumers continuous representation in Washington to compete with the lobbying efforts of producer groups in Congress and in the corridors of executive agencies. Nader has been involved in organizing so many groups as to become in effect a public interest conglomerate. It may no longer be true, as it once was, that even though "all citizens are consumers, their role as consumers is not nearly as important to them as is their role as producers." [13] Still, after reaching a high point in the early 1970s, the consumer movement seemed to recede, and an attempt to establish a specialized consumer protection agency was defeated in the House of Representatives in 1978.

Lack of cohesion in its clientele may also be highly disadvantageous for an administrative agency. Through much of its early history, the National Labor Relations Board suffered greatly from the split in the trade union movement between the AFL and the CIO. The agency often found itself caught in a crossfire between the rival labor organizations it was trying to protect even while it was attempting to fend off attacks from employers hostile to its very existence.

It might be assumed ordinarily that as the size of an agency's clientele decreases, its ability to provide the agency with effective support will diminish. This is not, however, always true, because a clientele that is dwindling may become, precisely because it is losing its own position of power in society, even more dependent upon a government agency and the services it provides, and hence more intensely devoted to it. The intensity of its clientele's commitment may thus be no less important to an executive agency than the size and cohesion of its following.

Of course, from the point of view of an administrative agency, no clientele is worse than one whose members are not included within the American voting population. In its successive incarnations in various organizational forms, the foreign aid agency has been gravely disadvantaged by the fact that it serves foreign groups that do not participate in American elections. That it has been subject to reorganization so many times testifies to the weakness of its support, because agencies like the Corps of Engineers that serve strong clientele groups have generally been able to resist having reorganization imposed on them. In an effort to counter this weakness, the agency's promotional efforts have stressed that many American economic interests benefit from goods produced in this country for eventual shipment overseas as part of foreign aid. In this way the agency seeks to transform its clientele of foreign nationals into an indigenous constituency.

At the opposite extreme is a clientele such as the agricultural population, which has always enjoyed high prestige in American society. The view that Jefferson first articulated has never been seriously challenged in American or for that matter in any other society: "The proportion which the aggregate of the other classes of citizens bears in any State to that of its husbandmen, is the proportion of its unsound to its healthy parts." The most remarkable aspect of this attitude is that it has so strongly persisted even though each decade has seen a steady decline in the size of the farm population.[14]

Certainly the strong position of the Department of Agriculture in American bureaucracy has not been appreciably weakened by this decline. The department's ability to maintain its strength even in the face of a sharp contraction in its clientele can partially be attributed to the prestigious position of the farmer in American life, and the image of farmers that so many urban residents share with them as a chosen people. For many Americans a sentimental tie with the country remained long after they had voted with their feet for urban life by moving to the city.

The structure of a constituency is also important in determining its value to an agency. We have seen that an administrative agency deriving most of its support from one outside group often finds itself excessively dependent upon the group for political support. As a result the group may acquire the power to prevent an agency from pursuing goals that the organization regards as professionally desirable. There is no certainty that the objectives of a bureaucracy will always mesh with the goals of an interest group upon which it depends for political support. Hence, an agency generally prefers to draw its support from a variety of groups, no one of which possesses substantial control over it. Interest groups, on the other hand, favor organizational arrangements that enable them to monopolize rather than share membership in an agency's constituency. Hence, they resist reorganization proposals that would force them to share an agency's attention with other groups. It was for this reason that the trade unions opposed so vigorously President Johnson's 1967 proposal to merge the Departments of Commerce and Labor.

The term constituency ordinarily includes all groups which perceive themselves or which are perceived by an agency as being affected by its activities. Some of these groups benefit from an agency's work — they are commonly referred to as its clientele. For other groups the agency may be a source of penalties or sanctions — they may look upon it with hostility, or even desire its elimination.[15] An agency's power thus rests on a favorable balance of attitudes toward it among the public. It needs not only to win friends but to avoid acquiring enemies. In this respect, regulatory agencies are usually worse off than agencies performing service functions. If it vigorously enforces the law it is charged to administer, a regulatory agency is bound to incur the displeasure of segments of the public upon which it imposes constraints. But if it fails to enforce the law aggressively, the groups on whose behalf regulation is being carried on may be peevishly critical of the agency for not doing more to advance their interests, or, as often happens, these friendly groups may leave the agency to fend for itself once it has been established.

A service agency, on the other hand, ordinarily generates benefits for the groups it serves, even though the eligibility rules and other requirements it imposes as preconditions for receiving these benefits may be hard to distinguish from the restraints of a regulatory body. From the perspective of its clients, a welfare organization may in fact look more like a regulatory than a service organization. This would certainly be the perspective of many of those receiving assistance under the AFDC program (aid for families with dependent children). Some of the state agencies administering this program include nocturnal visits as one of the methods by which they determine whether such families include a male breadwinner — a circumstance that would render a family ineligible for AFDC assistance. But in this case as in others the groups it serves usually constitute a solid core of support for an agency's survival and development.

Of course, there are great differentials in constituency support among such service agencies. Taxpayer opposition to increasing the costs of government programs is as high today as it has been at any time in the past, and this resistance is not evenly apportioned among government services. Educational agencies carry on activities designed to achieve an equality of opportunity that is one of the most highly cherished values in American society, and they perform this role for all strata of society. On the other hand, welfare agencies administer a function that sharply conflicts with the traditional American norm of individual self-reliance, and they perform it for lower income groups that are unorganized, demoralized, and often, as nonwhites, vulnerable to racial prejudice. Public opinion surveys customarily show that welfare expenditures enjoy less public support at the local level than any other government activity. Suggesting an element of racial prejudice in this attitude is one study which reports that "services whose clienteles are most widely thought to be racial minorities tend to be favored the least." [16]

The socioeconomic status as well as the geographic distribution of a clientele may thus be a strategic factor contributing to its influence. Eugene Lewis suggests that the impoverished sectors of the community can be more appropriately describd as "victims" than as clients, or constituents of the public organizations on which they depend — that is to say, they have little or no political clout through which they can influence the way in which these organizations treat them.[17] Such political weakness guarantees that the agencies serving their needs will also be fragile.

When all is said and done, the best situation for any agency may be to serve a constituency that might be called elite. This may be a group like bankers, who stand very high on the socioeconomic ladder. But, because prestige can accrue from occupation as well as social standing or wealth, the elite constituency may also be a professional group in high-status fields like science or medicine. The National Institutes of Health and the National Science Foundation derive much of their strength and standing as government agencies from the prestigious professional clientele with which they interact.

But for any administrative agency, the character of its constituency may vary greatly among governmental jurisdictions. A school system in a large urban center may be constantly embroiled in controversy resulting from conflicting demands by different neighborhoods for better services, a tension that is particularly acute today between white and nonwhite segments of the community. In a neighboring suburb, inhabited mainly by well-to-do citizens, the educational system may be at the pinnacle of the administrative pyramid — the system well financed, the teachers highly paid, and the clientele loyal and devoted to the welfare of the schools.

In summary, the ideal administrative constituency from the point of view of an executive agency is large and well distributed through all strata of society or in every geographic section of the community. It should include devoted supporters who derive tangible benefit from the services an agency provides. An administrative agency should not, however, depend excessively upon the support of any segment of the community, nor should it carry on activities that threaten the interests of substantial outside groups. Finally, the economic or social activities in which its clientele engages should be in accord with the highest-ranked values in the society. To the extent that it has these characteristics, an agency's constituency is in a position to give it effective support toward achieving its goals.

We have seen that agencies serving the poor are in a particularly vulnerable position in American society. This vulnerability contributes to a strong tendency in American public policy for activities initially set up exclusively for the benefit of lower income groups to be converted eventually into programs serving the middle class as well. This happened in higher education, where a system of financial assistance for economically disadvantaged students was gradually broadened to provide similar aid to middle-class students.[18] Only in this way, administrators argued, would the program enjoy enough political support to survive attacks from groups opposed to any federal intervention in higher education. A program serving only the poor would be in constant political jeopardy because of the weakness of its clientele. When the Reagan administration launched its stringent budget-cutting measures in 1981, it was most successful with programs designed to assist impoverished groups with little political clout. It eventually shied away from cutting programs with a substantial middle-class constituency.[19]

## ORGANIZATIONAL ESPRIT

During the Kennedy administration, no agency of the national government ascended more rapidly into the limelight or more quickly won the esteem of all sections of the community than the Peace Corps. Established in 1961 to help meet the need of the so-called emerging nations for trained manpower, the agency quickly established itself as one of the major successes of the Kennedy years. Talented young men and women whose aspirations would not normally be directed toward the public service flocked to the Peace Corps from all directions even though the remuneration they received was meager and the conditions under which they were expected to work abroad were uncomfortable and often hazardous. To be sure, this kind of organizational élan can be transitory. The attraction of the Peace Corps for young people was an early casualty of American involvement in Vietnam.

But it is nonetheless clear that an agency can derive enormous value by performing a function that excites the imagination of the community. Analyzing the structure and operation of bureaucratic systems, Amitai Etzioni identifies three kinds of power that organizations exercise over their members — coercive, remunerative, and normative.[20] Coercive power is the threat or actual use of physical control; remunerative control is the use of material rewards as incentives; and normative power rests on manipulation of "esteem, prestige, and ritualistic symbols."

From the perspective of this analytical scheme, the Peace Corps in its heyday was a striking illustration of a normative organization in the public service. Its power rested on the enthusiasm it was able to generate for its functions from both those who worked for it and the community at large. It is not, of course, the only example of a public agency with this kind of appeal. Elite military organizations, with a distinctive tradition and a membership drawn from volunteers rather than conscripts, have traditionally provided the most vivid displays of normative commitment in public bureaucracy. At various periods of American history the Marine Corps generated a great deal of zeal and dedication. The Green Berets, a special military force created during the Kennedy administration to combat guerrilla warfare, had similar organizational vitality until it was discredited by some of the roles it was called upon to play in Vietnam. The Peace Corps is an unusual demonstration of the capacity of a public agency to ignite enthusiasm without resort to regimental flags, legends of courage, feats of valor, or the other appeals of military life.

Another way to describe the power of an organization like the Peace Corps is to say that it is charismatic, insofar as it evokes a faith and enthusiasm that transcend rational calculation. This use of the term "charismatic," however, differs sharply from that of Max Weber, from whose work the concept of charisma in modern social science is largely derived. In Weber's view, bureaucracy and charisma were antithetical terms. Social movements that began under the leadership of a charismatic leader became bureaucracies as their functions were rationalized and routinized in formal organizations

— the sect in the end became a church. "In its economic substructure, as in everything else," Weber wrote, "charismatic domination is the very opposite of bureaucratic domination." [21]

It is possible to discern within bureaucratic organizations themselves a tendency to move from an initial period of enthusiasm and energy to a subsequent stage when the organization becomes routinized and gradually loses a good deal of its original élan. If this transition cannot, in Weber's terminology, be said to mark an evolution from charisma to bureaucracy, it certainly resembles such a transformation closely. Describing the "life cycle" of the independent regulatory commissions of the national government, Marver Bernstein shows that once such agencies have gotten past an initial stage of youthful zeal, they undergo a devitalization that culminates in old age and a period of debility and decline. "Complacency and inertia appear as inevitable developments in the life cycle of a commission. Although tradition, precedent, and custom can harden into blind routine in all types of social organization, the commission seems to be peculiarly susceptible to the disease of 'administrative arteriosclerosis.'" [22]

This tendency of established organizations to become wedded to routines and resistant to change has frequently been used to justify creation of new institutions to administer innovative programs. The establishment by President Franklin D. Roosevelt of "alphabetical" agencies such as the WPA and the CCC in the early 1930s has been widely interpreted as a step on his part to ensure that New Deal programs would be carried on with vigor and enthusiasm, rather than being smothered in the red tape and lassitude with which existing agencies might approach their administration.

For Roosevelt, this problem presented itself in a particularly acute form with the Department of Agriculture. Before Roosevelt's time, the department was strongly committed to a philosophy of confining the national role in agriculture to educational activities channeled through the state extension agencies. The new programs Roosevelt contemplated involved a direct relationship between the national government and the farmer in such fields as rural electrification and soil conservation. Faced with this dilemma, Roosevelt's characteristically diplomatic solution was to establish his programs initially in independent agencies such as the Rural Electrification Administration and the Soil Conservation Service. Then, as these agencies gained sufficient administrative experience and outside political support to ensure their viability, he allowed them to be incorporated into the department. By this time the agencies were too strong for the department to sabotage their mission. On the contrary, it was a reasonable expectation that the agencies might infuse the department with their own more enthusiastic attitude toward new agricultural programs.[23]

When the Peace Corps was being planned in the Kennedy administration in 1961, there was support for putting it in the Agency for International Development (AID). The head of the Peace Corps, Sargent Shriver, and his aide, Bill Moyers, strongly opposed this move. Moyers talked to Vice President Johnson about it:

> Moyers suggested to his former boss that the people who had been presiding over foreign aid pooh-poohed the idea that young Volunteers could contribute to a field which had been dominated by professional experts. Since they could not block the new President's special fancy outright, Moyers thought they were trying to do the next-best thing: absorb it. The result would be a stifling regulation and submersion of an idea which needed to be conspicuous in order to attract Volunteers and public support. The new wine should not be poured into an old bottle.[24]

Moyers asked Johnson to make the case for an independent Peace Corps with the president.

> Johnson responded immediately and made the case with such force that Kennedy finally agreed. The former Senate Majority Leader reminded the President of the foreign aid program's deep-rooted unpopularity in Congress and convinced him that the Peace Corps, with its fresh appeal, needed its special identity and a life of its own in order to have any chance to succeed.[25]

However, a cautionary note should be added. The Office of Economic Opportunity (OEO) was set up in the Johnson administration as an independent agency, and its autonomy seemed, if anything, an obstacle to the successful achievement of its goals.[26]

Organizational esprit depends very much upon an administrative agency's developing an appropriate ideology or sense of mission, both as a method of binding outside supporters to the agency and as a technique for intensifying its employees' loyalty to its purposes. Some of the conservation agencies have developed a very mystical sense of mission about their function in the administrative apparatus — preserving some priceless asset such as the forests, the soil, natural beauty, or historic monuments.[27] This ideology is a powerful force not only in maintaining the esprit of conservation agencies, but also in heightening their influence on the development of public policy. In modern times the Environmental Protection Agency (EPA) strongly exemplifies this traditional conservationist mystique in its efforts to prevent air and water pollution.

Of course, not all agencies perform functions that allow them to develop either a persuasive ideology or a sense of esprit. Any agency may seek by public relations activity to glamorize its role, but wholly artificial esprit is difficult to sustain. A great many agencies have a forceful sense of mission early in their history, but tend to lose this crusading spirit as they mature. A few agencies have managed to sustain it through much of their history, and cases of administrative renaissance are certainly not unknown. But when enthusiastic performance is sought in the public service, the common practice has been to create new agencies in order to achieve it. This is one of many reasons why bureaucracies tend to multiply.

Public organizations are subject to decline, but they rarely die. If nothing else, an agency provides a livelihood for its employees and a cluster of outside interests aggregate around its functions and support their continuance. Certainly compared to private organizations, public agencies have a very low mortality rate. Indeed, some failing private organizations — colleges and museums, for example — are taken over by the government and given a new lease on life as public institutions. Even though critics of bureaucracy often feel that many government agencies should declare bankruptcy, there is no record of any agency actually doing so and going out of business. (Some regulatory agencies, however, like the Civil Aeronautics Board, did support the steps taken during the 1970s to reduce their own regulatory authority and even initiated some of the deregulatory measures adopted.)[28]

The event that occurs most commonly with a devitalized public agency is not death but resurrection. A change in the political climate suddenly gives new life to its dormant functions. The U.S. Employment Service, having had a very active role in World War I finding workers for war industries, went into a state resembling suspended animation in the 1920s. But with the collapse of the economy and the depression of the 1930s, the employment service became an extremely important part of the Roosevelt administration's attack on poverty.

Faced with threats to their survival, public agencies often change their functions or alter the way in which they perform their traditional tasks. After long criticism from consumer groups that felt the agency had been captured by the business interests it was supposed to regulate, the Federal Trade Commission began in the 1970s to be much more vigorous in enforcing consumer protection legislation. During the same period, the Corps of Engineers, under heavy fire for neglecting environmental interests in its water resource projects, became much more environmentally conscious in planning and operating its dams and other facilities.[29]

## ADMINISTRATIVE STATECRAFT

The role of leadership in shaping the success of any organization is as elusive as it is important. On frequent occasions the ability of an administrative agency to achieve its goals and to secure the resources necessary for its survival depends directly on the identity of its leader. Early in the Truman administration, Congress made it very clear that the Federal Security Agency would never obtain the status of an executive department as long as Oscar Ewing was at the head of the agency. When Eisenhower became president, and Ewing was succeeded by Oveta Culp Hobby, the proposal to transform the FSA into the Department of Health, Education, and Welfare quickly won congressional approval.

The story of Jesse Jones as secretary of commerce during the Roosevelt administration provides equally compelling evidence of how important leadership is to an organization. During Jones's tenure as commerce secretary, his ability to command support in Congress and devoted allegiance from the business community was legendary. When Roosevelt removed Jones and appointed Henry A. Wallace as secretary of commerce in 1945, Congress immediately proceeded to remove from the department one of its most important constituent bureaus, the Reconstruction Finance Corporation. And the decisive factor in bringing about this reduction in the department's jurisdiction was the replacement of Jones by Wallace.[30]

Thus, personal antagonisms that its executive generates may be extremely costly to an administrative organization.

Of course, in appraising the role of leadership in an administrative agency, we must recognize that leadership in public administration, like leadership in any organizational context, is very much situational — dependent, that is, on factors in the environment other than the leader himself. Jones was successful as secretary of commerce in large part because his department served a business constituency which was strong in Congress, and still very powerful in the outside community, but which looked upon Jones as its only real protagonist in the executive branch. The influence Jones exercised was thus a product not only of his own capacities but of the circumstances that prevailed when he was in office. For the conservatives in Congress and the country, Jones was a solid and sensible figure in an otherwise radical administration. For President Roosevelt, Jones was a natural bridge to a constituency in which his administration was generally very weak. Jones's personal attributes thus fit perfectly the role he was called upon to play. He would have been far less successful as secretary of labor than he was as secretary of commerce, because none of his skills could have overcome easily the hostility in Congress and the business community toward the Department of Labor when he was in office.

During the Kennedy administration Sargent Shriver was widely heralded as the model of successful leadership while he was head of the Peace Corps, and many newspaper accounts celebrated the dexterity with which he handled relations with Congress and the public in advancing the cause of the agency over which he presided. After Johnson became president, however, Shriver took over responsibility for the Office of Economic Opportunity (OEO), an agency established to carry on "the war against poverty" in the United States. This assignment produced very little in the way of adulatory comment. But the presumption is strong that Shriver was no less able a leader in the OEO than he was in the Peace Corps. The critical change was in his assignment — from an agency carrying on generally popular activities abroad that threatened no important interests in the United States to an agency caught in the turbulence generated by radical militance and conservative backlash in major American cities.

In short, though an institution is often described as the lengthened shadow of a man, it may be equally correct to say that executives are the lengthened shadow of an institution, because their own prestige may primarily reflect the appeal of the organization they command. Consequently, executives who value their reputation for leadership must choose well the institution in which they exercise their talents, to make certain that their abilities and the institution's needs match. Or better yet, an institution can be one of those rare organizations which so well meets the mood of its time that it is assured of success. But in the end administrative executives, like Machiavelli's Prince, cannot escape the hand of chance upon the success of their career — being in the right place, at the right time, with the right tactic. As Machiavelli described the fate of leadership: "men are successful while they are in close harmony with Fortune, and when they are out of harmony, they are unsuccessful." [31]

Perhaps no executive career in recent years rose or fell more steeply than that of Robert McNamara, secretary of defense for both Presidents Kennedy and Johnson. Under Kennedy and in his early service with Johnson, McNamara was the very model of the modern executive: highly knowledgeable, sure of his decisions, and conveying an air of competence that overawed his opponents. But as the Vietnam War worked its inexorable way toward the top of the department's agenda and public attention, McNamara found himself in charge of a failure — whether of his own contrivance or not made little difference. His reputation waned steadily, and by the time he resigned very little was left of the original radiance in his image. Never was the power of Machiavelli's *fortuna* better exemplified.

But knowing this much about the accidental factors that help determine the success of leadership, we find it is nonetheless true that executives in quite similar positions in public bureaucracy often have varying success at their jobs. It seems reasonable to conclude, therefore, that the capacities of a leader can make a difference to an administrative agency and that we can identify some skills associated with the effective performance of the executive role in an administrative organization that contribute to a leader's success.

Leadership skills in the public bureaucracy are of principal value in two areas of an executive's responsibility: (1) externally, in ensuring a favorable response to the agency from the outside groups and organizations that control resources upon which it depends; (2) internally, in maintaining the morale of the agency's employees and their commitment to its goals. In large organizations, these external and internal responsibilities of leadership are so complex and demanding that they customarily require considerable specialization, and the organization is in effect run by an executive cabinet in which some individuals are given responsibility for handling external relations, and the duties of others relate primarily to the internal functioning of the institution. Even under this cabinet system, however, agency heads retain responsibility for the success or failure of the organization, as well as the privilege of choosing their executive associates and of deciding which of their responsibilities they will delegate and to whom.[32]

All studies on the external responsibilities of leadership stress that an executive must be able to create confidence in his or her own personal and technical capacities among those who control resources the agency needs. The executive must be a "trusted leader" upon whom others can rely. Fenno's work on the appropriations process suggests that the willingness of Congress to grant an agency the funds it needs to carry on its work is very much determined by the confidence legislators have in the head of the organization.[33]

Agency heads, therefore, need to know what techniques will help instill confidence in their abilities within their constituency. On this subject we have some guidelines, especially on an executive's relationships with legislators, a key elite with which the heads of public agencies normally deal. Studies in this field agree that at appropriations hearings and in other contacts with lawmakers, the head of an agency should display such qualities as honesty and clarity in presenting an agency's needs, a passion for economy in using public funds, and simplicity and affability of manner in personal contacts.[34]

In executive-legislative relations, it is essential for an agency executive to recognize that congressmen are in a highly vulnerable political position, subject as they are to removal from office by defeat at the polls. For a legislator, survival depends upon maintaining good relations with constituents. This is why so many members of Congress give top priority to their *ombudsman* role, helping constituents handle problems they may have with the federal government. The least agency heads can do is to avoid, whenever possible, decisions and actions by their agency that may be embarrassing to members of Congress in their own district.

On the more positive side, they can take steps to lend the legislator some forms of political support. The agency can routinely provide aid and information for members of Congress in handling questions that constituents bring to their office, or it may help legislators advertise themselves by arranging for a well-publicized trip to a field installation, or by allowing them to announce from their office the negotiation of a government contract, or the establishment of an administrative facility that will redound to their credit in their own district. If reciprocity is the unwritten if not altogether inviolable law of political life, an executive can reasonably expect that these investments will bring a high rate of political return.

As important as any skill an executive may possess is ability to communicate successfully with the agency's constituency. Very often the language in which an organization's policies are explained and defended is as important to their success as the policies themselves. In higher education, state university officials have frequently demonstrated great skill in using metaphors that will bring the distinctive needs of higher learning home to their agricultural constituencies. In a celebrated defense of academic freedom, the regents of the University of Wisconsin stressed their belief that "the great State University of Wisconsin should ever encourage that continual and fearless *sifting and winnowing* by which alone the truth can be found" (italics supplied). A similar sensitivity to the importance of using appropriate language in addressing a constituency was displayed in Texas where, in protesting against efforts to force the university to spend money from its reserve fund, an administrator vehemently declared that this policy would deprive the school of its "seed-corn." [35]

In dealing with their various publics executives must not only have the qualities associated with leadership but they must display these qualities as dramatically as possible. Victor Thompson has shown how dramaturgy is needed for the leader's role to be effectively performed.[36] Successful executives must be skilled in impression management — the ability to convey to others a sense of their own capacities. State university presidents have concentrated in recent years not only on being more efficient but also on convincing others that they are running an efficient institution:

> ... it is of vital importance that the state legislature and the taxpaying public ... be convinced of the soundness of univer-

sity operations. Under the pressures of competition from other state institutions, a large state university is often forced to put on a dramatic show of scientific objectivity in order to justify its requests for continued support, even though the dramatic props — elaborate formulas, statistical ratios, and so on — may have very little to do with the way in which decisions are actually made within the academic establishment. As one administrative vice-president remarked about the preparation of the university budget, "We simply use the displays that give us the best image...." [37]

As they have developed in recent years in higher education, techniques of scientific management may thus serve not so much to manage the university as to manage the impression that outsiders have about the university.

External relations occupy a good deal of the time and attention of the head of any administrative agency. Just as the duties of the president of the United States have increasingly focused on foreign affairs, so too executives in public agencies find themselves drawn more and more into community relations activity, negotiations with other organizations, and a variety of other roles that involve interaction between their organization and its environment. Herbert Simon writes:

> Observation indicates that, as the higher levels are approached in administrative organizations, the administrator's "internal" task (his relations with the organization subordinate to him) decreases in importance relative to his "external" task (his relations with persons outside the organization). An ever-larger part of his work may be subsumed under the heads of "public relations" and "promotion." [38]

One of the most interesting studies of leadership in American administration is by Eugene Lewis on the careers of three of the most eminently successful bureaucratic leaders in modern times: Hyman Rickover, J. Edgar Hoover, and Robert Moses.[39] Each of these nonelected executives was far more powerful than most of the elected officials with whom he dealt, and each was a leader whom elected officials dared to oppose only at great peril to their own political safety.

Perhaps the most striking characteristic these bureaucratic leaders shared was a genius for publicity. They did not confine themselves to the outskirts of power, remaining out of sight while making the decisions that elected officials announce, which is the role that bureaucrats have traditionally been expected to play in democratic government. Quite the contrary, Rickover, Hoover, and Moses were extraordinarily adept at publicizing themselves and their agencies' programs. Each became a highly visible figure in American public life, courted by the media and looked upon as government celebrities.

Two factors especially contributed to the ability of these leaders to attract so much public attention. For one thing, they alone seemed to command the expertise necessary to deal with problems the public regarded as both important and threatening. It is striking how much more confidence the public had in these bureaucrats than it did in elected officials, and how often it looked to them for leadership in defining and coping with major issues of public policy.

Along with their expertise in dealing with specialized problems, these bureaucratic leaders were also highly adept in using managerial strategies necessary either to advance their interests or to fend off adversaries within rival bureaucracies. None could have functioned as successfully as he did by policy expertise alone. In each case, such expertise was supplemented by a sure instinct for picking out advantageous and defensible organizational terrain and avoiding program assignments that might jeopardize either their own public standing or the autonomy of their agency.

Although external relations have thus become dominant in successful performance of the executive role, internal responsibilities have by no means disappeared. Apart from attending to the purely housekeeping chores of management, an executive has such major internal responsibilities as arousing the enthusiasm and energy of the organization's employees for its objectives; settling disputes and conflicts of interest within the organization; and generally serving as a catalyst for continuous appraisal of programs and inauguration, whenever necessary, of innovations in policy.

Of course, these external and internal dimensions of leadership are not altogether unrelated. If an executive comes to be regarded as politically weak in dealing with outside forces — a Cabinet member who has very little clout at the White House, for example — this external weakness will ultimately redound to an executive's discredit within his or her own organization. Hugh Heclo writes of political appointees who are not successful in building external support: "Experienced bureaucrats recognize that such appointees leave their agencies and programs vulnerable to more politically aggressive competitors elsewhere. In this sense, career officials will typically prefer a strong if unpleasant advocate to an amiable weakling." [40]

But very often, their internal and external responsibilities pull executives in opposite directions. Decisions they make to maintain harmony with the outside world may alienate the organization's employees. Conversely, the employees may push an executive in directions that make it more difficult to maintain good relations with outside groups. While he was secretary of state, Dean Acheson staunchly defended Department of State employees against attacks on their loyalty in Congress, a position that did little to endear him in influential circles of the legislature. On the other hand, his successor, John Foster Dulles, improved his relations with Congress by taking steps to tighten security procedures in the department. Because some of these steps were regarded as detrimental to their interests by Department of State employees, Dulles improved the department's external image at the price of drastically weakening his own standing with its career staff.[41]

Maintaining a good relationship with the White House generates especially strong cross-pressures upon the head of an executive agency. A president expects loyalty from agency executives both to himself and to his programs. This expectation may put the executive on the horns of a dilemma if the president's policies are unpopular with either the agency's employees or its constituents. They may expect instead that the head of their agency will become a protagonist of their goals and objectives, even if it means alienating the White House.

Two of President Nixon's appointees lost their Cabinet seats as a result of these cross-pressures. Robert Finch, HEW secretary, found himself caught between White House expectations that he would help reduce welfare expenditures and the strong view within the department that these programs should not be scuttled. As a result of this and other issues, the polarization between the White House and the agency became acute, and Finch resigned, escaping by his departure a face-to-face meeting with aroused departmental employees. A similar conflict led the White House to demand that Walter Hickel resign as secretary of the interior.

As these illustrations suggest, conflict with the White House has become the chief threat to a bureaucratic executive's survival in American national politics today. At midterm it has now become almost conventional for presidents to fire at least some of their Cabinet executives, as both Joseph Califano, President Carter's secretary of Health, Education, and Welfare, and Alexander Haig, President Reagan's secretary of State, were to discover in recent administrations.

The chief impetus for firing Cabinet members seems to come from White House staff members, who compete with departmental executives for control over presidential decisions and the direction of policy in every administration. Although Congress has often been viewed as the principal adversary with which the heads of executive agencies must cope, recent history suggests that getting on the wrong side of the White House staff is more likely than any other development to shorten an executive's career in Washington. It has become easier for a Cabinet member to be fired for real or assumed disloyalty to the White House than for incompetence on the job.

But quite apart from these problems of dealing with the White House staff, hard choices confront all executives in the day-to-day management of their agency, including the need to balance uncertain gains against certain losses, or perhaps to choose the lesser of two evils when which of the two is the lesser evil is precisely the issue in doubt. In national agencies, all executives are confronted by a board of directors in the form of a congressional committee that has many members who — for partisan reasons — wish them ill rather than well. The president, whom they nominally serve, may well abandon them if they get into trouble. The agency's employees are career bureaucrats who may choose to ignore the head of an agency or to undermine his or her authority, and they cannot easily be disciplined or dismissed. It is in this refractory environment that administrative statecraft must be carried on in the public service, and it is perhaps most remarkable not that many fail, but that some succeed.

## PURSUIT OF POWER

If the sources of administrative power are varied, so too are the motives that animate administrative agencies in their quest for primacy. Most clearly apparent is the desire of agencies to strengthen their position in order to enhance their ability to achieve such manifest goals as better medical care, a more effective system of crime control, or prevention of water pollution. The statutory objectives of public agencies today are wide-ranging, and in order to fulfill its mission, every agency requires an adequate supply of resources to employ personnel and meet the other expenses of organizational life. These resources are easier for the strong to obtain than the weak, and so power is sought not for its own sake but because it is prerequisite for carrying on an effective program.

But along with these manifest goals by which agencies are inspired in their quest for power, other latent objectives are also commonly present. At the upper reaches of the hierarchy, agency executives may have a strong desire for power as a means of gratifying a personal need for status and the other perquisites of office. For rank-and-file personnel, the pursuit of power may be primarily designed to ensure continuation of more tangible rewards important to them as civil servants, including adequate salaries, pensions, working conditions, and fringe benefits. As we saw earlier, the preservation and improvement of these remunerative incentives have become the special responsibility of public employee organizations.[42]

These varied motives for which power is sought are not necessarily incompatible, of course. An agency may be most capable of serving the public interest when it is led by an ambitious chief executive, who may, while using the agency as a springboard for advancing his own career, bring it to new levels of achievement in its capacity for public service. A private vice, as Adam Smith long ago saw, can often be transformed into a public virtue. The community may also be as well served if rank-and-file employees are allowed to gratify their continuing desire for improvements in remuneration and working conditions. It is certainly reasonable to expect that satisfied employees will be more efficient than those who cherish grievances. Public and private interests may thus dovetail neatly, in the best of all possible administrative worlds.

There are, however, less attractive possibilities. The personal goals of agency employees may gain a distinct priority over the purposes for which an organization was created. Public organizations and officials are often in a position to justify their pursuit of power by disinterested criteria like service to the public, when in fact power is sought only to advance the selfish interests of the organization's members. A general may launch a military campaign during a war at great cost in the lives of his own troops, which will contribute very little to the fortunes of his country but a great deal to the success of his own career. Staff members of any organization may push for adoption of policies that reflect not the needs of any significant segment of the public they service, but their own desire for power, prestige, or security. In this category are pessimistic assessments by the armed forces of a potential enemy's capabilities or intentions that are contrived in order to pressure the public into supporting an expansion in the strength of the military.

This kind of distortion occurs in its most flagrant form in cases of administrative corruption, where some members of a law enforcement agency may look upon its power not as a means of protecting the safety of the public, but as an instrument for extorting tribute from the individuals engaged in the illegal activity they are supposed to be suppressing. In situations of this kind, the needs of the public recede altogether, and administrative power is used merely to advance the private goals of agency employees.

Of course, the private interests that members of an administrative agency serve need not necessarily be their own. We have seen that many public agencies, either in their initial establishment or eventual development, are mainly satellite organizations for outside groups. A licensing board may be set up for the manifest public purpose of ensuring that professional standards are adhered to in the practice of a skill. But in fact the latent function of such an agency may be to limit entry into the profession to protect the economic position of present members of the group, thus inflicting costs upon the public it is supposed to serve.

Whatever its motives may be in seeking greater authority, an agency must constantly reckon with the fact that an expansion in jurisdiction does not always result in an expansion of power. Bureaucracies are often pictured as implacably imperialist in their desire to expand their jurisdiction, but there are occasions when an agency may increase its power by narrowing, or refusing to expand, its legal authority. According to Wallace S. Sayre and Herbert Kaufman, the agencies in New York City's government

> compete to avoid program assignments that are especially difficult and controversial. The Commissioner of Hospitals and the Commissioner of Correction have both tried to prevent lodging responsibility for treatment of narcotics addicts in their departments, and the Department of Health has been restive

under burdens of building inspection the Commissioner and the Board of Health would generally prefer to have placed entirely on the Department of Buildings.[43]

Thus, in the quest for power an agency's strategy has to be one of optimizing rather than maximizing its jurisdiction. Activities which have weak political support, are inordinately expensive, or which divert an agency from its essential purposes may be liabilities rather than assets from the point of view of an agency's power balance. As head of the FBI, J. Edgar Hoover was extraordinarily adept at keeping his agency from becoming involved in law enforcement activities — narcotics, for one — that might weaken its standing with the public.[44]

Sometimes the most significant limitation upon an agency's ability to grow comes not from external forces but from its own image of itself — its sense of its proper mission. In the United States the State Department has allowed other agencies to expand and occupy territory in the foreign affairs field primarily because the foreign service professionals who dominate the department take a narrow view of their role, confining it to diplomacy and excluding such matters as scientific research and economic forecasting that have become increasingly relevant to foreign policy.[45] The Defense Department, on the other hand, has been much more willing to recruit professionals in areas other than the military, or to upgrade the skills of military officers in order to protect its hegemony over the resolution of national security issues that increasingly turn on expertise in science and technology.

Perhaps the most embarrassing kind of jurisdiction an agency can acquire is control over an activity that is anathema either to its own sense of its mission or to its constituency. This was the unhappy fate of the Department of Labor in 1963, when it was put in charge of administering the Landrum-Griffin Act, a statute designed to protect union members from abuses of power by their own officers. Prior to its passage, this legislation had been bitterly fought by the labor organizations that are the department's chief source of outside support, and after its enactment the Department of Labor discharged its responsibilities in this area with minimal enthusiasm.[46] In cases of this kind, administration of the law may become in fact nullification of the law, or as some would put it, sabotage of its intent.

Executive agencies, like all contestants in the struggle for power, operate with imperfect knowledge of the kind of strategy that will advance their interests. An agency may strongly resist measures that it feels will reduce its authority, only to find, when the changes actually take place, that no such effects have occurred. In advancing or protecting its power interests, as on other matters, an executive agency thus operates within the limits of what Herbert Simon calls "bounded rationality." [47] The course of action best calculated to achieve its objectives is not always clear to it.

# *Notes*

1. Norton Long, *The Polity* (Chicago: Rand McNally, 1962), p. 50.
2. See Robert A. Dahl, *Modern Political Analysis*, 3rd ed. (Englewood Cliffs, N.J.: Prentice-Hall, 1976), pp. 25–53.
3. Burton R. Clark, "Organizational Adaptation and Precarious Values: A Case Study," *American Sociological Review* 21 (June 1956): 327–336.
4. Ibid., p. 335.
5. Edward Feit, *The Armed Bureaucrats* (Boston: Houghton Mifflin, 1973).
6. See Lucian W. Pye, *Aspects of Political Development* (Boston: Little, Brown, 1966), pp. 172–187.
7. Ronald Randall, "Presidential Power versus Bureaucratic Intransigence: The Influence of the Nixon Administration on Welfare Policy," *American Political Science Review* 73 (September 1979): 795–810.
8. For an argument that scientists are in a way a new "power elite," see Don K. Price, *The Scientific Estate* (Cambridge: Harvard University Press, 1965), and Ralph E. Lapp, *The New Priesthood* (New York: Harper and Row, 1965). Cf. also, however, the searching critique of this elitist thesis by Daniel S. Greenberg, "The Myth of the Scientific Elite," *The Public Interest* 1 (Fall 1965): 51–62.
9. Cf. the discussion of this point in Harold L. Wilensky, *Organizational Intelligence* (New York: Basic Books, 1967), pp. 106–107.
10. Hugh Heclo, "Issue Networks and the Executive Establishment" in Anthony King, ed., *The New American Political System* (Washington, D.C.: American Enterprise Institute, 1978), p. 119.
11. Arthur Maass, *Muddy Waters* (Cambridge: Harvard University Press, 1951). For the best general analysis of interest group influence in executive decision making, see Grant McConnell, *Private Power and American Democracy* (New York: Alfred A. Knopf, 1966).
12. George E. Hale and Marian Lief Palley, *The Politics of Federal Grants* (Washington, D.C.: Congressional Quarterly Press, 1981), p. 78. Project grants are here distinguished from formula grants, under which states and localities have automatic entitlement to financial assistance.
13. Mark V. Nadel, "Unorganized Interests and the Politics of Consumer Protection," in Michael P. Smith and Associates, *Politics in America* (New York: Random House, 1974), p. 149.
14. The literature bearing on this point is extensive. See, for example, Richard

Hofstadter, *The Age of Reform* (New York: Alfred A. Knopf, 1955), Henry Nash Smith, *Virgin Land* (Cambridge: Harvard University Press, 1950), and Leo Marx, *Machine in the Garden* (New York: Oxford University Press, 1964).

15. Cf. Matthew Holden, "'Imperialism' in Bureaucracy," *American Political Science Review* 60 (December 1966): 944. In Holden's view, the constituency of any agency head includes "those who support his ends, those who oppose his ends, and those who wish to intervene for what he regards as 'irrelevant' purposes." Holden also looks upon groups of employees within the agency as "internal constituencies" from the point of view of an agency executive. Murray Edelman, on the other hand, defines administrative constituencies as "the groups which have the power to remove the incumbents or kill the organization if it does not respond to their wishes." See "Governmental Organization and Public Policy," *Public Administration Review* 12 (Autumn 1952): 277. Unfortunately, from their own point of view, not many groups served by an administrative agency actually have the power "to kill the organization if it does not respond to their wishes," though they can certainly devitalize it by withdrawing their support.

16. David O. Sears and Jack Citrin, *Tax Revolt: Something for Nothing in California* (Cambridge: Harvard University Press, 1982), p. 49. On public attitudes towards various government activities, see also table 3.2, p. 48.

17. Eugene Lewis, *American Politics in a Bureaucratic Age* (Cambridge: Winthrop, 1977), pp. 20–24.

18. Sally A. Davenport, "Smuggling in Reform: Equal Opportunity and the Higher Education Act 1965–80" (unpublished Ph.D. dissertation, Johns Hopkins University, 1982).

19. "The biggest impact by far of the Reagan budget cuts was on the poor." So writes Richard P. Nathan, "The Reagan Presidency in Domestic Affairs" in Fred I. Greenstein, ed., *The Reagan Presidency: An Early Assessment* (Baltimore: Johns Hopkins University Press, 1983), p. 58. David Stockman, the Reagan administration's early spokesman on economic affairs made the same assessment. See William Greider, "The Education of David Stockman," *Atlantic Monthly*, December 1981, p. 50.

20. See Amitai Etzioni, *A Comparative Analysis of Complex Organizations* (New York: Free Press, 1961).

21. See H. H. Gerth and C. Wright Mills, eds., *From Max Weber: Essays in Sociology* (New York: Oxford University Press, 1946), p. 247.

22. Marver H. Bernstein, *Regulating Business by Independent Commission* (Princeton: Princeton University Press, 1955), p. 101.

23. An analysis of Roosevelt's strategy with respect to administrative organization may be found in Arthur Schlesinger, Jr., *The Coming of the New Deal* (Boston: Houghton Mifflin, 1959), pp. 533–552. See also Harold Stein, ed., *Public Administration and Policy Development* (New York: Harcourt Brace, 1952), p. 624. For a somewhat different view, see Theda Skocpol and Kenneth Finegold, "State Capacity and Economic Intervention in the Early New Deal," *Political Science Quarterly* 97 (Summer 1982): 255–278.

24. Harris Wofford, *Of Kennedy and Kings: Making Sense of the Sixties* (New York: Farrar, Straus & Giroux, 1980), p. 265. Wofford provides an interesting account of the enthusiasm surrounding the Peace Corps during the early days of this "anti-bureaucratic bureaucracy."

25. Ibid., p. 266.

26. See, in this regard, the excellent discussion of OEO's experience in Emmette S. Redford and Marlan Blissett, *Organizing the Executive Branch: The Johnson Presidency* (Chicago: University of Chicago Press, 1981), pp. 77–106.

27. Herbert Kaufman, *The Forest Ranger: A Study in Administrative Behavior* (Baltimore: Johns Hopkins Press, 1960).

28. Herbert Kaufman made a careful study of the longevity of bureaucratic organizations. See *Are Governmental Organizations Immortal?* (Washington, D.C.: Brookings Institution, 1976).

29. See Daniel A. Mazmanian and Jeanne Nienaber, *Can Organizations Change?* (Washington, D.C.: Brookings Institution, 1979).

30. For a brief but enlightening analysis of Jones's career as secretary of commerce, see Richard F. Fenno, *The President's Cabinet* (Cambridge: Harvard University Press, 1959), pp. 234–247.

31. See *The Prince* in Machiavelli, *The Chief Works and Others*, vol. 1, trans. Allan Gilbert (Durham, N.C.: Duke University Press, 1965), p. 92.

32. However, some businessmen complain strenuously that their power of appointment as government executives is too limited to permit them to control their departments. See W. Michael Blumenthal, "Candid Reflections of a Businessman in Washington," *Fortune*, January 29, 1979, pp. 36–49.

33. Richard F. Fenno, *The Power of the Purse* (Boston: Little, Brown, 1966), pp. 288–291.

34. See, in this regard, ibid., pp. 285–291, and Aaron Wildavsky, *The Politics of the Budgetary Process*, 3rd ed. (Boston: Little Brown, 1979), pp. 74–84.

35. Malcolm Moos and Francis E. Rourke, *The Campus and the State* (Baltimore: Johns Hopkins Press, 1959), pp. 24–25.

36. See Victor A. Thompson, *Modern Organization* (New York: Alfred A. Knopf, 1961), pp. 138–151.

37. See Francis E. Rourke and Glenn E. Brooks, "The 'Managerial Revolution' in Higher Education," *Administrative Science Quarterly* 9 (September 1964): 180–181.

38. Herbert A. Simon, *Administrative Behavior*, 3rd ed. (New York: Macmillan, 1976), p. 217.

39. Eugene Lewis, *Public Entrepreneurship: Toward a Theory of Bureaucratic Political Power* (Bloomington, Ind.: Indiana University Press, 1980).

40. Hugh Heclo, *A Government of Strangers: Executive Politics in Washington* (Washington, D.C.: Brookings Institution, 1977), p. 196.

41. See, in this regard, Norman A. Graebner, ed., *An Uncertain Tradition: American Secretaries of State in the Twentieth Century* (New York: McGraw-Hill, 1961), pp. 267–308.

42. The divergence between the goals of individuals and the goals of the organizations of which they are members is a recurring theme in organization theory. See especially the work of Chris Argyris, *Personality and Organization: The Conflict Between System and the Individual* (New York: Harper, 1957), and *Interpersonal Competence and Organizational Effectiveness* (Homewood, Ill.: Dorsey Press, 1962).

43. Wallace S. Sayre and Herbert Kaufman, *Governing New York City* (New York: Russell Sage Foundation, 1960), p. 262.

44. See James Q. Wilson, *The Investigators: Managing F.B.I. and Narcotics Agents* (New York: Basic Books, 1978), p. 169.

45. See Andrew M. Scott, "Environmental Change and Organizational Adaptation," *International Studies Quarterly* 14 (March 1970): 85–94, and John E. Haar, *The Professional Diplomat* (Princeton: Princeton University Press, 1969).

46. A similar case involving the failure of the Federal Power Commission to enforce the Natural Gas Act is cited by Holden, " 'Imperialism,' " p. 945.

47. See Herbert Simon, *Models of Man* (New York: John Wiley, 1957), pp. 196–206.

# Part Two

# *BUREAUCRACY AND PUBLIC POLICY*

# CHAPTER FIVE

# The Policy Process in Bureaucracy

We have examined some of the principal reasons why administrative agencies now play so large a role in the political system. The basic resources upon which administrative power has been shown to depend are (1) possession of a body of knowledge essential to reaching decisions in vital areas of policy, and (2) ability to mobilize an influential constituency. Both technical and political skill can thus help greatly in generating bureaucratic power. An agency's ability to exert influence in the policy process can also be traced to the esprit or vitality of the organization and how effectively it is led. In the more powerful administrative organizations, such as the Federal Bureau of Investigation in its heyday, a position of influence tends to reflect the simultaneous presence of all these assets: a valued skill, strong public support, organizational esprit, and adroit leadership.

In this chapter we will examine the way in which policy making is carried on within bureaucracy. We will look first at the principal groups in administrative agencies that participate in developing policy. Here we confront what might be called the internal politics of bureaucracy, where conflict may break out among individuals or groups inside executive agencies with different perspectives on policy issues. This system of internal politics does as much to shape the character of public policy as does the interaction between agencies and groups outside of bureaucracy. Much of it is hidden from public view and becomes visible only when conflict rises in intensity and "boils over." Participants who are losing out in the struggle over policy within bureaucracy leak information to the outside world in an effort to draw public attention to the dispute and change the outcome in their favor by widening the circle of those involved in the decision.

The second focus in this chapter is the nature of the policy process within administrative agencies. How does government decision making change in democratic societies, and what are its distinctive characteristics when its center of gravity shifts from legislative assemblies to the corridors of bureaucracy? We consider some of the significant ways in which policy making in executive agencies is shaped by the bureaucratic environment in which it is carried on.

## PARTICIPANTS IN BUREAUCRATIC POLICY MAKING

In much of the literature and folklore about bureaucracy, the image we see is that of a unified structure and a uniform perspective. Generalizations about the bureaucrat and the administrative role in government often seem to assume a totally homogeneous outlook among all those working in executive agencies. The word that outside observers most often use to describe bureaucratic organizations is "monolithic."

Viewed from within, however, the picture is far different. A government agency, like any other large and complex organization, can be seen to embrace a variety of points of view that produce diversity in perspective and often generate sharp disputes within its inner councils. Like a family or any other social organization that radiates an image of togetherness to the outside world, an executive agency shows itself on close inspection to be far from uniform in the attitudes and behavior of its members.

More specifically, the ranks of bureaucracy have four sources of cleavage that greatly affect policy development within administrative agencies. The first is usually a sharp difference in the role and attitude of political appointees at the top of the administrative pyramid and the career administrators beneath them. Second, within the ranks of career employees themselves there is frequently a wide divergence in outlook between the professionals who employ the skills with which the agency serves the community, and the administrators whose chief function is keeping the organization in existence. Third, in American bureaucracy there is a possibility for "lateral entrance" of outside experts who may take an advisory or consultative role in the agency's policy deliberations, or temporarily even serve full-time with the agency. These outsiders commonly bring perspectives to the framing of bureaucratic policy that differ from those of career employees. Finally, and quite apart from the varying roles officials play within bureaucracy, differences in personality or psychological orientation toward their work promote diversity in outlook among the staff members of executive organizations.

The power of bureaucratic organizations need not necessarily be exercised by bureaucrats themselves. The political officials who are legally at the helm of an executive organization, as well as the outsiders who may become temporarily involved in its operation, can have far more influence over the direction of an agency's policies than any of its career employees. Thus, the power that inheres in a bureaucratic organization because of its specialized functions and capacities is not always controlled by people who are actually bureaucrats in the true sense of being permanent employees of the agency for which they work. Such permanent employees often find themselves in the unhappy position of having no real voice in their own organization's major policy decisions. This is most likely to occur at the national level when a new president comes to power in Washington who is hostile to an agency's goals.

*Political Executives and the Career Staff.* A relationship that is fundamental to determining policy in any governmental bureaucracy is the interaction between political executives at the top of the administrative pyramid and career officials subordinate to them. In a democratic state political executives usually represent the political party that has been victorious at the polls. In nondemocratic societies they represent the ruling group that has taken power and presides over the destinies of the state. And in both democratic and nondemocratic states some tension and difficulty is a continuing characteristic of relations between career and political cadres.

The European interpretation of the relationship between the political executive and the career administrator has traditionally emphasized the career official's superior influence upon policy decisions. Max Weber contended that "the absolute monarch is powerless opposite the superior knowledge of the bureaucratic expert — in a certain sense more powerless than any other political head.... The Russian czar of the old regime was seldom able to accomplish permanently anything that displeased his bureaucracy and hurt the power interests of the bureaucrats." [1] A similar view was expressed by John Stuart Mill: "Where everything is done through the bureaucracy, nothing to which the bureaucracy is really adverse can be done at all." [2]

In American bureaucracy, however, the relationship between political and bureaucratic officials is far more subtle and complex than the comments of either Weber or Mill might suggest. Although the career official has advantages in this relationship, including continuity in office and greater familiarity with the work of the agency, the political executive is far from powerless. For one thing political executives preside over a hierarchic system in which their office is a primary source of legitimate authority. Whether elected or appointed, the political executive is in a way a symbol of public control over the governmental process. In a society highly impregnated with democratic ideology, as the United States certainly is, this is a formidable source of authority.

Consequently, the tendency is strong for career bureaucrats to tailor their recommendations to fit what they believe are the policy views of the political executive. And once the executive has made up his or her mind on a policy question, these career officials will ordinarily support the decision, even if they disagree with it. To be sure, mavericks in some agencies may publicly challenge their superior's decisions. But though these cases often receive great publicity, they are exceptions to the bureaucrat's general willingness to go along with policies decided upon at a higher level.

During the first term of the Nixon administration, there were several cases of public denunciation of official policy by organized groups of career civil servants. The war in Vietnam was the chief target of this bureaucratic rebellion, but other Nixon policies also came under attack, including a cutback in domestic welfare programs and an apparent weakening in the administration's commitment to vigorous enforcement of civil rights legislation. The protest movement was concentrated in the Department of Health, Education, and Welfare, but was visible in other national agencies as well. This bureaucratic defiance was part of a more general rise in political disaffection while the United States was directly involved in the Vietnam hostilities, but it never involved more than 2 percent of federal employees in Washington. [3]

Usually, bureaucratic opposition to official policy is covert rather than open — guerrilla warfare rather than a frontal assault. Career officials will confide their doubts about the wisdom of the policies being followed by their political superiors to friendly legislators or reporters, or they may alert pressure groups with which they have an intimate relationship that policy changes being contemplated by the administration in power are adverse to their interests. They thus convert disputes with political executives into conflicts between their superiors and outside organizations. In this way, they can pursue their objectives without jeopardy to the forms of bureaucratic life or the safety of their own position. Moreover, by avoiding an open break with their superior, they can continue to pass ammunition to a political executive's critics from the security of their intimate participation in the affairs and deliberations of the agency. In this surreptitious way, career officials can incite political conflict in the outside world without risking their own safety by directly participating in the combat. Many of these tactics were used by career employees at the EPA in their struggles with political appointees during the early years of the Reagan administration.

Such warfare is not a frequent occurrence. More commonly, the relationship between political executives and career officials can be described, in Charles E. Lindblom's terms, as one of "mutual accommodation." [4] Career subordinates have good reason for deferring to their political superior, who is invested with the authority of office in a bureaucratic environment in which rank is an impressive symbol of power. Members of Congress may be prepared to treat departmental executives with familiarity if not contempt. Ordinary bureaucrats are not.

Moreover, while representing the authority of the community in the agency, the political executive also represents the agency in the community. Bureaucrats cannot publicly undermine the executive without risking injury to the organization with which their personal fortunes are linked. They have a stake in his or her success. The political executive is the best salesperson they have for achieving the agency's goals and continuously replenishing its resources. An executive who is truly effective in speaking for the agency will be highly regarded by career officials, whether or not they agree with the executive on policy issues. As secretary of labor during the Nixon administration, George Shultz was greatly respected by departmental officials, even when they were not enthusiastic about the administration's labor policies. Though he remained friendly with the department's trade union constituency, Shultz had extremely good access to the president, and was thus in a strong position to advance and protect the department's interests at the White House.[5]

Of course, political executives cannot run roughshod over the views of their career subordinates. Even if they have the legal power to coerce these subordinates into obedience, they cannot force them to perform their duties enthusiastically, which is essential if the agency is to attain substantial effectiveness. Moreover, career subordinates have a formidable capacity to make trouble for executives in the outside community, as we have seen, and this threat requires political executives to exercise diplomacy in their dealings with these officials. Such diplomacy may sometimes lead a chief executive to call for improved salary and fringe benefits for an agency's staff as a means of purchasing their support for policy goals.[6]

In the formal theory of public administration, the role of the career staff is regarded as primarily that of ensuring competence in the design of policy — they are expected to see to it that the techniques used to achieve goals are the most effective available. In practice, however, the career staff also tends to develop a fine sensitivity to the political pressures to which an agency is subject. A political executive's best advice on how to operate politically may well come from career subordinates. They know their way around the political thickets that surround the agency; political executives may not. Moreover, legislators tend to seek advice on policy questions from career officials, because they often regard these officials as more knowledgeable and trustworthy in answering questions dealing with policy issues than political executives, who may try to defend or protect the party in power. The phrase Herbert Storing uses to describe the role of senior bureaucrats in the governmental process is that of "closet statesmen." [7]

On the other hand, the politically appointed head of an executive agency often has at least as much competence in the agency's area of expertise as the career staff. This happens especially often in agencies like the National Science Foundation, where outside professional groups insist that a top executive with first-rate scientific credentials be appointed. In situations of this sort, a political appointee is expected to take the lead in policy development, while the career officials help avoid political pitfalls in the agency's dealings with the community, Congress, and other executive agencies.

In democratic societies at least, it has traditionally been assumed that public policy should reflect both the needs and desires of citizens, and that the best expert advice and technical skill will be applied in satisfying these aspirations. The conventional wisdom has been that popular preferences should be reflected by political executives, while career civil servants provide the expertise needed to design ways of achieving policy goals. This is the arrangement in British and other parliamentary governments, and it has been endorsed in a number of proposals for reforming the American system. As indicated earlier, however, bureaucracy in the United States tends not to follow this neat division of labor. Career officials are often astute politicians and political executives may have impressive credentials as experts. But it has certainly not been demonstrated that policy decisions in American bureaucracy are any less responsive or less competent just because the actors do not always play the roles assigned to them in traditional democratic theory.

The steady expansion of unionization in the public service in recent years has significantly changed relationships between political executives and career civil servants. The trade unions' attention is mainly focused on "bread and butter" matters for civil servants: wages, working conditions, fringe benefits, and so on. But their power reaches into areas of public policy and executive decision making as well. Unions in New York City have fought efforts by civil rights organizations to restructure the organization and procedures of various agencies so as to make them more responsive to the needs of minority groups.[8]

As this union power continues to grow, particularly at the state and local level of government, it tends to create situations in which union members have dual and sometimes conflicting loyalty — to the department for which they work and the union to which they belong. Strikes, slowdowns, and other techniques available to trade unions are forms of bureaucratic power looming over the landscape of American politics. Of course, as the unsuccessful strike of air traffic controllers in 1981 revealed, political officials can bring lethal sanctions to bear against unions that defy governmental authority — at least at the national level. Most union members involved in this strike lost their jobs, and the union itself, the Professional Air Traffic Controllers Organization (PATCO), was decertified as a bargaining agent by the National Labor Relations Board (NLRB).

Moreover, cutbacks in financial support have now become the order of the day for executive agencies at all levels of government, making it more difficult for unions to bargain as vigorously and successfully as they once did.[9] In a climate of dwindling resources, career officials are not in a strong position to challenge or make demands on their political superiors. Indeed they may actually find themselves making concessions to protect their jobs, and political officials may as a result increase their authority over personnel issues affecting the career staff.

One striking characteristic of American bureaucracy is that, compared to many other political systems, the number of political appointees at the top of executive organizations is quite large. In the overall structure of bureaucracy the political layer is thus much thicker in this country than it is in many parliamentary democracies. As James Fesler writes:

> The United States outdoes all other modern democracies in its provision for change when party control of the executive branch shifts. About 1600 higher positions are filled by political appointment. This contrasts with the approximately 100 top officials in Britain and 360 in France — though 85 percent of France's are drawn from the civil service — that a new administration is entitled to choose afresh.[10]

This characteristic of American administration primarily reflects the successive efforts American presidents have made since at least the days of Dwight Eisenhower to tighten their control over the bureaucracies they confront when they take office by increasing the number of senior officials they can appoint to run the agencies under their jurisdiction. As a result American bureaucracies are commonly more "politicized" than their counterpart organizations in other societies, at least in being subject to heavier layers of control by political executives at the command centers of the organization. This arrangement makes it difficult for high-level career civil servants to play a major role in executive policymaking.

*Professionals and Administrators.* In many organizations in both the public and private sector so-called professional employees are assuming an increasingly strategic role. These are individuals with highly developed skills whose commitment to an organization arises essentially from the opportunity it gives them to practice their specialized craft.[11] Their primary loyalty remains, however, to their own profession, not to the organization, and their attitudes on

many questions are formed by and sometimes peculiar to their discipline. Many professions in the public service — city planners, foresters, social workers, and others — have a distinctive ideology about
policy in their own specialty that springs from a deeply rooted tradition of looking at social problems in a particular way.

City planners have a profound commitment to a city's having a
comprehensive design for its own development to which specific
proposals for urban land use can be related. Social workers often
have similar dedication to the necessity of taking care of the poor
and underprivileged in society, an attitude that, at least in its intensity, sets them apart from other groups in bureaucracy. Foresters,
like other conservationists, have an almost mystical reverence for
the natural resources under their jurisdiction. The founder of a
profession, such as Gifford Pinchot in forestry, may have a place of
honor in its development like that of the first patriarch of a religion.
Like a religious sect, a profession may also have its hallowed mar-
tyrs. Billy Mitchell, for the air force, is a notable example. J. Robert Oppenheimer, for the scientific community, is another.

There is, however, another group of employees within executive
agencies whose work is also essential to their successful operation.
The role and perspective of this group, who are generally described
as administrators, is shaped by the organization in which they function, not by a craft or skill in which they specialize. Within public
bureaucracy such administrators perform two particularly vital tasks.
The first is that of attending to auxiliary functions that are indispensable to the operation of any organization, such as handling
funds and maintaining physical plant and equipment. The second
and more prominent role is coordinating the work of professionals
within the organization and establishing effective liaison with the
community. The latter tasks have pushed administrators into executive leadership in a good many organizations.

Policy as it develops within executive agencies, and within the
government itself, is heavily influenced by pulling and hauling
between professional and administrative points of view. Professionals are primarily committed to attaining the goals that their skill
is designed to achieve. Administrators, if their function is that of
providing staff services, are likely to emphasize economy in use of
resources. This is the common perspective of budget officers and
purchasing officials. In a dichotomy of this sort, professionals care
about effectiveness of policy — achievement of objectives no matter

what the cost. Fiscal administrators, on the other hand, principally aim for efficiency in use of the organization's assets, attaining results with a minimum of the resources upon which there are multiple claims within the organization.[12]

Administrators with more general responsibilities in executive or public relations capacities are likely to be far more sensitive than professionals to the need for compromise in pursuing objectives — the necessity of settling for half a loaf, or of taking the views of other groups and organizations into account in reaching decisions. Such administrators are a force for moderation in the development of agency policies. The qualities needed in this kind of administrative role are a gift for negotiation and diplomacy, which contrasts starkly to the fanatical zeal with which professionals frequently pursue their distinctive point of view.

In looking at the evolution of policy within administrative agencies, it is clear that a great deal of the energy and innovative force in the policy process comes from professionals. True enough, the professional's perspective is often narrow. They commonly have difficulty in seeing a problem in its full breadth and complexity from the confines of their own specialty. Moreover, the inability of professionals to take costs into adequate account in pursuing policy goals, or to follow lines of authority and orderly procedure, is often a source of confusion and conflict within organizations.

But in the end it is professionals who are at the growing edge of policy. It is their skills that give agencies their problem-solving capacity; and their specialty often gives them foresight into the shape of things to come. Returning to the religious analogy, professionals frequently play the role of prophet in the policy process — seeing beforehand problems that lie far ahead. Scientists working in agencies that deal with nuclear energy, weapons development, and space exploration have been able to perform precisely this kind of prophetic function in recent years in developing national science and defense policy.

The importance of their own role often leads professionals to disparage the contribution that administrators can make to an executive agency. From the professional's perspective, the administrator is often looked upon as merely a bookkeeper or, that ultimate insult, a paper shuffler. The professional commonly regards administrative rules and procedures that are designed to promote organizational efficiency as stifling to both energy and imagination, though some professions, such as engineering, appear more comfortable in a governmental or bureaucratic setting than others. But as a rule, professionals believe that organizations should be subject to only loose and flexible supervision, rather than the tight rein that administrators characteristically prefer.

> Irritation over the approval of travel is typical of the administrative "tight rein" against which professionals often rebel. They complain that such controls consume time they should be spending on professional work. One regarded the review of scientific positions (required by the personnel officer) as "a waste of time." ... Still another professional complained of the requirement that he make out officer fitness reports. "[I] do not regard this type of report as relevant to the functions of a scientific research organization." [13]

The stereotype of the professional in the administrator's eye may be no less unflattering. Administrators in many agencies tend to look upon their role primarily as formulating policy with a realism and breadth of perspective that professionals by themselves could never provide. Although these contrasting outlooks engender tension and often conflict within executive agencies, both professionals and administrators have a vital and complementary role in developing policy. If professionals provide such useful ingredients as imagination and technical skill, administrators can help ensure that policy attains maximum results with the resources available, and that it is sensitive to the needs and interests of the community groups that will be affected by it.

The latter consideration is particularly important, since professional groups habitually frame programs in areas for which they are responsible in ways that may be more advantageous to themselves than to the groups affected by these policies. Administrators in city hospitals can represent patients or their families in developing policies governing medical care, and at state universities administrators can play a similar role in seeing that courses and schedules are designed with the interests of the student as well as the professor in mind.

Of course, administrators sometimes develop excessive attachment to formal rules and procedural regularity in ways that are highly disadvantageous to clients, such as the hospital administrator who insists that patients be properly checked in and their financial status determined before they are treated. In a context of this sort, clients may turn to professionals and obtain sympathy and help in breaking through organizational red tape.

The split between professionals and administrators has been examined here primarily as it operates between groups playing different roles within executive agencies. This cleavage in viewpoint can also characterize the relations between agencies themselves, however. In the national government, agencies that employ a high percentage of professional employees, such as NSF, NASA, and NIH, have a highly professional outlook that can generate sharp disagreement with an agency like GSA, which, by contrast, deals primarily with the housekeeping arrangements incidental to the work of other government organizations.

Of course, disparity in viewpoint between two professionalized agencies is equally possible. It is in fact such disagreement that provides the raison d'être for one of the most important roles that administrators play — mediating conflict between professional groups. Even in the United States, resources are not unlimited and priorities have to be established. Because all professional groups would regard the needs of their own area as having first claim in any decision on allocation, the role of the administrator in helping to determine the order in which needs will be met is a strategic source of influence over public policy. It is perhaps the greatest paradox of the policy-making process within bureaucracy that professionals, who have such great influence when program objectives are being determined, have so much less power over allocation of the fiscal resources that enable objectives to be realized.

One current trend that is bound to substantially influence the future role of professionals in organizations is their increasing tendency to divide in a very partisan way on policy issues. This tendency has been the source of acrimony and even disruption at meetings of professional societies like the American Association for the Advancement of Science, as dissidents demand that their professional association take a strong stand on such issues as population control, safety of nuclear reactors, or air and water pollution standards. One dimension of this dissent is the growing support among younger professionals for whistle-blowing. The practice may become even more common in the future, as more government employees take advantage of recent legislation encouraging whistle-blowing.

Among many professional groups a cleavage is also emerging

today between hard-liners and soft-liners. This is not unlike the distinction so often drawn during American involvement in the Vietnam War between "hawks" and "doves" — the hawks favoring a tough military posture as appropriate for the United States in dealing with the North Vietnamese, and the doves being more favorably disposed toward negotiation and accommodation. On many other issues of public policy one can discern a similar division among professionals. Some ecologists favor very strict measures to protect the environment and others are willing to modify standards of environmental control in order to achieve other policy goals — such as development of energy resources. Likewise in law enforcement, some hawks favor a very tough stand in dealing with criminals, while doves in the same professional area emphasize rehabilitating criminals and ameliorating the social and economic conditions such as unemployment out of which crime grows. In all these cases the direction of public policy is very much determined by the shifting balance of power between hawks and doves within a professional community.

*Bureaucracy: Insiders and Outsiders.* In the United States today, it is possible for many individuals with high standing in, say, one of the scientific professions, to participate directly in the process of policy making within executive agencies without committing themselves to full-time government employment. This is evident especially in the case of university scientists who can retain positions in academic life while having a voice in the development of policy within the inner councils of government agencies.

Commonly, the outsider gains this entree by serving in an advisory capacity to a government agency. The National Science Foundation and other professional agencies reach into private life to fill the membership of innumerable committees that help make governmental decisions on fellowships, grants to support scientific research, and the location of new laboratories or other research facilities. Many scientists thus serving as advisers have considerably greater eminence in their own professions than scientists who are full-time government employees. As a result, these outside scientists tend to be deferred to on policy questions by their professional colleagues in executive agencies.

Outsiders holding advisory positions within bureaucracy have been at the center of some of the most celebrated policy disputes within the national government since World War II. The struggle over whether the United States should attempt to develop a hydrogen bomb had its focus in the General Advisory Committee to the Atomic Energy Commission — a committee made up of distinguished scientists from outside the government. No event did more to trigger discussion and reappraisal of national security policy in the United States in the 1950s than the report of the so-called Gaither Committee, a presidential study group drawn from business and other institutions outside the government that President Eisenhower commissioned to study the defense needs of the United States.[14] Thus, the American system of government "has developed its public service in such a way as to avoid creating a closed bureaucracy." A variety of groups are given an opportunity "to help determine public policy and to assist in its execution through an elaborate system of advisory machinery." [15]

One agency that has made extensive and effective use of outsiders is the Social Security Administration. Martha Derthick, in her revealing analysis of the way in which social security policy has developed in this country, shows that advisory councils have played a critical role whenever major policy changes have been contemplated.[16] To be sure, the views of these outsiders were heavily influenced by agency executives, and the recommendations they presented were commonly those the agency wanted to have made. What the advisory councils did, however, was something the agency could not do for itself. They helped build political support for major changes in policy. This model was followed by the Reagan administration when in 1982 it established an advisory commission to draft proposals for reforming the Social Security Act, as well as in 1983 when the so-called Scowcroft Commission was established to rally support for some of the administration's more controversial defense strategies.

Several factors help to account for the expanding role of outsiders in the internal deliberations of executive agencies. To some extent, it is a product of necessity. In many of the more highly skilled fields, public agencies cannot recruit enough high-caliber personnel for full-time employment to meet their needs. The outsider, whether serving as adviser, consultant, or on temporary assignment with the agency, helps fill the gap created by this employment problem. Many talented outsiders will serve executive agencies on a temporary or ad hoc basis who could never be attracted to full-time government employment.

Moreover, the role of outsiders is such that they can contribute to the policy-making process qualities it would otherwise lack. Having a secure position in an institution other than the agency itself, outsiders can speak their mind without editing their thoughts for fear of reprisal by their administrative superiors in government. This independence of judgment helps promote diversity of opinion within a bureaucratic environment in which the pressures toward conformity may otherwise be very strong. A president or the head of an executive department may also bring in outsiders as a protection against domination by the vested interests and institutional ideologies of the agencies under their supervision. In this context, outsiders can play the devil's advocate, speaking for points of view that would not ordinarily enter the discussion were it not for their presence. There is, of course, no guarantee that outsiders will always exhibit such independence of judgment. The money or prestige that outsiders accrue from their consulting role may be very important to them, and they may hesitate to take positions too strongly critical of the agency from which they derive these benefits.

But at the very least these newcomers will not have been so thoroughly indoctrinated in the agency's institutional point of view as to be incapable of looking at problems in any but the traditional way. A chief disadvantage of the practice of confining policy positions to members of the career staff is commonly believed to be that they have spent their working lives in the service of the agency and their attitudes have been entirely shaped and limited by its norms and experiences.

To be sure, this lateral entrance may entail substantial costs. For one thing, any freshness of viewpoint that an outsider brings to an agency will almost certainly be accompanied by a lack of experience in dealing day-to-day with the problems that are its main interest. Originality may thus have to be purchased at some cost in practical judgment. Although long-time agency administrators may be inbred in their perspective, and have lost their zest for innovation, they may also have a keen eye for pitfalls in launching a new program.

The practice of allowing outsiders to make a lateral entrance into high-level positions without having served time in the ranks also negatively affects the morale of permanent employees who have spent their entire careers in the service of the agency and who see themselves being excluded from some of the most responsible jobs in the organization. In the long run lateral entrance can thus make it substantially more difficult to attract imaginative and capable personnel to permanent positions within the agency and in this way may actually reinforce mediocrity in the career staff. Some observers would cite the State Department as an example of an organization in which this development has occurred.

From an agency's perspective, there is also some irresponsibility attached to an adviser's position, because the outsider does not have to put a policy into effect in an often hostile environment, or live with the consequences of a decision once it has been made. Many advisers may also have private attachments or interests that color the advice they give the agency. The Dixon-Yates controversy, whose tremors shook American politics so heavily in the 1950s, had its origin in the fact that an adviser to the Bureau of the Budget was in a position to benefit personally from the recommendations he made to the government.[17]

"Conflict of interest" of this sort is an enduring problem in the use of outside advisers or consultants by executive agencies. The possibility that these outsiders may benefit personally from their privileged influence over decision making by membership on advisory committees has led to enactment of a number of statutes designed to regulate this role, such as the Federal Advisory Committee Act of 1972, requiring that the meetings of some 1,400 committees advising national agencies be open to the public.[18]

From the outsider's point of view, there are also liabilities attached to this position. Though you can give advice, you have no real authority to see that this advice is taken. As an adviser or consultant, the outsider may find that trying to get an agency to follow suggestions is a good deal like trying to push a boxcar uphill. It is this consideration that finally leads some outsiders to accept temporary government service in one of the agencies that provide employment opportunities through which outside professionals can exert some continuing influence at high levels of bureaucratic decision making.

An executive agency as well as an individual may find it difficult to exercise real influence when the authority for putting policy decisions into effect rests in other hands. Consequently, when an agency's power is primarily advisory, it may be forced to establish effective liaison with operating agencies in order to prevent its advice from being stillborn. The Council of Economic Advisers, established primarily to provide the president with competent advice on how best to preserve the health of the domestic economy, has also found it necessary to establish close and continuing relations with a number of executive agencies that wield important powers affecting economic stability. Chief among these agencies are the Bureau of the Budget, the Federal Reserve Board, and the Department of the Treasury. Ultimately, the economic advisory council's effect on monetary and fiscal policy depends upon its ability to exercise influence over these organizations as well as upon the president.

The practice of involving outsiders in the internal deliberations of executive agencies is a tradition in American bureaucracy. Its openness to outside penetration is in fact one of the distinctive characteristics of bureaucracy in the United States. As discussed earlier, this is most often seen as the problem of capture of a government agency by outside interests. But it also presents the danger of co-optation by the government of individuals who might otherwise be the best-informed critics of official policy. Taking a potential critic into the camp in this way may thus be regarded as an adroit technique through which the Department of State, for example, can muffle public debate in controversial areas of foreign policy. This is an illustration of Harold Lasswell's "restriction by partial incorporation," [19] buying off potential critics by giving them a place in court.

But the custom of bringing outsiders into government is more than a method by which officials may draw the teeth of their opposition. It is also a means of infusing official policy with the values and attitudes of the community, or at least informed segments of it. More than that, it is an avenue through which the long-term critical capacities of the community may actually be expanded rather than contracted. Sooner or later, many outsiders who are drawn into the policy-making councils of bureaucracy leave government employment. When they do, the inside knowledge they have gained in their government service enables them to become the most effective of all critics of official decisions. No one subjected the government's Vietnam policy to more searching or influential criticism than former officials of the Kennedy and Johnson administration. The criticisms of an outsider have much more credibility with the public if they come from a person who was once an insider, and who has had access to information available only to insiders.

This is not, of course, to deny the possibility that such bureaucratic migrants may also become apologists for, rather than critics of, official doctrine. Sometimes they may only appear to speak from an independent position as private citizens, for in fact they are drawing pay as consultants or advisers from the agency whose policies they are defending. At best, however, the public as well as the bureaucratic dialogue may be greatly improved by having outsiders participate in the internal deliberations of executive agencies. The bureaucratic dialogue may immediately become more spirited, and the public dialogue eventually may become better informed.

Albert O. Hirschman presents a stimulating analysis of the way in which the ability of members of organizations to leave or "exit" from their positions affects their capacity for independent thought on issues confronting the organization.[20] According to Hirschman, the possibility of such exit allows individuals to be much more vigorous in criticizing errors in the organization's established policies. Organizations are much less likely to become moribund when their membership includes individuals who can exercise this option. This is the core of the case that can be made for having outsiders as well as insiders play an important role in organizational decision making. By threatening to leave, or by actually doing so, outsiders can help alert organizations to problems which threaten their survival or vitality but which they might otherwise choose to ignore.

But the effectiveness of exit as a means of forcing an organization to reconsider the wisdom of its policies depends ultimately on the willingness of those leaving to make the reasons for their departure known. Unlike other democratic countries such as Great Britain, the United States has no tradition of resignation over disagreements on policy among executive officials. The costs of exile from the Court appear to be too heavy for many outsiders working for government agencies in this country to bear.

> To quit the club! Be outside looking in!
> This outsideness, this unfamiliar land,
> From which few travellers ever get back in . . .
> I fear to break, I'll work within for change.[21]

Thus, there were no high-level resignations during the Johnson administration in protest over the Vietnam War, even though many of those who left government service during this period were later to proclaim that they had in fact opposed the war. But silent exit certainly reforms neither policies nor organizations.

Perhaps the best case in recent times of resignation in protest was provided by Secretary of State Cyrus Vance, when in the last year of the Carter administration he strongly opposed the administration's ill-fated decision to rescue the American hostages in Iran. However, after leaving the government Vance did not thereafter criticize the decision he had opposed. His resignation was certainly a case of "minimum protest." [22] George Ball has presented a well-reasoned case for such quiet resignations. Ball, who himself resigned in disagreement with President Johnson's Vietnam policy, argues that "I could not share the confidence of my colleagues for a sustained period, then go out and denounce them." [23]

*Career Orientations.* Not all the differences in outlook among the participants in bureaucratic policy making spring from differences in the role that individuals play in organizations. If they did, we would be able to predict bureaucratic behavior entirely from the axiom that "where one stands, depends on where one sits." We know, however, that role is not always a reliable predictor of policy outlook. During the latter stages of the Johnson administration, Secretary of State Dean Rusk became the principal spokesman for military solutions to the conflict in Vietnam, while Secretary of Defense Robert McNamara was increasingly skeptical of their value.[24]

Consequently, interest has been growing in the use of psychological variables to explain behavioral differences among participants in bureaucratic decision making. This has led to construction of a number of typologies designed to relate differences in bureaucratic outlook to variations in career orientations or psychological predispositions. Anthony Downs presents a fivefold classification of bureaucrats as climbers, conservers, zealots, advocates, or statesmen, and each category has a distinctive set of motivations or behavioral patterns.[25]

Both climbers and conservers are motivated by self-interest. They see organizations as arenas in which they can achieve their personal goals. Climbers seek either advancement or an increase in the perquisites attached to their present job. They have a predilection for jumping from one bureau to another to improve their income or status. Conservers, on the other hand, care primarily about holding on to what they already have. They seek not to advance themselves, but to avoid changes that might jeopardize their personal security.

According to Downs, "the vast majority of officials . . . become con-servers in the long-run," because their expectations of improving their position eventually erode after long service in the bureau-cracy.[26]

The other three categories of officials in Downs's classification scheme are less self-regarding and at least partially motivated by concern for the public interest. One group of officials, whom Downs labels zealots, dedicate themselves to pursuit of a policy goal that they regard as essential to the national welfare. They are imbued with a sense of mission. Another group equates the public interest with preservation of the agency for which they work. These are called advocates and their identification is with an organization rather than a cause. Finally a group called statesmen takes a very broad and comprehensive view of all the factors and values that the public interest might seem to encompass. In Downs's view, statesmen "closely resemble the theoretical bureaucrats of public administration textbooks," [27] but their altruistic perspective does not fit well with the ambitious desires of most bureaus for expan-sion.

The Downs paradigm of career orientations is by no means the first of its kind. Much earlier, Dwaine Marvick set out a system based on a cleavage between "institutionalists" and "specialists" that parallels the distinction drawn earlier in this book between administrators and professionals.[28] He also includes a third "hybrid" type of bureaucrat whose characteristics and motivations are, as the term suggests, a mixture of the traits associated with the other two categories. Robert Presthus classifies career orientations in the cate-gories of upward-mobile, indifferent, and ambivalent — based essen-tially on variations in the degree of commitment that individuals have to achieving personal success in the organization in which they work.[29] The Marvick classification is notable because it is based on interviews conducted with federal employees, and is thus least sub-ject to the charge of being armchair psychology, and the outstand-ing characteristic of the Presthus analysis is that it links career orientations very closely to differences in specific psychological characteristics.

In any event it is clear that though a public agency seeks to mold employee behavior in ways that are functional for it, and some-times, as with the forest rangers that Herbert Kaufman describes, is very successful in doing so,[30] the energy and effectiveness that any organization exhibits is much affected by the personality characteristics its staff members already have when they begin working for the agency. An organization that needs zeal and dedication to achieve its mission is not likely to reach its goal unless it is successful in recruiting personnel with zealous temperaments. Moreover, the development of organizations may also be linked to changes in the temperament of the people working for them. The familiar tendency of reform agencies to lose their initial enthusiasm as they mature may be at least partially explained by their own employees becoming more conservative with age.

## CHARACTERISTICS OF THE EXECUTIVE POLICY SYSTEM

In many ways policy making within executive agencies is indistinguishable from the process that takes place within legislative assemblies. Agencies respond to group pressures by modifying existing policies or by developing new ones. Bargaining or adjustment of conflicting interests is as constant a feature of administrative politics as it is of the relations among legislators and legislative committees. Changes in policy tend to be, Charles E. Lindblom writes, "incremental" in character.[31] Bureaucrats, like legislators, are wary of sweeping innovations that may disturb existing programs or the groups that support and depend on these programs.

But though policy making within bureaucracy bears many similarities to the style of decision making within legislatures, there are differences also. To some extent these are differences in degree rather than kind, but they are nonetheless far from unimportant — as we will show. Three characteristics of bureaucratic policy making are particularly significant: (1) the fact that authority in executive agencies is hierarchically structured; (2) the strong influence of professional or technical as distinct from political criteria in arriving at decisions; (3) the fact that the policy process is considerably less public in bureaucracy than it is in the legislature.

*Hierarchy and Decision Making.* One of the most prominent characteristics of bureaucracy as a form of social organization is the distribution of authority by hierarchical rank. In a bureaucratic setting officials at higher echelons normally expect to receive obedience from their subordinates. Hence, though policy deliberations in the legislature take place among elected officials who are equal in power in the salient respect that they all have but one vote on the questions that come before them, the policy dialogue in bureaucracy takes place among officials who are unequal in rank and in consequent authority over final decision.

In recent times there has been a strong tendency in some of the more sophisticated appraisals of American public administration to discount hierarchy in bureaucracy. Emphasis has been placed instead on the extent to which subordinate officials can in fact determine policy outcomes — often in defiance of the views held by the heads of their own executive department. In the past, this weakness of hierarchy in American administration has commonly been explained in terms of political factors. Subordinate units are able to organize such strong constituency support that their hierarchical superiors are reduced to mere figureheads. Witness this description of his own managerial impotence by a former director of the U.S. Employment Service:

> I started as director with a naive idea that I ran it, but I discovered that there was a part of the service that no director ran. This was the Veterans Employment Division, which did not even receive its mail in our mailroom. It had a special post office box downtown. When I tried to do something about the division, I learned that it took orders mainly from the Employment Committee of the American Legion. From then on I discussed the work of the division regularly with a committee of the American Legion in Indianapolis.[32]

One agency long famous for the autonomy it enjoyed within the executive apparatus is the Federal Bureau of Investigation. This attitude of independence from hierarchical control was given vivid expression by one FBI agent — responding angrily to the suggestion that his bureau follow the same policies in disclosing information as those practiced by the department in which the FBI is located:

> Don't tell me about the Justice Department. I don't care how they handle things. They do things their way, and we do things our way. They don't tell us how to handle our affairs, and we don't tell them. And another thing, when you have any questions about our work, don't call the Justice Department! Call us! We handle our own policy, not them. They don't tell us what to do![33]

Another major factor helping to undermine hierarchical authority in administrative decision making in recent years is the growing power of skilled professions in the work of public bureaucracy. "Especially is the hierarchical procedure weakened," Herbert A. Simon, Donald W. Smithburg, and Victor Thompson write, "as the social division of labor turns more and more people into indispensable and recondite specialists." [34] Professionalism is rapidly succeeding politics as the principal source of decentralization of authority in American bureaucracy. A subordinate who is a master of esoteric skills is no easier to dominate than one backed by a strongly entrenched group of political supporters.

Even in the face of these obstacles, however, hierarchy has become increasingly important in the operations of national bureaucracy in the United States as in other societies. The growing scope and complexity of bureaucratic activities engenders an irresistible need for coordination of effort that can be achieved only by vesting authority over decision making in the higher ranks of bureaucracy. Left to themselves, subordinate units cannot escape duplication of effort or pursuit of contradictory objectives. [35]

Moreover, the location of decision-making power at higher echelons makes it possible to achieve more efficient allocation of resources among subordinate units. Certain activities can be centralized to conserve manpower, expenditures can be subject to more rigorous scrutiny by overhead agencies, and priorities can be established to ensure that resources are directed toward the organization's more important goals. Considerations of economy thus favor an increase in hierarchical authority, a factor of no small importance when we consider the mounting awareness of the need to find some way of cutting back on public expenditures. If professionalism pushes organizations toward decentralization, fiscal imperatives pull them toward centralization of authority.

The doctrine of party government also supports an aggrandizement of hierarchical influence in bureaucracy. A political party that has won an election can control the reins of government only if it can name its own partisans to the commanding heights of bureaucracy where they can oversee and direct the activities of the permanent and professional employees of government. Victor Thompson writes a searching critique of the practice of subordinating skilled specialists to the commands of hierarchical superiors who do not have equal technical competence. [36] The objectives of a democratic society often require such subordination, however. Civilian control of the military can be achieved only if military professionals are subject to hierarchical control by civilian officials who, though less knowledgeable about military matters, are also less insulated from the preferences of the electorate.

Moreover, most proposals for reform in American politics reveal great faith in the benefits that will come from an increase in hierarchy. Studies of Congress or of American political parties generally stress the need to bolster the leadership role within such institutions. A traditional remedy for the ills of metropolitan life is to replace the present multiplicity of governmental units with one authority having jurisdiction over all or a major part of the public functions being performed in the region. Presidential reorganization proposals usually concentrate on the idea of transferring power in a hierarchical direction — by moving authority upward from the bureaus to the departments or by strengthening the capacity of the White House to monitor decisions being made within subordinate executive agencies.

The presence of hierarchy as a dominant characteristic of bureaucracy has significant consequences for the policy process. For one thing, it enhances the likelihood that discrete policy decisions will be consistent with each other. Hierarchy is thus an instrument for coherent policy making, and in this sense at least, an aid to rational calculation in governmental decisions.[37] Activities that cannot be geared together by a more or less self-regulating system of mutual adjustment can be consciously coordinated. Moreover, under a hierarchical system it is much less likely that the policy process will be stalemated. The exercise of hierarchical authority can break the logjams created by conflict between two irreconcilable and equally powerful points of view at lower levels of decision. The growth of hierarchy thus reduces the necessity of relying upon interminable bargaining processes to arrive at policy decisions.

Not all the consequences of hierarchy contribute to rational calculation in policy deliberations, however. The inequality of power inherent in hierarchy means that the views of highly placed individuals carry immense weight, not because their arguments are persuasive but simply because of the exalted status from which they speak. Subordinates may have to go along with policy decisions reached at higher levels even when they know that their superiors are wrong. Or they may find that their own advice, however well founded, tends to be discounted because of their low standing in the hierarchy. The rationality of policy under a hierarchical system is thus constantly threatened by the disjunction between power and knowledge.

Some critics of bureaucracy would question whether a decision-making system subject to the constraints of hierarchy is capable of meeting the requirements of a democratic society committed, in theory at least, to full and frank exploration of all options as a prerequisite to rational decision. It is not unfair to say that more of the literature on policy failure focuses on the pathologies in bureaucratic communications brought on by hierarchy than on any other subject.

Ways of dealing with this problem do of course exist, but they are more palliatives than antidotes. As we saw earlier, subordinates can go over the head of their superior and betray their doubts on the wisdom of his judgment to other highly placed persons.[38] This is a course of action not without risk, open only to the venturesome. An advisory group made up of individuals having independent status outside the agency can also serve as a check upon folly in high places. But the difficulty here is that, as Dahl and Lindblom point out, people at the top of a hierarchy "decide when, in what conditions, and with whom consultation takes place." [39] Hierarchical superiors, from the president on down, have a penchant for selecting as advisers those who will give them the advice they want to hear.[40]

Hierarchy can thus be an immensely important factor inhibiting discussion and free exchange of ideas in bureaucratic policy deliberations. In the past, it has been less a problem in American than in other bureaucratic systems. Bureaucracy in the United States was traditionally characterized by pluralism rather than hierarchy in its organizational design, reflecting the character of the political culture of which it is a part. Whatever disadvantages this system may have had, it presented small possibility that debate might be stifled by deference to the views of a superior. The growth of hierarchy in American bureaucracy in recent years thus presents a continuing challenge to develop ways of dealing with the repressive effects it may have upon the policy dialogue.

Some students of organizations now argue that hierarchy has outlived its usefulness and that in the future organizations will be structured more like teams of equals sharing responsibility for decision making than pyramids of authority linked by a chain of command. Warren Bennis is conspicuously identified with the view that "temporary" organizations of this sort will be the dominant bureaucratic model of the future — organizations put together to solve particular problems and then dissolved.[41] The impermanence of these organizations provides protection against the vices that arise when bureaucracies furnish people with lifetime careers and fixed interests that any change threatens to disturb.

But though such temporary organizations, which Alvin Toffler calls "adhocracies," [42] have been created in the public sector and have dealt effectively with many special or emergency problems, they tend in government at least to supplement rather than to supplant permanent agencies. Indeed, they are often staffed with career officials drawn from the regular executive apparatus and the behavior of these officials must be guided by the expectation that they will some day return to their bureaucratic home. Although they serve many useful purposes, adhocracies do not, therefore, seem likely to bring an end to either hierarchy or bureaucracy in government.

One characteristic of public administration in the United States that helps mitigate the negative effects of hierarchy is the prevalence of governmental programs carried out through private institutions. Banks administer government loan programs, localities frequently rely on private contractors for garbage collection, and much of the research that government funds is carried out by universities or specialized institutions. This is part of what Lester Salamon calls "third-party" government, which is sometimes referred to as private federalism.[43] A new domain has emerged, alongside the private and public sector in which private organizations carry out tasks that are wholly or partially funded by the government. Many private welfare agencies depend heavily on the financial support they receive from public agencies to achieve their goals.

*Professionalization of Policy.* As we have discussed, bureaucracy is a governmental habitat in which expertise finds a wealth of opportunities to assert itself and to influence policy. Don K. Price wrote that "the development of public policy and the methods of its administration owed less in the long run to the processes of conflict among political parties and social or economic pressure groups than to the more objective processes of research and discussion among professional groups." [44] This is the sense in which bureaucracy contributes to the influence of expertise upon policy decisions. It provides a setting in which experts in and out of government can get together to work on policy problems. Sometimes this exchange occurs long before these problems become legislative issues or matters of public debate. In national security policy, controversies over the feasibility of a hydrogen bomb, the need for greater expenditures on civil defense, and the wisdom of constructing an antimissile system, were issues in bureaucracy long before they became matters of general public concern.

This is not, however, to suggest that political considerations are unimportant in bureaucratic deliberations. Nothing could be further from the truth. Executive agencies are part of the political system and their activities inevitably reflect the values and interests of outside groups. Certainly an agency's calculations on the views of its own constituency have a major part in the positions it takes on policy questions. It is rare to find an agricultural agency, for example, coming up with policy recommendations that are highly disadvantageous to the groups it serves merely because its own impartial analysis leads it to inevitable and irresistible professional conclusions.[45]

Moreover, an executive agency commonly has political interests of its own that may greatly affect the positions it takes on policy issues, and these interests may be quite distinct from the needs of its constituency.

Questions involving administrative jurisdiction, or allocation of appropriations among programs, will inevitably touch an agency's sensibilities about its own organizational stature. No agency can be expected to preside enthusiastically over its own liquidation, and its perspectives on policy are bound to be shaped to some degree at least by considerations of its own organizational self-interest. Otherwise, an agency may find itself in the unhappy position of the Department of Labor in the 1930s, when the labor programs of the federal government greatly expanded, but the scope of the Labor Department's own administrative authority remained stationary, and even, after a time, began to decline.

It is also important to guard against the fallacy — so dear to the American reform tradition — that a policy issue can be depoliticized by turning it over to bureaucracy. It is clear that most policy issues have a zero-sum quality — gains by some groups will have to be offset by losses for others. The decision of bureaucrats, no less than those of politicians will involve redistribution of costs and benefits, and will as an inevitable result be political. Moving authority for decision from politicians to bureaucrats may mean only that decisions will be made by different people and will result in a different allocation of resources among conflicting groups.

At the same time, however, it is equally vital to avoid the opposite fallacy of assuming that all policy making in bureaucracy is entirely politicized — that technical and professional considerations have no weight whatsoever except perhaps as window dressing. The truth of the matter is that a great many policy judgments hinge on technical advice that only professional personnel can supply. A health agency cannot make policy decisions or recommendations on the smoking of cigarettes as a health problem until it has obtained the best scientific advice available on the relationship between smoking and a variety of illnesses now linked with use of tobacco.

Likewise, a president, involved in the critical choices he has to make in national security policy, will want to have the best advice he can get — whether from scientific or military sources — on the technical feasibility of certain courses of action. If a president chooses to ignore professional opinion altogether, the political consequences for his own interests can be highly disadvantageous if not disastrous. Consequently, from the point of view of self-preservation alone, politicians are obliged to lean heavily upon the advice of bureaucratic experts in making policy decisions.

The importance of preserving the independence and integrity of certain kinds of expertise in government is thus very great. Traditionally, public agencies performing educational functions, like state universities, or at the national level governmental organizations engaged in research, like the Bureau of Labor Statistics or the Bureau of Standards, have been granted — by law or custom — a great deal of administrative autonomy. This freedom has been justified on the practical grounds that performance of such functions as education and research demands an atmosphere completely free from political pressure.

But as more and more agencies play a policy-making role that requires reliance upon expert or at least nonpolitical standards, the need for professional autonomy begins to assert itself in all phases of bureaucratic policy making. If policy decisions are to be effective, they must be informed by honest technical advice. This candor can be secured only if professionals are protected from reprisal for policy findings or recommendations that may be offensive to politically potent groups.

An executive agency may sometimes choose to isolate a unit within its own organization from outside pressures, or even visibility, and charge it with making recommendations on politically sensitive issues. In this way an agency can at least be certain that nonpolitical criteria are taken into account in making policy decisions, even though political constraints may prevent decisions from being made on these criteria alone. This was the strategy followed by the Office of Price Administration during World War II, when it set up a Gasoline Eligibility Committee within its own organization to make recommendations to policy-making officials on objective factors in the highly inflammable issue of allocating gasoline among domestic consumers.[46] With such a unit, an agency has some assurance that its policy deliberations are not being completely politicized.

In view of the roles that both political and nonpolitical criteria play in the bureaucratic policy process, the framing of public policy in a bureaucratic setting can be seen to involve constant interplay between two quite different sets of factors. It becomes in effect a mixed system of politics and professionalism. Clearly political considerations have to be taken into account in bureaucratic policy making in measuring the effect of decisions upon the outside community. At the same time, however, policy decisions certainly cannot fly in the face of professional advice when experts agree on the technically sound course of action.

The way in which political and administrative criteria interact in executive agencies can be seen in a decision to close four field offices of the Department of Commerce. The forty-six field offices maintained by the department were first ranked by the number of requests for information they received each month. The secretary of commerce then selected four offices for elimination from the fourteen that ranked lowest on this quantitative scale. Although purely administrative criteria had determined which fourteen offices would be considered for elimination, political considerations were prominent in deciding which four of the fourteen would actually be abolished.[47]

Under the system followed in the Department of Commerce field service case and in similar situations such as choosing locations for waste-treatment facilities, a decision must not clearly flout professional or nonpolitical criteria. Other considerations can enter the decision-making process only when a decision is defensible on technical grounds. Agency heads would leave themselves highly vulnerable to criticism if they made decisions that were altogether indefensible by professional standards. At the same time, any objective criteria used would ordinarily allow an executive to take other factors into account as well. An executive's options are not usually foreclosed by the findings of professionals within his organization.

The need to free executives from control by their professional staff in framing policy is certainly clear. In many areas of policy it is impossible to develop quantitative criteria as a basis for decision. Judgments must be made using incomplete evidence or qualitative factors for which there is no evidence whatsoever. To be sure, this procedure sometimes permits decisions to be affected by political considerations of a crude kind. At worst, agency decisions may even be used to reward friends and punish enemies.

At the same time, however, restraints on the influence of professionals also make possible decisions that take into account a much broader range of considerations than are always encompassed within the perspective of a professional group in bureaucracy. Military officials may not see the diplomatic implications of a course of action they are recommending. Or doctors considering the location of a new city hospital may not give adequate weight to the needs and interests of the patients who will use this medical facility.[48] It is thus possible to see and to find examples of "politics" as corrupting the process of professional decision in bureaucracy. It is also possible to see it as greatly expanding the horizons of bureaucratic decision makers and enabling policy to satisfy the needs of much wider or more diverse segments of the public.

*Secrecy and Public Policy.* The policy process as it is carried on within legislatures is not entirely public. In spite of a number of steps taken by Congress in the 1970s to open all legislative hearings to outside scrutiny, these measures have sometimes been circumvented by the legislative practice of holding private meetings to bargain over difficult issues.[49] At the same time, however, the legislature is primarily a public institution. The public, and increasingly the private activities of its members are open to constant scrutiny from the outside world. Its debates are conducted in public. Most of the investigations and interrogations of its committees are visible on a day-to-day basis and are eventually printed in exhaustive detail as a public record. Whatever disadvantages the legislative policy-making process may exhibit, it has a striking asset — its delibera-

ons and concerns are so easily known to those who will be affected
y them. Citizens thus have an opportunity to make their views
nown on pending legislative issues before final decisions are made.

The bureaucratic policy process is, by contrast, a quite invisible
art of government. The environment of bureaucracy is a cloistered
inctuary compared with the limelight in which a legislative assem-
ly normally operates. Though an executive agency may hold public
earings, conduct press conferences, or release news bulletins of one
ind or another, it controls, far more than does the legislature, the
iformation available to the public on its internal deliberations and
ecisions. The meetings, conferences, negotiations, and agreements
hrough which bureaucratic policy decisions are reached can be but
imly seen through the opaque exterior that an administrative
gency presents to the outside world. In some administrative activ-
ties information is made available only through leaks, interviews
vith "informed" sources, or an unexpected disclosure of secrets that
vere meant to be kept by a departing member of the inner circle.

To be sure, the bureaucracy did not invent secrecy in American
overnment. The Founding Fathers found it expedient to conduct
he deliberations of the Constitutional Convention at Philadelphia
n 1787 in private long before there was an administrative establish-
nent of any consequence in the United States. And presidents have,
hrough the high development and use of "executive privilege,"
ontributed a great deal to the secrecy surrounding executive activ-
ties.[50] Sometimes bureaucrats have actually enhanced openness in
overnment by disclosing information that the White House would
orefer to have concealed, as during the Watergate era. But it re-
nains true that the growth of bureaucracy in American government
as brought about an enormous expansion in the secretiveness with
vhich public policy is made.

As we have seen, this secrecy contributes to the effectiveness of
overnmental decisions in important respects. At least in the early
tages of policy development, a good many proposals benefit from
orivate discussions. It is possible to explore some courses of action
n private that could much less easily be discussed in public, such
is use of the American government's funds to disseminate information on birth control at home or abroad. Except for a few hardy
ndividuals, "thinking about the unthinkable" (Herman Kahn's revealing phrase) is an enterprise much more easily conducted in private than in public.

Because privacy is conducive to candor in policy deliberations administrative policy making may permit more honest exploration of alternatives than is possible in the legislature. People are less often compelled to edit out of their discussions "dangerous thoughts" that might get them into trouble if they were widely known. Such privacy would be an unqualified benefit to rational calculation in policy deliberations, except that it also constricts the number of alternatives considered by excluding many informed individuals from the discussion.[51]

But it is true that the greater privacy characteristic of bureaucratic operations does promote accommodation and compromise in the development of public policy. Participants in administrative discussions can back down more easily from positions they have previously taken if they have not put their earlier point of view on public record. Compromise solutions that may be difficult to explain to constituents can be agreed to more easily in private than in public, because the responsibility for decision in this case is obscure. Because stalemate would be a worse alternative for the group whose interests are involved, privacy may have a constructive effect upon the policy process by encouraging such mutual adjustment of interests.

Even though there are advantageous aspects of privacy in policy deliberations, the costs of this characteristic of bureaucratic policy making are also high. Because of the restrictions of secrecy many executive officials make decisions on policy questions without having full access to the facts possessed by the government that are relevant to these decisions. Secret information does not circulate any better within the government than it does to the public. Moreover when policies are determined in private, the sources of influence on these decisions may be unknown, and many groups whose interests are affected may not be consulted at all.[52]

Finally, it is much more difficult to identify and reverse mistakes when policy deliberations and decisions are made in secret by some chosen few — the saints rather than the sinners. This is particularly a problem in foreign affairs, where the possibility of irreversible error — of a fait accompli that cannot be undone — is heightened because so much of policy formulation takes place in the cloistered corridors of bureaucracy. In domestic policy, on the other hand, interaction among executive agencies, legislative committees, and community groups is so constant that very little of what is decided can be long concealed. It is hard to escape the conclusion that the more widely a policy proposal is discussed, the more likely it is that its defects will be exposed.

Congress has made innumerable efforts to limit the secrecy in which executive agencies engage, including periodic investigations and passage of laws attempting to establish the public's right to obtain information from the executive branch. But even this reform legislation has permitted withholding of information in specified situations, as when legitimate claims to privacy by citizens might be endangered by release of data in the government's files. These so-called exemptions from the principle of disclosure have often been seized upon by administrative agencies to justify secrecy. Consider this description of the way in which the Freedom of Information Act was administered after its first enactment in 1966:

> The bureaucracy did not want this law ... this attitude of opposition has manifested itself during the first years of the act's operation in excessive processing fees, response delays, and pleas of ignorance when petitioned for documents in terms other than the exact title or other type of precise identification.[53]

Congressional opponents of executive secrecy saw the way in which the 1966 law was being administered as a clear case of bureaucratic sabotage of legislative intent. Consequently, the Freedom of Information Act was greatly strengthened in 1974 and reenacted after President Ford's veto of the bill initially submitted to him.

The amount of secrecy that prevails in American bureaucracy should not, of course, be exaggerated. Pressures toward an open government are very strong in American society. The power of the news media, the wide-ranging investigative activities of Congress, and the infinite variety of ways in which executive agencies and the public interact in this country all conspire to make it as difficult to keep governmental secrets in the United States as it is anywhere in the world. But the growing tendency to resort to secrecy in the practice of American government since World War II has been unmistakable, and it has significantly affected policy making, especially, as we have seen, in matters relating to national security and foreign affairs.

One final paradox appears in policy making as it is carried on within a bureaucratic setting. Although Max Weber and other early students of the subject saw the coming of bureaucracy as the ultimate triumph of rationality, many of its modern critics see bureaucracy today as having characteristics that contribute instead to irrationality in decision. As indicated earlier, bureaucratic organizations provide societies with a capacity to handle problems and to provide services that are indispensable for the functioning of a civilized society in a modern industrialized environment. They do so by providing organized, reliable procedures through which such problems can be handled. Yet, as we have also seen, in the eyes of many people today, bureaucratic organizations are closely associated with irrationality — with having hierarchical distribution of authority and a penchant for secrecy that severely handicap their ability to arrive at sensible decisions on issues of public policy. As Martin Albrow writes, "Two incompatible concepts — bureaucracy as administrative efficiency and bureaucracy as administrative inefficiency — compete for space in twentieth-century theory." [54]

# *Notes*

1. H. H. Gerth and C. Wright Mills, eds. *From Max Weber: Essays in Sociology* (New York: Oxford University Press, 1946), p. 234. For a revealing analysis of the more subtle interplay of influence between political executives and career administrators in the American system of government, see Hugh Heclo, "Political Executives and the Washington Bureaucracy," *Political Science Quarterly* 92 (Fall 1977): 395–424. Cf. also by Heclo, *A Government of Strangers: Executive Politics in Washington* (Washington, D.C.: Brookings Institution, 1977).

2. John Stuart Mill, *On Liberty* (New York: Appleton-Century-Crofts, 1947), p. 115.

3. For a full account of the factors and forces underlying this rebellion, see Gary Hershey, *Protest in the Public Service* (Lexington, Mass.: Lexington Books, 1973).

4. See Charles E. Lindblom, *The Intelligence of Democracy* (New York: Free Press, 1965). A study of the attitudes of career officials toward political appointees showed that these appointees are generally held in high esteem. See M. Kent Jennings, Milton C. Cummings, Jr., and Franklin P. Kilpatrick, "Trusted Leaders: Perceptions of Appointed Federal Officials," *Public Opinion Quarterly* 30 (Fall 1966): 368–384.

5. See Jonathan P. Grossman, *The Department of Labor* (New York: Praeger, 1973), pp. 82–85, 230–231.
6. As we saw earlier, however, an agency executive often has to tread a tightrope in wooing his subordinates without alienating important constituency groups. In contemporary urban politics, a police commissioner faces the difficult task of handling the "police brutality" issue to satisfy both the members of his own department and civil rights organizations in the city.
7. See Herbert J. Storing, "Political Parties and the Bureaucracy" in Robert A. Goldwin, ed., *Political Parties, U.S.A.* (Chicago: Rand McNally, 1964), pp. 137–158. This article presents the clearest picture ever drawn of the relationship between political and career officials.
8. A thorough and absorbing account of some vital chapters in the New York experience is presented in Gerald Benjamin, *Race Relations and the New York City Commission on Human Rights* (Ithaca, N.Y.: Cornell University Press, 1974).
9. See Charles H. Levine, ed., *Managing Fiscal Stress: The Crisis in the Public Sector* (Chatham, N.J.: Chatham, 1980), esp. pp. 3–30.
10. James W. Fesler, "Politics, Policy, and Bureaucracy at the Top," *The Annals of the American Academy of Political and Social Science* 466 (March 1983): 24–25.
11. For an illuminating discussion of the role of the professional in organizations, see Amitai Etzioni, "Authority Structure and Organizational Effectiveness," *Administrative Science Quarterly* 4 (June 1959): 43–67. An analysis of the attitudes and behavior of professionals in more specifically governmental organizations may be found in John J. Corson and R. Shale Paul, *Men Near the Top* (Baltimore: Johns Hopkins Press, 1966), pp. 77–102.
12. Cf. the distinction between efficiency and effectiveness in Amitai Etzioni, *Modern Organizations* (Englewood Cliffs, N.J.: Prentice-Hall, 1964), pp. 8–10. Herbert Simon, *Administrative Behavior*, 3rd ed. (New York: Free Press, 1976) presents a similar contrast between "efficiency" and "adequacy."
13. Corson and Paul, *Men Near the Top*, pp. 90–91. The best study of professionals and their role in government is Corinne L. Gilb, *Hidden Hierarchics* (New York: Harper and Row, 1966).
14. See Morton H. Halperin, "The Gaither Committee and the Policy Process," *World Politics* 13 (April 1961): 360–384. The list of committee members is given on pp. 361–362, notes 5, 6.
15. Don K. Price, *Government and Science* (New York: New York University Press, 1954), p. 200. See also the discussion of "in-and-outers" in Richard E. Neustadt, "White House and Whitehall," *The Public Interest*, 2 (Winter 1966): 59–61. In a very interesting analysis of national security policy making, Bert A. Rockman identifies a split between "regulars" and "irregulars" similar to the distinction drawn here between insiders and outsiders. See "America's *Departments* of State: Irregular and Regular Syndromes of Policy-Making," *American Political Science Review* 75 (December 1981): 911–927.
16. Martha Derthick, *Policymaking for Social Security* (Washington, D.C.: Brookings Institution, 1979), pp. 89–109.
17. See Aaron Wildavsky, *Dixon-Yates: A Study in Power Politics* (New Haven: Yale University Press, 1962).
18. See Mark V. Nadel,"Corporate Secrecy and Political Accountability," *Public Administration Review* 35 (January/February 1975): 16.
19. See Harold Lasswell, *Politics: Who Gets What, When, How* (New York: Whittlesey, 1936), p. 166.

20. Albert O. Hirschman, *Exit, Voice, and Loyalty* (Cambridge: Harvard University Press, 1970).

21. Barbara Garson, *MacBird!* as quoted in Hirschman, *Exit*, p. 115.

22. Cyrus Vance, *Hard Choices: Critical Years in America's Foreign Policy* (New York: Simon and Schuster, 1983), pp. 410–412.

23. George W. Ball, *The Past Has Another Pattern: Memoirs* (New York: W. W. Norton, 1982).

24. See David Halberstam, *The Best and the Brightest* (New York: Random House, 1972), for one of the best accounts we have of the role of personality in shaping decisions at high levels of executive policy making.

25. Anthony Downs, *Inside Bureaucracy* (Boston: Little, Brown, 1967). For an interesting classification of different types of bureaucrats in the private sector, see Michael Maccoby, *The Gamesman: The New Corporate Leaders* (New York: Simon and Schuster, 1977).

26. Ibid., p. 99.

27. Ibid., p. 89.

28. Dwaine Marvick, *Career Perspectives in a Bureaucratic Setting* (Ann Arbor: University of Michigan Press, 1954).

29. Robert Presthus, *The Organizational Society* (New York: Alfred A. Knopf, 1962).

30. See Herbert Kaufman, *The Forest Ranger: A Study in Administrative Behavior* (Baltimore: Johns Hopkins Press, 1960).

31. "Incremental" decision making is a main theme in David Braybrooke and Charles E. Lindblom, *A Strategy of Decision* (New York: Free Press, 1963).

32. Marver Bernstein, *The Job of the Federal Executive* (Washington, D.C.: Brookings Institution, 1958) pp. 94–95.

33. Allen Weinstein, "Opening the FBI Files: An Interim Report," *Smith Alumnae Quarterly* 66 (February 1975): 14. I am indebted to Lynne Brown for calling this reference to my attention.

34. Herbert A. Simon, Donald W. Smithburg, and Victor Thompson, *Public Administration* (New York: Alfred A. Knopf, 1950), p. 200. A perceptive discussion of how hierarchy affects decision making is in Harold L. Wilensky, *Organizational Intelligence* (New York: Basic Books, 1967), pp. 42–48.

35. Cf. also, on this point, the discussion on p. 163.

36. Victor A. Thompson, *Modern Organization* (New York: Alfred A. Knopf, 1961).

37. For an analysis of the advantages of hierarchy as a form of social organization, see Robert A. Dahl and Charles E. Lindblom, *Politics, Economics, and Welfare* (New York: Harper, 1953), pp. 236–243.

38. See pp. 128–129.

39. Dahl and Lindblom, *Politics, Economics, and Welfare*, p. 227.

40. See the earlier discussion of this point on pp. 21–22.

41. Warren G. Bennis, *Changing Organizations* (New York: McGraw-Hill, 1966). Cf. also Frederick C. Thayer, *An End to Hierarchy! An End to Competition!* (New York: New Viewpoints, 1973).

42. Alvin Toffler, *Future Shock* (New York: Random House, 1970), pp. 112–135.

43. Lester Salamon, "Rethinking Public Management: Third-Party Government and the Changing Forms of Government Action," *Public Policy* 29 (Summer 1981): 255–275.

44. Price, *Government and Science*, p. v. See also the discussion of the "professional state" in Frederick C. Mosher, *Democracy and the Public Service*, 2nd ed. (New York: Oxford University Press, 1982), pp. 110–142. Mosher's analysis

is far and away the best account we have of the growth of professionalism in the public service.

45. For an interesting account of the troubles that beset one agricultural agency when it pursued research to conclusions that were disadvantageous to a group that considered itself part of the agency's constituency, see Charles M. Hardin, "The Bureau of Agricultural Economics Under Fire: A Study in Valuation Conflicts," *Journal of Farm Economics* 28 (August 1946): 635–668.
46. Harold Stein, ed., *Public Administration and Policy Development* (New York: Harcourt Brace, 1952), pp. 749–759.
47. See Kathryn Smul Arnow, "The Department of Commerce Field Service," *The Inter-University Case Program* (University, Ala.: University of Alabama Press, 1954).
48. Decisions on the location of facilities such as schools and hospitals often generate such conflicts between professional and community groups. See, for example, Edward Banfield, *Political Influence* (New York: Free Press, 1961), pp. 15–56, 159–189.
49. As a result of pressures from Common Cause and other public interest organizations, as well as the growth of reform sentiment within Congress itself, there has been a marked decline in the number of committee meetings conducted in secret.
50. Raoul Berger, *Executive Privilege: A Constitutional Myth* (Cambridge: Harvard University Press, 1974).
51. See p. 6.
52. An analysis of the influence of administrative secrecy upon policy decisions may be found in Wilensky, *Organizational Intelligence,* esp. pp. 66–74.
53. Harold C. Relyea, "Opening Government to Public Scrutiny: A Decade of Federal Efforts," *Public Administration Review* 35 (January/February 1975): 4. Of course, a great deal of administrative secrecy is designed to serve the interests of outside groups rather than bureaucrats themselves. See Francis E. Rourke, "Bureaucratic Secrecy and Its Constituents," *The Bureaucrat* 1 (Summer 1972): 116–121.
54. Martin Albrow, *Bureaucracy* (New York: Praeger, 1970), p. 31. See also Eugene P. Dvorin and Robert H. Simmons, *From Amoral to Humane Bureaucracy* (San Francisco: Canfield Press, 1972).

# CHAPTER SIX

# Improving
# Administrative
# Performance

As indicated in earlier discussion, the design of the system through which executive agencies participate in policy making has been structured by two not always consistent objectives — responsiveness and effectiveness. Bureaucrats are expected to serve the needs of the public — as the public reveals its needs or as they are defined by its representatives — and to use the most effective means available for achieving the goals set by these outside authorities for each government organization.

Today as in the past, continuing efforts are being made to enhance the likelihood that bureaucratic decisions and behavior will meet these standards of responsiveness and effectiveness. Administrative reform has been a high-priority objective in the United States since the 1930s, when the executive apparatus reached new heights of power in modern American politics. In this chapter we will look at some of the main areas in which these reform efforts have been concentrated — administrative reorganization, the quantification of decision making, and the attempt to find new ways of curing the inertia to which all large bureaucratic organizations seem inevitably to be subject.

## REFORM AND REORGANIZATION

Much of the history of administrative reform in the United States has centered on the search for a style of organization that would broaden the perspective of executive agencies.[1] As public administration was shaped by the forces ascendant in nineteenth and early twentieth-century politics, it seemed to many reformers that policy decisions tended to reflect too narrow a set of interests. Authority for designing programs was widely dispersed among subordinate units of the executive branch, and their decisions responded not to the needs of broad segments of the public, but more commonly to the pressures of small clientele groups that held individual bureaus in captivity.

Beginning in the 1930s, it thus became a primary objective of administrative reform to restructure the executive branch so that power would be centered, not at the lower and seemingly more parochial echelons of bureaucracy, but in the hands of high-level executives, where it was expected that the interests of wider segments of the public would be taken into account in making policy choices. The location of decision-making power in subordinate agencies and bureaus was thus identified in the traditional reform theory of administrative organization with a limited perspective in policy making, and the centralization of power in the hands of top-level executives was looked upon as a method by which the horizons of policy could be greatly broadened.

The effort to achieve an executive-centered system of administrative organization was vigorously pursued at all levels of government in the United States. As is usually true in matters of administration, however, the national government took the lead in organizational reform and the states followed. The report of the President's Committee on Administrative Management in 1937, as well as the findings and recommendations of two Hoover Commissions in 1949 and 1955, led the way toward a very substantial expansion in executive authority in national administration. This administrative reorganization had a variety of objectives, including the saving of money by eliminating duplication of effort, and the grouping of related activities into cohesive units. But at the heart of the traditional reorganization movement was the belief that policy making could be more farsighted and comprehensive in outlook when responsibility for decision rested with higher rather than lower authority. This movement toward reorganizing government organizations was heavily influenced by organizational theories and practices being developed in the private sector.[2]

The movement toward a more hierarchical system of organization was part of the long quest for administrative arrangements that would enable agencies to promote the "public interest" in their decision-making processes. To be sure, there has never been agreement in the literature of public administration on the meaning of so elusive a concept as the public interest. Some have seen it as signifying no more than the sum of the private interests affected by particular administrative decisions; others have regarded it as embodying collective interests that transcend the needs of particular groups in the community. But there would certainly be widespread agreement with the proposition that this public interest standard requires administrative agencies to take the needs of broader as well as narrower publics into account in designing their policies and procedures.[3]

Even as the reorganization movement was mostly successful in centralizing authority for decision making in the heads of departments or in the office of the chief executive, however, voices were increasingly heard suggesting that the old-fashioned system of dispersed authority in administrative organization was not altogether without value for public administration. A "revisionist" critique thus emerged at the very moment when the traditional reorganization movement had largely won the day and become the "conventional wisdom" on questions of organization design.

Revisionists pointed out, for example, that a structural pattern under which administrative authority is widely dispersed has the advantage of promoting varied points of view and a more spirited dialogue among executive agencies in policy development. In his analysis of President Franklin D. Roosevelt's style as an administrator, Arthur M. Schlesinger, Jr. argues that the secret of Roosevelt's success was his ability to keep administrative authority scattered so as to permit disputes among his subordinates that would broaden his own options while preventing any one adviser from gaining excessive influence over him. Roosevelt, writes Schlesinger, "deliberately organized — or disorganized — his system of command to insure that important decisions were passed on to the top. His favorite technique was to keep grants of authority incomplete, jurisdictions uncertain, charters overlapping." [4] However, if Roosevelt derived advantages from a system of decentralized administrative authority, he also, as president, did a great deal to enhance administrative centralization by the appointment of the President's Committee on Administrative Management in 1936, and the steps he subsequently took to carry out its centralizing recommendations.

That dispersion in administrative authority may enliven the process of discussion within bureaucracy is not the only ground on which it can be defended. It may also be argued that such fragmentation helps to link authority with knowledge, insofar as the professional personnel in subordinate bureaus and agencies commonly know more about the technical aspects of the policy issues with which they are dealing than do departmental executives. From this perspective, the traditional reform effort to shift authority from bureaus up to departments can be looked upon as widening the split between knowledge and power that is endemic in modern bureaucracy.[5] Under a system of centralized authority, subordinates inevitably find themselves being overruled by superiors whose professional competence is far less than their own. Though these upper-echelon officials may have a broader perspective on the problems under consideration, they lack the depth of knowledge on particular issues that their subordinates possess.

Moreover, it is not always certain that officials who are more highly placed in bureaucracy will actually have a clearer view of the public interest in administrative decision making than their subordinates. Aaron Wildavsky, for one, argues to the contrary.

> ... the partial-view-of-the-public interest approach is preferable to the total-view-of-the-public interest approach, which is so often urged as being superior.... The danger of omitting important values is much greater when participants neglect the values in their immediate care in favor of what seems to them a broader view.... A partial adversary system in which the various interests compete for control of policy (under agreed-upon rules) seems more likely to result in reasonable decisions — that is, decisions that take account of the multiplicity of values involved — than one in which the best policy is assumed to be discoverable by a well-intentioned search for the public interest for all by everyone.[6]

Wildavsky's argument here parallels very closely the defense by Charles E. Lindblom of fragmented as opposed to comprehensive approaches to policy development: "different points of view taken by the different groups in government serve to make each group something of a watchdog for certain variables against others." [7]

But though such revisionist views have been increasingly prominent in the literature of public administration, official studies and reports at all levels of government still recommend an increase in hierarchy as the standard way of improving the organizational design of the executive branch. How far some of its most enthusiastic proponents would take the theory of centralization has not been altogether clear. Carried to an extreme, it seems to imply that at the national level the best system of policy making for the executive branch would be to place authority for all decisions in the hands of the president. Clearly, this would be excessive centralization even for the most ambitious tenant of the White House, and this overload at the top would quickly paralyze the development and effective administration of all government policies below.

Practical limitation on such extreme centralization are still strongly entrenched in the United States, however. Federalism disperses authority over decision in many areas of domestic policy by requiring national agencies to negotiate with the states or localities in developing policy. The long practice of executive agencies catering to the groups they serve is also a staunch barrier against undue centralization, as is the common tendency of congressional committees to take agencies in whose activities they have a special interest into "protective custody."

Finally, the movement (discussed earlier) toward professionalism within the ranks of government employees provides the best of all guarantees that decentralization will always be alive and well and living in American bureaucracy. As long as subordinate agencies are important repositories of specialized skills, with close ties to professional associations outside of government, and as long as knowledge is widely distributed at lower levels of the hierarchy, power must in large measure follow suit. Agencies in which one or all of these fundamental sources of independence are strong — clientelism, alliance with a congressional committee, or professionalization — have commonly been able to exempt themselves from the real effects of centralizing proposals.

Of course, it is not inevitable that a choice must be made in designing a policy system between a decentralization that allows for articulating specialized and intense interests, and a centralized structure that reflects the needs of broader and less self-interested publics. It is possible to establish an administrative system that incorporates both perspectives in making decisions in any area of policy. In public higher education in the states, the individual colleges and universities have been left with substantial autonomy to promote their own goals, and at the same time it has become increasingly common to establish a coordinating agency or "superboard" to look at higher education from the perspective of the needs and problems of the entire state. In this way, both Wildavsky's "partial-view-of-the-public interest" and a "total-view-of-the-public interest" may simultaneously inform and guide policy development in the governor's office or in the state legislature. Incremental and comprehensive ways of looking at policy issues need not always be mutually exclusive.

An alternative to conventional reorganization strategy that came to the fore in the 1960s is the proposal to decentralize authority in executive agencies, and to allow those for whom services are being provided to participate in decisions in which they have a stake. This proposal was pushed with particular vigor in services designed for low-income groups in cities, perhaps because the cultural gulf between the middle-class bureaucrats who furnish these services and the impoverished urban clientele who receive them was both wide and visible.[8]

A decentralized administrative structure in which the citizens being served have a voice in decision making has particular appeal for agencies that are trying to effect some basic transformation in their clients, rather than simply providing them with a service for which they have a need. For agencies dealing with an economically deprived clientele, for example, it can be argued that the poor will enhance their own sense of personal efficacy if they participate in administrative decisions affecting them. Such participation may help overcome the demoralization and dependence that so often accompany economic deprivation and perhaps enable a poverty agency to restore more of its clients to an independent and productive role in society.

In addition to cases where such clientele transformation is a real possibility, there is also strong justification for citizen involvement in agency decision making when the side effects, which economists call the "externalities" of decisions, are particularly acute, and when an agency is dominated by a professional group that may not always be sensitive to these side effects. Consider the highway department in a state or locality whose designs for a new road may have grievous, but unanticipated, consequences for some of the neighborhoods through which the agency's traffic engineers have routed it.

The technique of allowing the members of affected groups to become involved in policy decisions is far from a new departure in American administration. It has traditionally been standard practice in rural America. Farmers have long been granted the right to participate in deciding many questions on agricultural policy either by direct vote or by representation in advisory groups that have a dominant role in policy decisions. Techniques of representing the public in policy development have also been prominent in the Selective Service System, as well as in the system of grazing administration carried on by the Bureau of Land Management in the West.

It is not always self-evident, however, what form citizen involvement in policy making should take even where it does seem appropriate. In some areas of policy citizen groups have been granted a virtual veto power over policies affecting their interests. This has long been true in certain aspects of agricultural and conservation administration, and some supporters of antipoverty programs advocated a similar arrangement for programs affecting the urban poor. More common, however, is the practice followed by many planning departments of holding public hearings at which they present proposals for new highways or changes in land use, and citizens or neighborhood organizations can appear and offer objections to these projects. If these objections seem well founded, or are backed by substantial community pressure, then the planning department may be forced to abandon or revise its initial proposals.

Although some revisionists are trying to make executive agencies more sensitive to the special needs of the groups they serve, a radically different orientation toward organizational reform is taken by public interest groups. These groups seek instead to broaden the perspectives of the regulatory agencies in which they are strongly interested by making them less responsive to their immediate clientele and more sensitive to the needs of the public at large, whose interests as consumers of transportation, energy, and other goods and services are greatly affected by the decisions of these regulatory bodies. A major paradox of contemporary public administration thus is that while some reformers are trying to make agencies more responsive to the specialized constituencies they serve, others are trying to make them less so.

Watergate perhaps did as much damage as any other event in modern times to the conventional reform belief in the merits of a centralized executive structure. It demonstrated very clearly that decentralization of authority provides some protection against corrupt use of power at the top of any organization. In the Watergate episode, subordinate agencies with some tradition of autonomy, like the Federal Bureau of Investigation and the Internal Revenue Service, resisted White House efforts to involve them in illegal activity. Instead they became important sources of information on the misconduct of presidential aides for the press and eventually the Special Prosecutor's Office.

Looking back on Watergate, it is ironic to recall that three decades earlier the Brownlow Commission on executive reorganization had recommended to President Roosevelt that he create the first full-fledged White House staff to assist him in centralizing control over the executive branch. The primary attribute of this staff, the commission urged, should be a "passion for anonymity." Little could Brownlow and his colleagues have anticipated in 1937 that the passion for anonymity of one White House staff member would lead him in 1972 to procure dark glasses and a red wig to carry out his assigned tasks, which included breaking into the national headquarters of the Democratic party in the dead of night.

One thing should be clear: As a technique of administrative reform, reorganization provides no royal road to economy and efficiency in government. It has often been advertised in this way, principally because its supporters sought to mobilize support in conservative circles for reorganization on the illusory grounds that it would reduce the costs of government and thus lighten the burden of the taxpayer. No evidence exists, however, that reorganization has ever had much if any effect in this direction.[9]

Historically, the chief beneficiaries of conventional reorganization theory appear to have been chief executives at all levels of government, particularly the president. To no one's surprise, it is these chief executives who have been the principal sponsors of reorganization studies and proposals. Reorganization has helped to centralize control over the executive branch in their office, or in the hands of their own political appointees. Moreover, when chief executives put forward a grandiose reorganization scheme, it helps create the public impression that they are in fact in charge of the executive apparatus, though in reality the conduct of most government programs may be little affected by structural changes brought about by reorganization. Chief executives may thus pursue reorganization for its dramatic value rather than its intrinsic administrative utility, even though, as with President Jimmy Carter, it may ultimately prove to have neither. Harold Seidman accurately described Carter's reorganization efforts: "The results . . . are disproportionate to President Carter's huge investment of political capital, time, and staff resources." [10]

Other presidents have varied a great deal in the interest and importance they have attached to reorganization. Some chief executives, President Truman for one, have seen it as a useful avenue for extending their control over the executive apparatus. President Kennedy, on the other hand, tended to disparage the importance of organization. The key to effective government from his perspective was recruiting talented people to work for his administration — the "best and the brightest," as David Halberstam somewhat ironically described them — rather than the search for an ideal organizational structure.[11] President Nixon saw reorganization as a weapon against the entrenched power of the bureaucracy. He proposed wholesale revamping of the executive branch — changes that would have detached executive agencies from their patterns of clientele and congressional support and subjected them to closer White House control.

If chief executives, most especially presidents, have been the chief beneficiaries of reorganization, the groups that have long regarded themselves as most threatened by it are the interest groups representing the various publics dependent on the work of executive agencies affected by reorganization. From the point of view of these groups, any alteration in the status of their agency endangers their interests and may ultimately weaken their access to the executive branch and their influence over policies that are extremely important to them. These fears are not always warranted — an agency may be as strong an advocate of their interests in one organizational setting as another. But neither are they idle fears: reorganization is often aimed at changing the patterns of group influence to which agencies are subject.

It can be argued that one reason government executives put so much faith in reorganization as an avenue of reform is that traditional personnel regulations make it very difficult to upgrade the quality and the performance of the civil servants who work for the agency. Executives change organizational structures because the option of making changes in personnel is not open to them.

Perhaps the boldest effort to reform public administration by altering personnel practices rather than redesigning organizational systems, was the enactment, during the Carter administration, of the Civil Service Reform Act of 1978. This legislation established a system of merit pay to provide incentives for improved performance by mid-level managers. The Act also made it easier for political executives to reward successful performance by subordinates, while eliminating career employees whose work was regarded as unsatisfactory. There are those who feel that these changes concentrate too much power over career administrators in the political sector, but, at the very least, the Carter Civil Service Reform Act represents an unusual recognition by a president that the way to reform bureaucracy is to improve the quality of the government's personnel rather than its machinery.[12]

## DATA AND DECISIONS

A second major direction of reform efforts in public administration in recent years has been toward more effective use of quantitative data in making policy decisions. This push toward quantification in decision making partly reflects new management techniques that greatly enhance the capacity of administrators to base their decisions upon more solid ground than speculation and hunch. Moreover, the vast sums of money now being spent by executive agencies create strong public pressure for greater economy. Because it promises to bring about more efficient use of financial resources to achieve program goals, quantified decision making thus has wide appeal for political officials as well as management specialists.

The changing technology of management that has given rise to the new vogue for quantification mainly reflects innovations in software, in the sense of techniques such as cost-benefit analysis that make it possible to link data to decision more effectively. But it rests upon changes in management hardware as well, particularly the coming of data-processing equipment. Computers have the capacity to sort out large masses of information and to do so with a speed that enables data to be compiled soon enough to influence decision. To be sure, most employment of computers to date in public as well as in private administration has been in the routine areas of decision: helping administrators keep track of payrolls, clients, and other management records. Use of computers at more complex levels of policy decision is as yet very limited, although they are necessary for the econometric models now being used to test the impact of high-level budgetary decisions before they are put into effect.[13]

The budgetary process has in fact been at the heart of reform efforts to put policy decisions on a more quantitative basis, for the budget is in a sense the expression of policy in numerical terms. Attempts were made as early as the 1930s to find better methods of relating the use of budgetary resources to the achievement of policy goals through a system of program budgeting that would link agency expenditures to the objectives they were designed to achieve rather than — as in traditional line-item budgeting — to the services and equipment they would be used to purchase.[14] These efforts reached something of a climax during the 1960s, when a comprehensive form of program budgeting called PPBS, a planning-program-budgeting system, was established in the national government. Under PPBS, it was hoped, the costs of alternative ways of achieving a policy objective could be clearly identified, and resources could be concentrated on programs best calculated to achieve this goal at the lowest cost.

PPBS was initiated in the Department of Defense in 1961 in an effort to obtain maximum return on the vast sums of money being expended to achieve national security objectives. It enjoyed at least the image of success in that area of policy, perhaps because achievement of defense goals is so easily linked to the construction and procurement of weapons systems. Alternative ways of ensuring the nation's security through armaments could be expressed in dollar figures and subjected to comparative evaluation on a quantitative basis. In 1965 PPBS was extended by President Johnson to a wide variety of domestic programs as well. Thereafter, it began to languish, until it was finally replaced in the Nixon administration as an executive panacea by "management by objectives" — MBO — a technique designed to point executive agencies toward achieving their goals rather than comparing different ways of using their resources.[15]

The troubles PPBS encountered are typical of the difficulties that confront all efforts to apply the magic of managerial science to public administration. Many programs proved stubbornly resistant to quantification under PPBS. Foreign policy objectives cannot readily be converted into budgetary alternatives. Cost-benefit ratios are difficult to work out in areas of international policy where pursuit of program goals is not primarily a matter of spending money.[16] Similar difficulties confront efforts to apply quantitative methods to domestic programs. Hard facts on which measures of achievement can be based are not easy to come by. Who can calculate the long-term benefits that may accrue to society from a federally financed program of educational enrichment designed for slum children in the elementary grades? The task of measuring the costs of a course of action can also be extraordinarily difficult, especially because it is usually necessary to bring nonmonetary costs within the sphere of calculation. Moreover, calculations of future costs and benefits depend on methods of forecasting that are as yet far from perfect.[17]

In any case, no system of quantification now available permits comparisons of the relative payoff of achieving disparate goals such as welfare, education, or public health. The hard choices of policy, allocating scarce resources among widely different programs, still remain essentially a matter of public decision. No set of quantitative techniques can transform policy making into a purely managerial process. Whether it is more important to use resources to achieve national security objectives, or to spend them on one or more of a variety of domestic programs that also contribute to the national welfare, are questions that defy purely quantitative analysis.

To be sure, the fact that quantification does have such limitations provides reassurance for those who fear that some new managerial technology will strip power from the public and its elected representatives and shift it to a technocratic elite skilled in both quantitative analysis and use of the new computer hardware. From this perspective it is comforting to know that politics plays a central role even in a computerized policy process. Major policy decisions invariably involve a choice between conflicting values — the relative importance of, say, rehabilitating slum areas as opposed to a highway construction program. The larger decisions of a society thus remain inextricably a matter of public preference. Indeed, it has been argued that the rise of quantitative technologies that improve our ability to make choices makes us more aware of choices that can be made and thus actually increases the public role in decision making.[18]

Moreover, with or without managerial science, pressures from community groups, or politicians' calculations on the possible reactions of these groups, will always represent salient factors in making policy choices in a democratic society. A program may rank very low on the scale of cost-benefit ratios, but if it enjoys extensive public support, or if the president or members of Congress calculate that it has broad public appeal, then its adverse standing in terms of economic rationality is not likely to be a fatal defect. Now as in the past, policy responds to the balance of forces within the community, or politicians' perceptions of this balance, as well as to the analytical data generated by quantitative systems of management. Hence, political considerations, in the sense of both value conflicts and the play of conflicting forces within the community, continue to have a major influence upon administrative decisions even in a setting of managerial science.

Moreover, from the point of view of an executive agency itself, it is often imperative to follow a strategy of organizational opportunism in pursuing its goals, no matter what priorities strict adherence to cost-benefit data may seem to require. A program for which a great deal of community support exists at a particular time may have to be vigorously pursued even though costs are high and benefits relatively low, in order not to miss the opportunity created by an immediately favorable climate of opinion. The arrival of managerial science does not abolish the need for adroit administrative statecraft.

But at its best a quantitative technique of management can serve as an important instrument of clarification in the design and development of an executive agency's program. It may not always provide answers in making policy choices, yet it certainly concentrates attention on the important questions and provides a framework within which the pursuit of many objectives can be most intelligently carried on. As one observer put it: "What the new intellectual techniques, such as those used in PPBS, attempt to provide are methods by which those who make the decisions about how the government should direct its efforts can increase their awareness of the conditions and consequences of their choices and can clarify the elements that, explicitly or implicitly, enter into their judgments." [19] Certainly, it is clear that a great many agencies have very little information about how well they are doing on the mission on which they are embarked.

Again, however, political realities may have to be taken into account. Investigations conducted in the 1960s by Congress and the press disclosed that the Subversive Activities Control Board was accomplishing very little in achieving its statutory objective of identifying and deterring subversive activity. But in spite of this evidence of its ineffectiveness, the agency continued to command strong support in Congress and elsewhere. As the work of Murray Edelman brings out, an agency can have enormous symbolic value for its adherents quite apart from its tangible accomplishments.[20] The symbol of opposition to Communism that the Subversive Activities Control Board represented far outweighed in the eyes of its supporters the fact that it was not doing anything of consequence. The agency was abolished only in 1973 when changes in the political climate finally made it politically safe for Congress and the president to withdraw financial support and thus liquidate it.

The greatest danger that these quantitative techniques of analysis present is the possibility that they may arm error with the seeming support of scientifically established fact, giving ill-advised policies greater credence. When this occurs, the finely honed rationalizing instruments of managerial science can become dispensers of irrationality measured out with mathematical precision.[21] During the Vietnam War, managerial specialists were constantly inventing and using quantitative measures of American success in the effort to suppress the Vietcong and pacify the countryside — such as the ill-famed "body count" that measured military success by the number of enemy troops slain in battle. These measures had great influence with policy makers, even though they proved in the end only to be instruments of self-deception.

One situation in which quantitative data may have extraordinary weight is where most of the considerations involved in decision making are intangible. Here numerical measurements may command a great deal of deference simply because they are precise quantities in a sea of uncertainty. To preserve rationality in decision, it is essential, therefore, that the use of data be hedged about with a sense of the limitations as well as the possibilities of such factual information. A balanced perspective of this kind can be most confidently expected when sophistication in the use of quantitative techniques of analysis is widely distributed throughout the government, so that weak arguments in a policy discussion do not gain an unwarranted advantage merely because they are put in the language of managerial science.

Interest has been growing in recent years in applying quantitative techniques to administrative regulation, in the hope that such techniques may help distinguish between rules and regulations that have a positive effect, and those which do not. During the past decade interest has been strong both in Congress and the White House in having regulatory agencies weigh the costs (especially in inflationary impact) as well as the benefits to be derived from any new rule they are considering, and to put into effect only regulations whose benefits exceed their costs. This cost-benefit technique is modeled on a procedure long practiced by the Corps of Engineers, which is required to use cost-benefit analysis in evaluating proposed water resource projects and to undertake only projects whose benefits exceed their costs.

Strong efforts were made in both the Ford and Carter administrations to induce regulatory agencies to subject their rules and regulations to the cost-benefit test, and those efforts were redoubled after President Reagan took office in 1981.[22] Putting this technique into practice has proved to be difficult mainly because there is very little consensus on the factors to be taken into account in devising cost-benefit ratios in regulation. Opponents of regulation tend to emphasize its costs and supporters try to highlight its benefits; the numerical values assigned to both costs and benefits are more often the product of imagination than of mathematical skill.

Thus, although the effort to introduce cost-benefit analysis into administrative regulation in recent years points up the enduring attraction of quantification as an instrument of administrative reform, the ultimate fate of this kind of evaluation in the regulatory field remains very much in doubt. One member of Congress, Albert Core, Jr., from Tennessee, expressed considerable skepticism. When the goal of public policy is to protect consumers from deceptive practices in the marketplace or workers in hazardous occupations, he doubted whether "any kind of ethereal academic analysis can adequately value the benefit of lives saved by regulations." [23]

As we have seen, recent presidents have tried to increase White House influence over regulatory decision making by establishing an executive office unit in charge of monitoring decisions to make sure that they are more beneficial than costly to the public. Since Richard Nixon, all presidents have taken steps in this direction, but executive order 12291, issued by the Reagan administration in 1981, established the most stringent system of White House control yet devised (including OMB clearance of all proposed regulations).[24] The new system was meant to eliminate regulations that impose burdensome costs without commensurate benefits. At the same time, it opened up the possibility that regulated industries would use access to the White House as covert pressure against regulations they dislike.

## Overcoming Bureaucratic Inertia

Among the many ways in which the American experience with bureaucracy differs from the European, none is more striking than the fact that executive agencies in the United States have so often been looked upon as major instruments of change in social and economic policy, whereas in Europe bureaucracy has historically been regarded as a chief source of institutional support for the status quo. Indeed, it is no exaggeration to say that public bureaucracy has been a revolutionary force in American society insofar as it has provided a channel through which submerged groups could use the powers of government to enhance their power. Farmers in the last century and more recently trade unionists and the urban poor have looked to executive agencies for redress of their grievances against more powerful segments of society, and the services of these organizations have provided the means by which the welfare and status of these disadvantaged groups have been greatly improved. In Europe, on the other hand, such groups more commonly have identified bureaucracy as part of the political system that must be overcome if public policy is to be changed in ways that are advantageous for them.

In the 1930s, public bureaucracy was a principal instrument through which the New Deal revolutionized American society. Agencies such as the Securities and Exchange Commission, the Social Security Board, and the National Labor Relations Board quickly became identified as major institutions through which the power of the mighty could be put down, and the welfare of the humble exalted. Certainly it was in this light that these agencies came to be regarded by business groups hostile to the New Deal. From the point of view of American conservatives, bureaucracy was both the symbol and the source of radical change in American society in the 1930s. Fulminations against bureaucratic power dominated conservative rhetoric, while defense of the role of administrative agencies in government came to be a conditioned reflex for the American liberal.

More recently, however, a new reform perspective on the relationship between bureaucracy and change has begun to appear. Increasingly, the established bureaucracies in welfare, education, foreign affairs, and a variety of other areas have come to be looked upon as obstacles to imaginative and creative thought in their own area of policy responsibility. Liberal reformers interested in taking bold new steps in dealing with the problems of the "permanently poor," or raising the aspirations of children in the slum schools, or in achieving a breakthrough in international relations that would reduce the possibility of nuclear war have frequently found that a major source of resistance to change is the executive agency chiefly responsible for developing and carrying out official policy. Witness this description of the role that public bureaucracy has come to play in the modern history of New York City:

> The leaders of the city's bureaucracies are a conservative force in the political contest. The stakes they seek are primarily those that minimize innovation and change. Their drive for autonomy is largely an effort to reduce the influence of the outside "movers and shakers" upon settled routines. . . . The policy and procedural *status quo* of today, or perhaps yesterday's in some matters, is their accepted milieu. . . . In the city's political process the leaders of the organized bureaucracies are an anchor, not a force driving forward.[25]

No agency better exemplifies the shift in the reform perspective on bureaucracy than the Tennessee Valley Authority. When it was established in the 1930s, TVA was the supreme organizational expression of the liberal belief that a public agency could serve as an instrument of change. The agency was created to invigorate the economy and elevate the welfare of the entire valley region by comprehensive planning and control of the development of its water and other natural resources. It was expected that TVA would not only harness the area's natural power for human purposes, but that it would also spread the benefits of that enrichment more equitably among the people who lived there. Thus, TVA's initial goals were both developmental and redistributive. Though bitterly opposed in its early years by private power companies and other conservative interests in the valley area, the agency eventually won a secure standing as a successful public agency, especially after World War II, when the less-developed countries came to see it as a model for the way in which they might quickly industrialize themselves by governmental development of hydroelectric power resources.

By the 1970s, however, TVA was no longer a beacon for change. In the eyes of reformers, it had transformed itself into one of the major vested interests in the valley region. Environmentalists were particularly incensed because the agency's ever-expanding quest for new sources of energy led it to give strong support to strip mining and other practices considered hazardous to the environment. Ecology groups even took the agency into court in an effort to prevent it from constructing a dam that they alleged would do substantial damage to recreational use of adjacent land.

As the TVA experience so clearly reveals, bureaucracy today is as frequently a target of criticism from the left in politics as it is from the right. Although the burden of complaint from conservatives is likely, however, to be the charge that executive agencies are exceeding their authority, liberal groups more frequently complain that agencies are doing far less than their responsibility requires them to do. On one point, however, viewpoints very often converge — the belief that bureaucrats are unimaginative, reluctant to accept new ideas, and extraordinarily slow to abandon policies that are clearly unsuccessful. These complaints against bureaucracy have been made by critics from all over the political spectrum.

As a result there has been a continuing search for ways of overcoming the alleged inertia of public organizations. Historically, the preferred option of those seeking to have an innovative program administered imaginatively and aggressively has been to have it carried out by a new agency. This new start allows for recruiting a fresh group of administrators to achieve the program's objectives, rather than having to face the troublesome task of trying to convert old hands to new ideas. A new agency is also free from some of the constraints that limit the flexibility of established organizations, such as long association with pressure groups, or mutual accommodation with legislators upon whom an agency may depend for fiscal support. Moreover, such an agency has not yet acquired the administrative habits and experience that it may eventually come to regard as the sum total of human wisdom in its own area of policy. But it is no small irony that a major remedy for the ills of bureaucracy should be creation of additional bureaucracies.

Similar in its energizing effect on bureaucracy is a significant change in the jurisdiction or resources vested in an administrative organization. In the 1960s, a flood of educational legislation greatly broadened the responsibilities and funding of the U.S. Office of Education. This led to an influx of new personnel as well as to reorganization of the agency, which altered not only its internal structure of power, but also the pattern of influences to which the agency was subject from outside groups.[26] Though not all observers would agree that such measures genuinely improved the character of the Office of Education, this experience does point up the possibility of administrative renaissance — an old agency may be given new life through administrative reorganization, the influx of new personnel, or a dramatic shift in the scope of its activities.

A livelier approach to policy development and administration can also be promoted by having executive agencies contract with organizations outside of government to undertake studies and make proposals on policy issues. In recent decades arrangements have proliferated at all levels of government under which private organizations perform research at the request of public agencies for the guidance of policy makers. Much of this kind of activity has been delegated to universities, but in addition a number of sidecar corporations like the Rand Corporation or the Institute for Defense Analyses exist almost entirely on the revenue they receive from conducting studies for government agencies under contractual arrangements.

A number of advantages accrue from the use of outside organizations for research purposes. For one thing these organizations are free from the restrictions that surround government hiring procedures and can, as a result, often recruit a very high caliber of professional personnel. They have no vested interests to protect in arguing for one line of policy rather than another, so that the conclusions they arrive at are often regarded as a good deal more reliable than the findings of a research unit under the jurisdiction of a line agency. Within government itself, research is often used not so much to find answers to questions as to build support for solutions that policy makers have already decided upon, or to advance the jurisdictional interests of an agency. Policy studies conducted by outside organizations are less susceptible to this tendency, though they are not immune to it. One study of RAND suggests that findings in its reports are prestructured by their governmental sponsors.[27]

Outside organizations can be used not only for advisory or consultative purposes but also for the direct operation of governmentally supported activities. The atomic energy program as well as a wide variety of research and development projects sponsored by agencies like NIH and NASA, are carried on mainly by government contracts with outside organizations or business firms. The Office of Economic Opportunity administered most of its antipoverty activities through private, nonprofit corporations called community action agencies. This system, which Don K. Price calls "federalism by contract," [28] is to a large extent motivated by the belief that nongovernmental organizations can be considerably more imaginative in their approach to policy problems and much more flexible in their day-to-day operations than public agencies.

One very widely criticized way in which bureaucratic inertia manifests itself is when government organizations fail to deal vigorously and imaginatively with problems that are high on the agenda of public concern. In part this is simply a matter of bureaucrats choosing to ignore problems that lie within their official responsibility, because executive agencies do have an enormous capacity for "nondecision." [29] They can see to it that issues do not arise in areas in which, to an outside observer, action may seem to be urgently needed. In part also executive agencies may find it difficult to shift their sights when past policies are no longer appropriate to present conditions.

The latter aspect of bureaucratic inertia — the difficulty administrative officials have in admitting and reversing mistakes — sharply contradicts one of the major justifications traditionally offered for transferring power over policy development from legislative assemblies to executive agencies. This was the expectation that administrative agencies would be considerably more flexible than legislatures in their response to changing environmental conditions — mainly because they were organizations continuously in existence, which could use the discretionary authority given them to adapt old policy to meet new needs. In fact, however, public bureaucracies frequently have proved to be quite rigid in their policy commitments, unable to change courses of action with which they as institutions or the reputations of their leaders have become identified.

Some resistance of bureaucracy to new outlooks may be simply a function of the slow movement of large organizations. A broad and complex pattern of consensus must be developed before change can take place in vast organizational systems with many centers of power and innumerable points at which decision can be blocked. It is also possible, however, for organizations to acquire vested interests in policies that are, from the point of view of society at large, dysfunctional, and to resist change, not because it is difficult for them to move in response to new stimuli, but simply because they have acquired a stake in the policies they are already following. If existing programs serve the comfort and convenience of a public agency's employees, or conform to their own professional view of what should be done, then they may develop deeply entrenched resistance to any alteration in such policies.

Private organizations can, of course, exhibit this same tendency toward organizational inertia.[30] By so doing, though, they run the risk that the public will cease to purchase, or otherwise support, the goods and services they supply, and a private organization's survival may be quickly threatened by its failure to adapt to the needs of the community it serves. Public agencies, on the other hand, perform functions that a community cannot do without, and they frequently hold a monopoly in providing such services. Except with agencies that enjoy only precarious political support, citizens cannot directly threaten the existence of a public agency as a means of forcing it to put their needs before goals it may choose to set for itself. Their efforts to change an agency's behavior must be confined to political channels rather than the threat to withhold economic patronage.

Some critics of bureaucracy would change this situation and subject public organizations to the same pressures of competition that organizations in the private sector experience. They contend that public agencies lack incentive to perform effectively because the consumers of their services have nowhere else to go to obtain a more satisfactory product. Hence, critics of the public schools argue for an educational voucher system, which would permit parents to choose among a variety of schools on which to spend their tax dollars. Such a system would encourage development of alternative schools that would compete with one another for enrollment. It would thus subject public agencies to the discipline of the market. Schools which satisfied a public demand for the kind of education they provided would thrive; those which did not would suffer a loss of resources. This voucher system has not been used extensively enough to know how well it would work in education, and it is difficult to see how it could be applied in many other areas of policy.[31]

But is is certainly clear that in the absence of market penalties for poor performance, public bureaucracies often seem to be most rewarded when they are not accomplishing their objectives and to be least rewarded, if not actually punished, when they are. A police department is much more likely to receive an increase in appropriation in a crime wave, much more likely to have its budget cut when the streets are comparatively serene. An internal study of the operation of New York City's public hospitals showed that the lion's share of appropriations went to hospitals that were doing the poorest job in terms of eighteen performance criteria. Under this skewed incentive system, it can be argued that it pays a public agency to do poorly the task it is asked to undertake.

These considerations have led some observers to conclude that society should try to avoid whenever possible using bureaucratic organizations in trying to cope with social and economic problems. A searching critique of bureaucratic organizations and of the programs and activities they carry on has come to the fore in recent years through the work of neoconservatives, a school of social scientists and philosophers who generally take the pessimistic position that government efforts to improve the human condition serve only to worsen it.[32] To support this jaundiced view of governmental effectiveness, which has had great intellectual force and influence, neoconservatives point to alleged failures in the war on poverty programs enacted with high hopes during the 1960s as part of President Lyndon Johnson's Great Society.[33]

At the grass-roots of American politics there has been a parallel development with even greater practical political significance. A strong taxpayers' revolt has erupted against public expenditures that have risen steadily since World War II. During the 1970s this movement had its most stunning success with enactment of Proposition 13 in California, a measure aimed at drastically reducing the financial burden on the state's taxpayers. Inevitably, it also forced a trimming back in the scale and scope of government activities in California. Similar measures have been pushed in other states, as well as at the national level, where a constitutional amendment has been proposed that would require the federal government to balance its budget annually.[34]

Finally, recent years have seen extensive and primarily successful efforts toward administrative deregulation, cutting back on government intervention in the decisions and activities of business firms in many industries. Deregulation has been supported by both conservatives and liberals: conservatives, because of their traditional distaste for government interference with business, and liberals because of the growing belief that government regulation of a number of industries has resulted in higher prices and poorer services for consumers.

With such a political consensus behind it, deregulation quickly won the day in the late 1970s in the airline industry, and enjoyed similar success in such other areas as government regulation of banking, transportation, and telecommunications. The ultimate influence of the deregulatory movement on consumers' welfare remains to be seen. Certainly not all consumers were immediately benefited by airline deregulation, which led to higher air fares and allegedly poorer service for travelers in many of the nation's smaller cities.[35]

Moreover, the political consensus in support of deregulation prevails only with the traditional areas of economic regulation such as transportation, where the restraint of market competition was missing. Liberals and conservatives commonly part company, however, when attention shifts to the newer kind of social regulation: government actions designed to achieve such goals as safety in the workplace, protection for the environment, or purity of foods and drugs. Many conservatives feel that regulation in these areas is excessive, but liberals commonly argue for even tougher enforcement of the existing laws.

Be that as it may, varied forces have converged, pressing strongly in recent years toward debureaucratization, a governmental system in which the role and power of bureaucracy is greatly reduced. As indicated above, these forces include the ascending influence of the neoconservative critique of bureaucracy and all its works; cutbacks in the funds available for government services by measures like Proposition 13 in the states and localities as well as a general pattern of national budget reductions; and last but not least a wave of deregulatory measures aimed at trimming the power of regulatory agencies.

Does this mean that we are at a turning point in American political history following which the cure for the ills of bureaucracy will be seen more and more as doing away with the bureaucracy altogether? [36] This outcome is not likely. In many sectors of governmental activity like foreign affairs and national defense we have no choice but to rely on the talents of public organizations, however critical we may be of the results they achieve. And in a number of domestic policy areas our dependence on bureaucrats is equally apparent.

The ultimate effects of debureaucratization may be quite different than its sponsors intend. While pruning away some of the services and regulatory activities provided by executive agencies, it may also sharpen public awareness and appreciation of the governmental functions that remain, even strengthening their position in American society. With the benefit of hindsight it was ultimately recognized that the reform agencies established by the New Deal in the 1930s won real legitimacy as public institutions only when their functions were finally administered by a Republican as well as a Democratic president in the 1950s. In the same way the agencies established in the second great period of bureaucratic expansion in American politics in the last half-century — the activities launched during Lyndon Johnson's Great Society — may acquire a similar legitimacy and permanent footing only after undergoing the trial by fire they experienced during the great wave of debureaucratization during the 1970s and 1980s. In this sense at least, debureaucratization may ultimately consolidate the position of large sectors of the welfare and environmental protection bureaucracy that had not previously enjoyed a public consensus of support.

The strong support given debureaucratization in recent years reflects wide public perception of bureaucratic failure, a growing sense that the performance of executive agencies has fallen far short of the promise of the programs they administer. But when a government policy or program fails to live up to expectations, the fault may lie elsewhere than in the organization charged with putting it into effect. Sometimes policies fail because bureaucratic organizations are given ends to achieve, for which we do not yet have the requisite means or the appropriate technologies. When agencies seek elusive goals such as "clientele transformations" in fields like education and welfare, we enter areas with many more "experts" than demonstrable expertise. Bureaucratic organizations are bound to fail if they are given tasks that are beyond human competence to perform at the time they are assigned.

In other cases policies may fail because the sacrifices required or the resources allocated for their achievement are insufficient to obtain successful results. As Paul Schulman notes in his analysis of large-scale policy making, success in the war on poverty might have been within the country's grasp if it had been prepared to make the necessary commitments or spend sufficient resources, but it proved unwilling to do so.[37] In any of these failures of policy, the fault may lie not with bureaucratic incompetence, but with elected officials who promise more than they can deliver, or the public itself, which is unwilling to pay the costs necessary to attain some of its goals.

# *Notes*

1. For a comprehensive look at the whole subject of administrative reform, see Gerald E. Caiden, *Administrative Reform* (Chicago: Aldine, 1969).
2. See in this regard Alfred D. Chandler, Jr., *The Visible Hand: The Managerial Revolution in American Business* (Cambridge: Harvard University Press, 1977).
3. For a discussion of efforts to use the public interest as a touchstone in appraising administrative decision making, see Pendleton Herring, *Public Administration and the Public Interest* (New York: McGraw-Hill, 1936), esp. pp. 377–399; Emmette S. Redford, *Ideal and Practice in Public Administration* (University, Ala.: University of Alabama Press, 1958), pp. 107–137; Glendon Schubert, *The Public Interest* (New York: Free Press, 1960), esp. pp. 64–74, 106–123, 173–186; Frank J. Sorauf, "The Public Interest Reconsidered," *Journal of Politics* 19 (November 1957): 616–639; and Norton Long, "Bureaucracy, Pluralism and the Public Interest" (Paper delivered at the annual meeting of the American Political Science Association, Aug. 31–Sept. 3, 1979).
4. Arthur M. Schlesinger, Jr., *The Coming of the New Deal* (Boston: Houghton Mifflin, 1959), pp. 527–528. Cf. also on this point the discussion in Richard E. Neustadt, *Presidential Power: The Politics of Leadership from FDR to Carter* (New York: John Wiley, 1980), pp. 115–118.
5. The best treatment of this problem is by Victor Thompson, *Modern Organization* (New York: Alfred A. Knopf, 1961).
6. Aaron Wildavsky, *The Politics of the Budgetary Process*, 3rd ed. (Boston: Little, Brown, 1979), pp. 166–167.
7. Charles E. Lindblom, "Policy Analysis," *American Economic Review* 48 (June 1958): 306. More distantly, Wildavsky's viewpoint corresponds to the concept of "piecemeal" social planning developed in the work of Karl Popper, *The Open Society and Its Enemies* (New York: Harper & Row, Torchbook edition, 1963), esp. I: 157–168.
8. See also the earlier discussion of decentralization on pp. 8–9. One of the best studies of the decentralization movement is by Alan A. Altshuler, *Community Control* (New York: Pegasus, 1970). For an analysis and bibliography on citizen participation techniques, see Robert K. Yin, William A. Lucas,

Peter L. Szanton, and J. Andrew Spindler, *Citizen Organizations: Increasing Client Control over Services* (Santa Monica, Calif.: Rand Corporation, 1973).

9. See Harold Seidman, *Politics, Position, and Power: The Dynamics of Federal Organization*, 3rd ed. (New York: Oxford University Press, 1980), for a very illuminating analysis of the theory and practice of reorganization in the United States. For an analysis of the influence of reorganization on government expenditures, see Kenneth J. Meier, "Executive Reorganization of Government: Impact on Employment and Expenditures," *American Journal of Political Science* 24 (August 1980): 396–412.

10. Seidman, *Politics, Position, and Power*, p. 132. For a critique of the whole procedure through which reorganization is carried out in the United States, see Louis Fisher and Ronald C. Moe, "Presidential Reorganization Authority: Is It Worth the Cost?" *Political Science Quarterly* 96 (Summer 1981): 301–318.

11. David Halberstam, *The Best and the Brightest* (New York: Random House, 1972).

12. For critical views of the Carter civil service reforms, see Mark W. Huddleston, "The Carter Civil Service Reforms: Some Implications for Political Theory and Public Administration," *Political Science Quarterly* 96 (Winter 1981–82): 607–621, and Dick Kirschten, "Administration Using Carter-Era Reform to Manipulate the Levers of Government," *National Journal* April 9, 1983, pp. 732–736.

13. Some of the more advanced uses of computers in administrative decision making are explored in Herbert Simon, *The New Science of Management Decision* (New York: Harper & Row, 1960). See also Martin Greenberger, ed., *Computers, Communications, and the Public Interest* (Baltimore: Johns Hopkins Press, 1971).

14. The historical development of program budgeting is traced in Allen Schick, "The Road to PPB," *Public Administration Review* 26 (December 1966): 243–258. See also the letter by Frederick C. Mosher in *Public Administration Review* 27 (March 1967): 67–71.

15. For a review of the decline and fall of PPBS, see Allen Schick, "A Death in the Bureaucracy: The Demise of Federal PPB," *Public Administration Review* 33 (March/April 1973): 146–156. The most ambitious attempt to evaluate MBO is by Richard Rose, *Managing Presidential Objectives* (New York: Free Press, 1976).

16. See, in this regard, the initial memorandum of the Senate Subcommittee on National Security and International Operations, *Planning-Programming-Budgeting*, 90th Cong., 1st Sess., committee print, August 11, 1967.

17. Some of the pitfalls that confront forecasting are explored and explained in William Ascher, *Forecasting: An Appraisal for Policy-Makers and Planners* (Baltimore: Johns Hopkins University Press, 1978).

18. See Victor C. Ferkiss, *Technological Man* (New York: George Braziller, 1969), pp. 136–137. Cf. also Daniel Bell, *The Coming of Post-Industrial Society* (New York: Basic Books, 1973), pp. 341–367.

19. Virginia Held, "PPBS Comes to Washington," *The Public Interest* 4 (Summer 1966): 114.

20. See Murray Edelman, *The Symbolic Uses of Politics* (Urbana: University of Illinois Press, 1964), esp. pp. 44–72.

21. For some reservations on the role of PPB in national security policy making, see Klaus Knorr, "On the Cost-Effectiveness Approach to Military Research and Development," *Bulletin of the Atomic Scientists* 22 (November 1966): 11–14.

22. For an excellent review of recent presidential efforts to monitor regulatory decision making see Lester M. Salamon, "Federal Regulation: A New Arena for Presidential Power?" in Hugh Heclo and Lester M. Salamon, eds., *The Illusion of Presidential Government* (Boulder, Colo.: Westview Press, 1981), pp. 147–173.

23. See Timothy B. Clark, "Do the Benefits Justify the Costs?" *National Journal* 13 (August 1, 1981): 1386.

24. These developments are traced in Salamon, "Federal Regulation."

25. Wallace S. Sayre and Herbert Kaufman, *Governing New York City* (New York: Russell Sage Foundation, 1960), p. 407. Other studies that point up the obstructive role of bureaucratic organizations in policy development include Gilbert Y. Steiner, *Social Insecurity: The Politics of Welfare* (Chicago: Rand McNally, 1966), and David Rogers, *110 Livingston Street* (New York: Random House, 1968).

26. See Stephen K. Bailey, "The Office of Education and the Education Act of 1965," *Inter-University Case Program, No. 100* (Indianapolis: Bobbs Merrill, 1966). In 1979 the office was given departmental status.

27. See Philip Green, "Science, Government and the Case of RAND: A Singular Pluralism," *World Politics* 20 (January 1968): 301–326.

28. Don K. Price, *Government and Science* (New York: New York University Press, 1954), pp. 65–94. See also the earlier discussion on p. 150.

29. This is a term introduced to guide the analysis of political power in urban communities by Peter Bachrach and Morton S. Baratz, *Power and Poverty* (New York: Oxford University Press, 1970). Matthew Crenson has used this concept with great skill in analyzing the development of air pollution policy in American cities. See *The Unpolitics of Air Pollution* (Baltimore: Johns Hopkins Press, 1971).

30. For a systematic analysis of factors affecting innovation in public and private organizations, see James G. March and Herbert A. Simon, *Organizations* (New York: John Wiley, 1958), pp. 172–210.

31. The literature on "public choice" is the best exploration of the possibility of using market forces to control bureaucratic behavior. See Vincent Ostrom, *The Intellectual Crisis in American Public Administration* (University, Ala.: University of Alabama Press, 1971). Cf. also William A. Niskanen, *Bureaucracy and Representative Government* (Chicago: Aldine Atherton, 1971), and Gary L. Wamsley and Mayer N. Zald, *The Political Economy of Public Organizations* (Lexington, Mass.: Lexington Books, 1973).

32. For a comprehensive overview of neoconservative thought, see Peter Steinfels, *The Neoconservatives: The Men Who Are Changing America's Politics* (New York: Simon and Schuster, 1979).

33. See, in this regard, Daniel P. Moynihan, *Maximum Feasible Misunderstanding: Community Action in the War on Poverty* (New York: Free Press, 1970).

34. For an excellent study of the factors underlying the tax revolt in California and elsewhere, see David O. Sears and Jack Citrin, *Tax Revolt: Something for Nothing in California* (Cambridge: Harvard University Press, 1982).

35. See Michael Wines, "Verdict Still Out on Deregulation's Impact on U.S. Air Travel System," *National Journal* 10 (March 6, 1982): 404–409.

36. For some suggestive comments see James Q. Wilson, "The Bureaucracy Problem," *The Public Interest* 6 (Winter 1967): 3–9.

37. Paul R. Schulman, *Large-Scale Policy Making* (New York: Elsevier North Holland, 1980), pp. 77–100.

# *Bureaucracy as a Power Elite*

A specter that has haunted political life throughout this century is the possibility that bureaucrats will come to occupy so commanding a position in the policy process as to become in effect a power elite, dominating all government decisions in which they participate.[1] Growing reliance upon the skills of bureaucrats in the operation of modern government has thus been coupled with pervasive distrust of bureaucratic power. For conservatives this fear has mostly been of civilian bureaucrats taking over areas of social and economic decision that ought to be left in private hands. From the liberal side, fear of bureaucracy concentrates on the growing power of national security agencies — not only the military establishment but also such organizations as the CIA and the FBI.

Concern over bureaucratic power is closely akin to the fear of technology that has loomed so large in contemporary political thought. Critics of technology are alarmed by the possibility that modern civilization will be dominated by the machines that have been its most conspicuous product. There is continuing apprehension that mankind will be transformed and ultimately dehumanized by intimate association with its own mechanical and electronic contrivances. A cinematic expression of this fear is the movie *2001*, which depicts a voyage to Jupiter in which the crew manning the spacecraft are virtually robots and a computer is the only one aboard capable of real feeling. But conforming to the traditional fear of technology, the computer eventually becomes the instrument of the crew's destruction.

From this perspective, bureaucracy can be viewed as part of the technology of modern life, a way of organizing human efforts so that

189

people can replicate the efficiency of the machine. Just as some fear that the instruments men construct will go out of control, attacking and perhaps destroying their human creators, so others are apprehensive that the organizations people devise to achieve their goals may eventually become their masters rather than their servants. The ancient Greeks attached the name *hubris* to the excessive pride men often take in their own capacity for invention and achievement. The wide reaction against technology and bureaucracy in more recent times suggests that human beings can also be quite fearful that their creations may be a threat to them.

Fear of bureaucracy has sometimes taken extravagant form in modern society, exaggerating beyond all bounds of possibility the capacity or likely intention of particular agencies to assume a controlling voice in governmental decisions.[2] Paradoxically, this fear of bureaucracy often coexists with another attitude with which it sharply contradicts — the belief that bureaucrats are timid, unimaginative, and reluctant to make hard decisions. The stereotype of a bureaucracy that is boundless in its appetite for power may thus coexist with an image of bureaucracy paralyzed with indecision when confronted with an opportunity to exercise authority.

It is clear that even if bureaucrats had the inordinate appetite for power commonly attributed to them, their role in the governmental process is hedged about by a wide variety of constraints that limit their ability to exercise influence. These limitations arise partly from sources external to executive agencies, the fact that bureaucrats do not rule alone in any area of public policy. They rest also upon factors indigenous to bureaucracy itself — "inner checks" built into the structure of administrative organization and the behavior of bureaucrats. As we saw earlier, many bureaucrats look upon power as a burden rather than an opportunity, and shift it from their hands whenever possible.

If bureaucrats do not have a monopoly over policy making, however, it is clear that they have a strategic role in the process by which decisions are made. Although they are unable to rule alone, no one in modern politics can rule without them. And when administrators cannot achieve their own goals, they may be able to prevent others from achieving goals to which they are opposed. It is as a "veto group," or perhaps through its ability to keep some matters from coming to decision at all, that an executive agency may actually exercise its most formidable influence. In this chapter we examine both the pattern of contraints to which bureaucratic power is subject, and the extent to which executive agencies yet manage to play a leading role in determining public policy.

## COMPETITION AMONG ELITES

A fundamental restriction under which bureaucrats operate is that they share control over decisions with other elites in the political system. Whatever else it may be, theirs is not an exclusive power. Among the most important groups with which they compete for influence are the political elites in both the executive and legislative branches of government. In addition, the leaders of nongovernmental organizations with continuing interest in the issues over which executive agencies have jurisdiction strongly influence their decisions. In some areas of policy public agencies may be little more than pawns in the hands of the private groups with which they are associated. Equally critical is the periodic participation by the media of communication and the courts in the processes of policy making. Both of these institutions have long helped to define and set boundaries upon the power of bureaucrats.

Interaction of bureaucrats with each of these elite groups in developing public policy will be examined in the section that follows. Bureaucratic influence, however, is by no means a constant factor in the policy process. As pointed out earlier,[3] bureaucrats may exert measurably more influence in one policy setting than they do in another, or the influence of a group of bureaucratic professionals may be much greater in one governmental jurisdiction than it is in an adjacent community. Significant variations in the balance of power between bureaucrats and other elites may also occur at different periods as a result of changes in the context in which policy is being made. "Power in America," David Riesman wrote, is "situational and mercurial." [4] Clearly, this is no less true of bureaucratic than it is of other forms of influence in the United States. Of course, in Western European democracies and elsewhere in the world, the balance of power between bureaucratic and other elites is tilted much more strongly in favor of bureaucracy.

*Political Elites.* The relationship between bureaucratic and political elites in the United States is enormously complicated by the fact that varied sets of political leaders simultaneously occupy positions of authority with respect to administrative agencies. On the one hand is a set of executive politicians with which agencies must share power — a chief executive such as the president, a governor, or a mayor, and his or her appointed or elected administrative subordinates. On the legislative side, there are, under the bicameral system of representation that generally prevails in the United States, two or more sets of legislative leaders who may participate with bureaucrats in making policy decisions.

The presence of these varied political elites in the policy process helps to create a system of multiple constraints upon bureaucratic behavior and decision. Executive agencies in the national government operate within limits set by the president and his agents with respect to budgets, personnel, and policy, as well as restrictions imposed by Congress through statutes, appropriation acts, or the threat of investigation. In addition, these agencies are subject to a continuing pattern of informal political pressure from both legislative and executive leaders because they depend so heavily upon these officials for fiscal and other resources necessary to sustain their programs.

Of course, by winning favor with one political elite, bureaucrats can limit the authority of another. By assiduously cultivating support from key legislative groups, administrative agencies have been able to reduce, sometimes to the vanishing point, the controls exerted over them by executive politicians. An agency can also use one group of legislators as a shield against another.[5] The Pentagon can always rely on strong support from its congressional allies whenever it comes under criticism from other sources in the national legislature. Political elites compete with each other as well as with bureaucrats, and executive agencies often serve as valuable allies in the struggle for power among politicians. It is questionable, however, if bureaucrats always increase their influence in the policy system by playing one political elite against another. When they decrease the control exercised over them by executive politicians, they may do so at the price of increasing their subordination to legislative elites, so that they become in effect "legislative agencies."

A much more promising strategy for any administrative agency is to build up sources of public support to which political leaders in both the executive and legislative branches of government will defer. The power of political leaders in a democratic society ultimately depends on their ability to stay in tune with public opinion.

Hence, they are quick to defer to an agency carrying on activities they perceive to be popular, whatever their private feelings about such programs may be.

In many countries, bureaucrats derive their greatest advantage in their interaction with political elites from both their expertise in technical policy and their continuity in office. However, in the American political system, these assets of expertise and continuity are not always the exclusive possession of the bureaucrat. Legislators in the United States tend to specialize in certain policy areas — a tendency that is encouraged by the strong power vested in legislative committees — and to enjoy long tenure in office. These characteristics of the legislative role help to offset the superiority in formal professional qualifications that bureaucrats ordinarily bring to policy deliberations.[6]

In short, it is incorrect, as we have seen, to regard a political elite's influence as resting solely upon the power of numbers, upon the ability of the politician to reflect and generate public pressures, while bureaucratic influence is attributed entirely to the professional skills of administrators. Politicians, too, may in time acquire formidable credentials as experts, if they do not bring such credentials with them when they come to office. At the same time, bureaucrats themselves are quite capable of mobilizing public support in behalf of their own policy positions. The competition between bureaucratic and political elites is thus one in which either side can bring to bear both political and professional resources.

Recent years have seen mounting efforts by political elites in the United States to monitor and control the activities of bureaucrats. At the national level both the president and Congress have greatly strengthened their capacity to oversee the work of excutive agencies. As a result, each institution has significantly changed the way in which it operates. The rise of bureaucratic power in American politics thus not only adds a new institution to the governmental structure, but also transforms the institutions already in place.

For the White House, the need to interact with a bureaucracy of vastly expanded size and complexity has forced presidents to call on the services of many types of political intermediaries to help supervise activities in the executive branch. Many of these aides work in the White House itself or in the adjacent units of the Executive Office of the President. The president thus comes to share his power with a variety of other White House officials, and a presidency intended in the Constitution to be singular becomes in effect a plural office.

Along with the assorted aides who are now part of an ever-expanding White House entourage, an increasing number of the president's men and women are now appointed to run the various agencies and departments of the executive branch. These presidential surrogates extend the reach of White House influence over the bureaucracy, because they help keep agency programs from deviating too sharply from the president's policies. When a president takes office, it is commonly expected at the White House that the bureaucracy will be quite resistant to his authority.[7]

At the same time, his executive agency appointees can create significant problems for the president. They can, as is so often charged by White House aides, "marry the natives" — that is, care more about the needs and problems of the agency whose work they are directing than they do about representing the president's views in developing the organization's policies.

Settling disputes among these various appointees at the White House and in the executive departments may also consume a great deal of the president's time and attention, as well as creating a public image of disarray within his administration. Many of the fiercest struggles in American politics during recent years have been between rival presidential appointees competing for power and primacy within the government. Not the least of the ironies of the modern presidency is thus that the officials appointed to help the president curb the bureaucracy may generate more trouble for the White House than the bureaucracy itself does.

For Congress, the chief effect of its growing effort to control the executive bureaucracy has been the "bureaucratization" of the legislature as well. Legislative staffs in congressional offices and legislative committees have expanded, and four main legislative staff organizations have been created: the Congressional Research Service, the General Accounting Office, the Congressional Budget Office, and the Office of Technology Assessment. All these staff officials and organizations help members of Congress oversee the activities of the executive organizations under their jurisdiction, but through their involvement in this oversight role, themselves become powerful actors in the political system. They help members of Congress develop policy guidelines for executive agencies, assist them in determining appropriate levels of financial support for agency activities, and investigate areas of executive activity where controversy has arisen.

The way that both the president and Congress have thus had to bureaucratize their own operation in order to control the bureaucracy illustrates the contagion effect of bureaucracy. Institutions that carry on extensive and continuing interaction with bureaucratic organizations are eventually compelled to hire their own bureaucrats to assist them in performing this task, a tendency that is visible in the private as well as the public sector when institutions like universities interact with federal agencies. The chief question that this development raises about the president and Congress is whether it further shifts power from elected to nonelected officials. Politicians in these institutions now face the task of supervising their own staffs in addition to managing or controlling the work of executive agencies. It thus becomes somewhat uncertain whether the growth of staff at the White House and Congress weakens or strengthens political elites in their efforts to bring public needs and concerns to bear on the technical issues with which government bureaucracies commonly deal.

*Public and Private Power.* The leaders of nongovernmental organizations also are an elite whose power bureaucrats cannot safely ignore. This stature is obvious in nongovernmental organizations that have an adversary relationship with an executive agency. If a government agency administers laws that restrict the discretion of, for example, business organizations, these outside organizations will in turn bend every effort to see to it that the powers of such a regulatory agency are confined within narrow limits.

It is less obvious that the leaders of nongovernment organizations that are allies rather than antagonists of an executive agency may also limit its freedom of action. But in international politics alliances often limit the options open to states that participate in such arrangements, preventing them from following certain courses of action and requiring them to fulfill commitments that they might well prefer to forget. Similarly, the alliances forged by the Departments of Agriculture, Commerce, and Labor with their farm, business, and trade union clientele, though of great value in enhancing the constituency strength of these agencies, nonetheless require that each department defer to the views of its nongovernmental allies in adopting policy positions. The development of political support by negotiation of alliances with outside organizations is thus a means by which the power of executive agencies is circumscribed as well as extended.

In some areas of the economy the decisions of administrative agencies may have life-or-death consequences for the business firms under their jurisdiction. A television station requires a license from the FCC in order to operate, a utility cannot raise its rate without permission from a public service commission, no drug company can market a new product without approval by the Food and Drug Administration, and all large firms face the constant possibility of antitrust prosecution by the Justice Department.

But even in relationships where such apparent administrative hegemony exists, the business firms subject to regulation have a great deal to say about the direction and development of policy in the agency under whose jurisdiction they lie. They can exert great influence on legislation affecting the agency's power, the fate of its requests for appropriations, or the appointment of political executives who will have ultimate control over the agency's decisions. In such patterns of reciprocal influence, the balance between public and private power in American society is not easy to discern.[8] In the worst scenario, an agency may allow the private groups most attentive to its work to determine the way in which it exercises its legal authority. The bureaucracy in question can then be said to be controlled, in the sense at least of not setting its own course. But this control may be purchased at a very high price, if it denies agencies the independence they need to carry out the tasks assigned them by the president or Congress in behalf of the public.

It is also possible for agencies themselves to capture outside groups for whom they provide benefits and use this support to insulate themselves from control by legitimate sources of authority in the White House or Congress. "Capture" may thus come in two forms. An administrative agency may be taken into captivity by outside groups (the regulatory agency syndrome), or, if these groups depend heavily on it, the agency may itself be the captor (the distributive agency syndrome), as exemplified by the Corps of Engineers. The result in either case is an agency whose policies executive and legislative officials will not easily control.

*The Media and Bureaucracy.* In some areas of policy, it is representatives of the media of communication who generate the most substantial outside constraint upon the decisions and activities of government officials. The news media have a powerful role in the development of policy because they both reflect and on occasion shape public opinion.[9] Nowhere is the influence of the media more keenly felt than in the agencies dealing with foreign policy, for only news organizations have the capacity to gather and disseminate information that may challenge the viewpoint of government officials on areas remote from the average citizen's power of observation.

To be sure, it is always possible for an executive agency to capture representatives of the media, and to use them to purvey the agency's point of view. Reporters can be given preferential treatment by access to official sources, provided with advance information on pending developments, or given by leaks (surreptitious disclosures) inside information not available to less friendly journalists. In these and other ways some representatives of the news industry may be corrupted into a relationship of faithful adherence to official policy doctrines. Russell Baker writes an amusing account of the way in which reporters at the State Department and the Pentagon take on the manner and even the dress of the bureaucrats whose work they cover.[10]

Reporters, however — at least in the United States — strongly resist a captive role in their relations with executive agencies. For one thing, American journalists have a status of parity with government officials that reporters abroad seldom enjoy. This high standing gives them a professional pride that ensures some independence in their dealings with the government. Moreover, in accordance with the muckraking tradition of American politics, the reporter in this country ordinarily conceives of his or her appropriate role as that of exposing the misdeeds of public officials, and this perception itself strongly inhibits subservience to the government.

Finally, representatives of the media as a group commonly cultivate a cynical disbelief toward statements and activities at "city hall," a term embracing executive agencies at all levels of government. This attitude creates a built-in, substantial credibility gap between media personnel and government officials, and strongly reinforces the independence of reporters. True, reporters are sometimes manipulated by executive agencies into disseminating policy viewpoints that the agency wants the public to accept. They may become in effect mouthpieces for the officials or agencies they cover. At the same time, however, there is no more effective instrument than the news media for ferreting out information that agencies are trying to conceal because it contradicts the tenets of official policy.[11]

This ability to expose information that agencies would prefer to conceal makes news organizations a threat to the power of bureaucracy. And yet the media can also augment the power of agencies by providing them with channels through which they can reach and mobilize the support of a constituency. The reporters' hunger for news — a commodity essential to the performance of their professional task — makes them very vulnerable to being used by an agency to disseminate information that will reflect favorably upon it. For the public information or public relations personnel of executive agencies this is one of their chief functions — feeding the media stories that will enhance the public standing of their agencies. An agency may also use the media to release, or more likely, to leak information damaging to another organization with which it is competing in a struggle over jurisdiction or some other bureaucratic resource.

Although agencies and the media thus have a common stake in disseminating news, they differ radically in their perception of what should be disclosed, and this difference is at the root of much of the antagonism that crops up between the media and the bureaucracy. The news that reporters often pursue is information that agencies are reluctant to divulge, because it contains items that cast them in an unfavorable light. Public officials would of course prefer that reporters let them decide what information should be released. When, as it sometimes happens, reporters are willing to accept so passive a role for themselves, the news media function not as a check on bureaucratic power, but as a major conduit through which it is exercised.

But even if this kind of capture does not take place, other factors may weaken the role of the media as a constraint upon bureaucratic power. At the state and local level of government, reporters often pay very little attention to the activities of executive agencies. Delmer Dunn found that reporters in Wisconsin spend most of their time covering legislators, even though administrative agencies are at the center of policy making in that state as elsewhere.[12] Reporters seek out stories of general interest to a mass audience, and executive organizations commonly deal with specialized subjects that reporters have neither the time nor the energy to master.

Still, Dunn also discovered that administrators much more than legislators look to the media for clues on public attitudes. Legislators tend to feel they have a direct pipeline to public opinion through elections and continuing contacts with their constituents. Executive agencies are somewhat more isolated from the public and often rely on the press to mirror public opinion for them, a reliance that cannot help but give the press strong influence over their behavior and decisions.

In national administration, even if reporters from the major news outlets ignore the work of specialized administrative agencies, the work of these organizations is still subject to very close and intensive coverage in segments of the trade press. *Broadcasting Magazine* follows the activities of the Federal Communications Commission very closely, and it is a valuable source of information on what the agency is doing and where its policies are tending. Over the years this communications journal has had an excellent record at predicting presidential choices to fill commission vacancies. The journal *Science* tracks very carefully the size of the government's budget for scientific research as well as other developments of interest to the scientific community that occur within the bureaucracy. Thus, the medium about which many administrative agencies worry is not the evening news on the major television networks, but the news that appears in specialized journals that few members of the public ever read or are aware of.

Of course, when the media of mass circulation do actually zero in on the activities of an administrative agency, they can do so with telling effect. Nothing more quickly focuses the attention of administrators than being identified on evening news telecasts as having neglected their duty or abused their authority. Other institutions interested in controlling bureaucratic behavior and decisions often use the media of communication to amplify their own criticism of bureaucracy. A legislative committee will turn over to reporters information on alleged cases of bureaucratic misbehavior, hoping that the ensuing publicity will bring an end to the practices in question. Although the media are thus an important instrument of control over bureaucracy in their own right, because of their zeal for investigative reporting, they are also important in facilitating the ability of other institutions like Congress to exercise such control.

*Judicial Control over Administration.* The judicial elite's role in restraining the power of bureaucrats varies from one policy sector to another. In many areas of policy, the decisions of executive agencies can be appealed to the courts. The possibility of such appeal is greatest for agencies exercising regulatory power, because their decisions may have so negative an effect on the constitutionally protected rights of individual citizens to life, liberty, and property. An agency like the Department of State, on the other hand, may (except for passport cases) seldom have occasion to find itself in court. But the possibility of being haled before a judge and having their decisions overruled is real and is a noticeable check upon all executive agencies.

Reform groups now make considerable use of the courts as a means of controlling bureaucratic decisions and behavior. In the early part of this century, reformers looked upon the courts as hidebound institutions that blocked social and economic regulation by insisting upon adherence to due process of law and being excessively preoccupied with protecting property rights. In modern times, however, the reform perspective has shifted. Reformers today routinely go to court to challenge decisions by executive agencies that they regard as damaging to the public, or to force agencies to protect the public by using powers that are lying dormant in their hands. Where once they were seen as obstacles to change, the courts have now become major channels through which reform groups can pursue regulatory goals such as environmental and consumer protection.

To be sure, a vast area of administrative action is, in legal terms, nonreviewable. Partly it is exempt because of procedural considerations, such as the fact that much of administrative policy making does not generate cases or controversies that can be taken to court. Partly, however, it rests upon the need for caution by those subject to regulatory authority. When an agency has a continuing supervisory relationship with a private organization or individual, this relationship often breeds acquiescence even to agency actions that are regarded as challengeable in court, for the agency's capacity for reprisal against those who challenge its power often deters assaults upon its authority.[13]

Moreover, the outlook is not always promising for individuals who choose to contest agency actions in court. On balance, it is better in state and local than it is in national administration, because judges at these lower echelons have tended to construe the powers of government more narrowly than jurists in the federal court system. From a study of U.S. Supreme Court decisions affecting ten executive agencies over the decade 1947 to 1956, Joseph Tanenhaus concluded that "the Court and its individual members favor federal agencies more frequently than they oppose them to a statistically significant degree." [14]

In recent years, however, there has been a growing tendency for the courts to intervene in the administrative process and reverse administrative decisions when they appear to infringe the basic constitutional rights of citizens. This intervention has been particularly striking when exercised on behalf of people who have been called "captives of the administrative state" — individuals locked away in prisons or mental institutions, for example.[15] In several recent cases involving such captives, the courts have required the administrative agencies in charge of these inmates to provide them with better treatment or living facilities. The courts have also been increasingly solicitous of the rights of individuals who depend on government benefits, reversing the position they once took that such benefits were privileges that administrative agencies could grant or withhold at their own discretion.

In the constantly evolving relationship between the courts and administrative agencies in this century, we can thus identify three quite distinctive historical periods. In the first period, prior to Roosevelt's New Deal in the 1930s, the courts were suspicious of a bureaucracy that looked as if it was poaching on their territory, and they were quick to overrule administrative decisions on the grounds that they suffered from one legal defect or another. Administrative agencies established in this early period, like the Federal Trade Commission in 1914, commonly found themselves losing out in the courts when they tried to assert powers that Congress had seemingly granted them.

Beginning in the 1930s, however, the attitude of the courts toward the exercise of administrative power shifted radically, as judges began to accept the fact that such agencies had an expertise to which they should defer. They might not always agree with what agencies decided, but judges should nonetheless face the reality that administrators had superior knowledge in the areas in which these agencies specialized. The findings of administrative agencies should thus prevail unless there was some conspicuous defect in the procedure by which they reached their decision. The substance of a decision was left to administrative determination, but the procedure by which it was reached was subject to judicial review.

We are now living in a third period, when judges appear more cognizant of the fallibility of administrative expertise and more willing to question whether this expertise is the last word on subjects in dispute before the courts.[16] As we saw earlier, the resurgence of judicial power has been particularly evident in cases involving individuals who charge that their rights have been violated by administrative actions. Critics of this new activist phase in the judicial relationship with the bureaucracy complain that the courts are overreaching themselves by second-guessing administrators who are operating facilities like schools and prisons — in some instances, judges are even taking over supervision of such facilities themselves. The argument is that these judges have neither the personal skill nor the institutional capacity to handle such specialized and continuing responsibilities.[17]

The quest for balance in the relationship between courts and administrative agencies thus continues. No formula for maintaining an equilibrium between these two institutions has long endured, such as the fact-law distinction and "substantial evidence" rule that sought in earlier years to differentiate the role of the courts as guardians of the law from that of administrators as servants of the public interest. The fact-law distinction put questions of fact under the control of administrators and left issues of law to the judgment of the courts. The substantial evidence rule gave finality to administrative decisions, even when judges disagreed with them, as long as the record included a reasonable amount of evidence that might lead administrators to reach such conclusions.

At all levels of government, one of the most important effects of judicial review of administrative decisions is to enlarge the role and influence of lawyers in the policy-making process within bureaucracy. Because advice on the legality of proposed courses of action is their specialty, lawyers are in a position to discourage policy measures they consider undesirable by declaring that these policies are certain to invoke judicial veto.[18]

The structure of influence over decision making within executive agencies is thus affected by the fact that bureaucrats share power in the policy process with outside elites. Moreover, lawyers are not the only group inside bureaucracy who benefit from the necessity that agencies face of negotiating with external forces. The role of budget officers in policy decisions is buttressed by their primary role in the bargaining with political elites that is necessary to obtain fiscal resources. The influence of legislative liaison officials in an executive agency is derived in no small measure from their close association with the legislators whose goodwill is vital to the agency's development and even survival. And public information officers can use their intimate contacts with outside groups and the news media to expand their own influence in policy deliberations within bureaucracy. The participation of outside elites in the policy process in which agencies are involved thus has a major effect not only upon the decisions made within executive organizations, but also upon the identity of those who make these decisions.

## The Inner Check

Limitations upon the power of bureaucracy stem not only from the competitive pressures of outside elites but also from factors related to the way in which organizations operate and bureaucrats behave within their own habitat. Even if there were no forces in the external environment to restrict their power, executive agencies would still find themselves limited in the scope of their discretion and the extent of their influence by restraints originating in the internal life of bureaucracy itself.

*Competition Among Bureaucracies.* Not least important in this respect is the struggle for primacy that is so constant a characteristic of relationships among executive agencies. Although the overt objective of this struggle is to strengthen the agencies that participate in it, an unanticipated consequence of such interbureaucratic combat is that the agencies involved become much more susceptible to outside control.

In the United States, the branches of the armed forces have long competed vigorously for financial support as well as jurisdiction over weapons systems and combat missions. This interservice rivalry was weakened by amalgamation of the separate services into one military establishment in the Department of Defense, but it was not ended. This competition has had a large part in facilitating civilian control over the military primarily because it has incited each branch of the service to criticize the defense policies advocated by the others, thus preventing growth of a monolithic military point of view on national security matters and enabling outside groups to make their own influence felt by siding with one military organization or another.

American presidents have never had much difficulty in finding support among military organizations for whatever defense policies the chief executives wished to adopt.[19] On one occasion, a president was even able to use the views of a foreign bureaucracy to counter the recommendations of his own military establishment. Early in World War II, President Franklin D. Roosevelt came under strong pressure from the American armed forces to authorize establishment of a second front in Europe. He was aided substantially in his resistance to this pressure by simultaneous opposition to such a venture from the British military organizations with which the American high command was then working very closely.[20]

Competition as a restraint upon bureaucratic power functions within executive agencies as well as between them, in the form of a struggle for power among the various professional groups that play a role in the operation of an agency. As we have shown, there are multiple forms of expertise in bureaucratic organizations in advanced industrial societies, as well as many areas of policy deliberation within these agencies where decisions are shaped by competitive pressures from different clusters of professionals.

In modern American bureaucracy such natural rivalries in controlling bureaucratic behavior have been supplemented by deliberate creation of executive organizations whose major function is that of monitoring other agencies to see that their decisions conform to specified policy goals. The Commission on Civil Rights has the task of seeing to it that national agencies do not discriminate against women, blacks, and other disadvantaged groups in their personnel policies, and the reports of the commission have often severely criticized the practices of various agencies. In a similar way the Environmental Protection Agency (EPA) seeks to have all executive agencies abide by standards designed to protect the natural environment from deterioration resulting from, among other things, air or water pollution. Both the Commission on Civil Rights and the EPA thus function as what might be called adversary bureaucracies — set up to bring the decisions and actions of other agencies under greater scrutiny and to deter them from malpractice.

Thus, although it may come as a surprise to critics of bureaucracy who see it only as a source of excessive regulation of private citizens, bureaucracies are themselves highly regulated organizations.[21] Indeed the chief function of a growing number of administrative agencies is that of regulating the activities of other executive bodies. Some administrative executives complain that the burden of complying with all the internal regulations to which they are subject severely limits their ability to attain their agency's policy objectives. State agencies are particularly vociferous in their complaints against the numerous rules imposed on them by the federal agencies monitoring their programs. National agencies like the TVA, with a long tradition of administrative autonomy, looked upon early attempts by the EPA to get them to conform to environmental standards as a threat to their organization's independence. Paradoxical though it may be, bureaucrats can regard themselves as major victims of bureaucratic regulation. And, like business executives in the private sector, they often complain that these regulations ask them to do contradictory things.

One form of adversary organization much used in European societies to control bureaucracy is the office of ombudsman, an administrative agency charged to help citizens obtain remedies for decisions by executive officials that inflict unjustified injury upon them. This institution, developed initially in Sweden, has spread to many other countries, and it is being urged as the solution to the general problem of controlling the unwarranted exercise of bureaucratic power. A major factor leading to creation of the ombudsman office is the expectation that it will make agency decisions more sensitive to the needs and interests of individuals whose circumstances may not always fit neatly into the classes or groups into which bureaucrats tend to categorize the population.[22]

*Internalized Restraints.* Perhaps the best kind of "inner check" upon bureaucratic power is not interagency rivalry, which requires, after all, a vigorously competitive relationship between two or more executive organizations, but restraints that operate within the personalities of bureaucrats themselves, preventing them from unlawful or excessive use of the power placed in their keeping. Such internalized restraints have the great advantage that, when they are effective, they are a constant presence — exercising a restraining influence in areas of decision known only perhaps to the bureaucrats themselves.

Ideally, the bureaucrats' conception of their own role in the governing process can be structured to constitute by itself a substantial check upon the extravagant use of power.[23] If bureaucrats themselves feel it is necessary to defer to the preferences of citizens in framing public policy, or regard it as reprehensible to use power in ways that infringe upon the liberties of individuals subject to their jurisdiction, then the problem of controlling bureaucratic power is very largely solved at the source. The bureaucrat's own inhibitions may be an effective substitute for external controls.

Codes of ethics adopted by administrative groups such as city managers characteristically accept a subordinate role for bureaucrats in the governmental process. To be sure, this acceptance may be mere lip service, designed to disguise the extent to which city managers as well as other bureaucrats actually control policy decisions. At the same time, however, it seems fair to assume that there will always be some strain toward consistency on the part of administrative officials, and that bureaucrats' conception of their role as limited will restrain their behavior in office.

Certainly it is true that in a country like the United States, bureaucrats are, like all other citizens, subject to education as children, and continuing indoctrination as adults, which stress adherence to fair play in relations between government and the citizen, as well as the obligation of public officials to defer to the will of the people.[24] And if bureaucrats were to forget that their proper role is that of the public's servant and not its master, a variety of institutions — including legislative bodies, the courts, and the press — would be quick to remind them of their subordinate role.

Moreover, many executive agencies have developed their own ways of keeping themselves in touch with public opinion. They follow the results of public opinion surveys taken by polling organizations and may even conduct their own polls. Agencies may also monitor editorials in newspapers on the policy issues with which they deal, as well as letters to the editor. They can also respond to complaints filed with the special service some segments of the media now provide, where citizens may send in complaints about a grievance they have for which an administrative agency may either be responsible or able to provide a remedy. Through these and other techniques, agencies may establish direct links with public opinion, and thus acquire a capacity to anticipate the reactions of the public in designing official policy — to avoid doing things that they know beforehand will bring an adverse public reaction.[25]

Of course, a system under which executive officials themselves take public opinion into account in their policy decisions differs from a genuine system of representation or citizen participation in which the public has an opportunity to speak for itself either directly or through officials it elects. When public opinion filters into executive agencies only through bureaucratic perceptions, the image may be grossly distorted, reflecting not the actual contours of opinion but the image that it is convenient for the bureaucrat to see.[26]

An old dispute in the literature of public administration is whether the more effective way of containing expansion of bureaucratic power is through the various internal restraints just discussed or through the competition among elites outlined in the earlier sections of this chapter. The argument for primacy of the inner checks rests essentially on the grounds that these controls are more pervasive and effective than the efforts at surveillance over bureaucratic behavior by external elites. Considering the complexity of modern government, it is impossible to avoid leaving large amounts of power in the hands of bureaucrats to be used at their discretion.

The chief disadvantage of these purely psychological inner checks, however, is that they rely upon inculcation of virtue, operating through either conscientious scruples on the part of the individual official, or a code of honor or ethics prevailing among an administrative group to which bureaucrats feel they have a professional obligation to conform. Carl J. Friedrich once argued in favor of relying on bureaucrats' own sense of responsibility to deter any abuse of power on their part.[27] But as Herman Finer pointed out in response, "reliance on an official's conscience may be reliance on an official's accomplice," because "the political and administrative history of all ages ... has demonstrated without the shadow of a doubt that sooner or later there is an abuse of power when external punitive controls are lacking." [28]

The competition among elites, on the other hand, rests upon the solid bedrock of human selfishness — the ambition of political and bureaucratic elites alike to pursue and protect their own power interests. It was just such motives that the authors of *The Federalist Papers* saw as the most dependable base on which restraints on power could be built realistically into the American constitutional system: "Ambition must be made to counteract ambition. The interest of the man must be connected with the constitutional rights of the place ... the constant aim is to divide and arrange the several offices in such a manner as that each may be a check on the other — that the private interest of every individual may be a sentinel over the public rights." [29]

*A Representative Bureaucracy.* It has long been felt, not only in the United States, that the surest way of ensuring that a bureaucracy will be truly responsive is to require it to follow recruitment practices which ensure that its personnel will have the same characters as demographic character of the community it serves. Thus, throughout American history there has been a continuing effort to open up employment opportunities in bureaucracy to all segments of the country. In part this effort has been motivated by a commitment to equality of economic opportunity. In the United States as elsewhere, public bureaucracy has become an increasingly significant source of jobs. Approximately one out of every five employed Americans works for the government today. And in some Third World countries, the bureaucracy is the principal employer in the society.

But beyond this desire to use bureaucratic employment as a means of promoting equal economic opportunity is the belief that a bureaucracy that mirrors a society in its social, economic, and cultural composition will be much more sensitive to the needs of citizens of that society, and much less likely to be arbitrary or abusive when it is exercising power over "its own kind" of people. It is precisely this premise that lies behind recruiting of blacks by urban police departments in the United States today, but at least since the days of President Andrew Jackson the idea of a representative bureaucracy has had great appeal in the United States as a logical implication of the American commitment to an egalitarian democracy.

This representative bureaucracy concept has been strongly criticized when it has appeared to conflict with the modern attachment to the standard of merit in recruiting public servants — the belief that preferment should be given in all decisions on public employment to the most able and qualified applicants in society. As in other ways mentioned earlier, a step taken to ensure a more responsive bureaucracy comes into apparent conflict with the need to maintain the effectiveness of public agencies. A compromise sometimes reached in a number of countries, including the United States and Israel, is to adhere to the standard of merit in filling positions wherein skill is an indispensable requirement in public bureaucracy, but to attempt to satisfy the need for representation of all segments of society in recruiting for other positions requiring somewhat less technical skill.[30] When this occurs, disadvantaged groups are much more strongly represented at lower than at higher echelons of bureaucracy.

The quest for a representative bureaucracy can help to achieve goals besides economic and political equality. One very important role is helping to overcome divisions and alienation within a society, especially one as fragmented as the United States. In the days of Jackson prior to the Civil War, access to public employment helped to overcome friction between inhabitants of the newly settled regions in the West and the more established Eastern Seaboard. After the Civil War, assimilation of newly arrived immigrant groups such as the Irish was greatly facilitated by the availability of jobs in the public sector, especially in the large cities where many immigrants clustered. In contemporary American culture, public employment has become more and more important in satisfying the aspirations of disadvantaged groups, especially blacks. In appraising the value of representation as a goal in recruiting public servants, we must remember that it can serve latent functions like political integration as well as more manifest goals like equality of economic opportunity or bureaucratic accountability.

## Enduring Problem of Bureaucracy

Extensive as the controls over bureaucracy may seem, both from external and internal sources, the power of executive officials remains an object of intense concern in modern politics. To some extent this anxiety reflects the persistent political mythology in many countries that credits bureaucracy with a good deal more power than it actually has. It also tends to be forgotten that although the power of bureaucracy can threaten the traditional freedoms of a democratic society, this power can also be used to protect and extend those freedoms.

Witness the fact that a number of civil rights agencies in the United States have the chief purpose of seeing to it that minority citizens are not denied the rights guaranteed them by the constitution. Moreover, as we have seen, when the Nixon administration began carrying on the illegal and covert activities that were eventually to lead to its removal from office, it quickly became clear that bureaucratic organizations could help to strengthen rather than weaken democracy by exposing if not actually opposing the plans of their political superiors.

At the same time neither the Watergate episode nor any other recent development can erase the fact that a decisive power of initiative now lies in the hands of career bureaucrats. Apprehensions over the power of executive agencies are well grounded in the realities of modern politics. There is always the nightmarish possibility that military organizations may use their power over disposition and use of weapons to precipitate a thermonuclear war that would destroy modern civilization. Against such a holocaust, the controls discussed in this chapter may seem pitifully inadequate, even though the outbreak of war today is as likely to stem from miscalculations of politicians, or the passions of the public, as it is from precipitous actions by bureaucrats.

Fear of bureaucracy is not altogether relieved by the fact that public agencies do not wield monopoly power, but are linked instead in a policy system with other bureaucratic or nonbureaucratic elites. Some observers would argue that relations among these groups can more closely resemble oligopoly than they do competition. These separate elites may be able to find common interests in developing policies that will satisfy all their interests rather than those of the public. The military-industrial complex in the United States is often identified as just such an arrangement under which military bureaucracies, defense contractors in private industry, and political elites, such as congressmen connected with military affairs, are linked in support of a high level of defense spending from which each group derives substantial benefits. In a situation of this sort, it is argued, the belief that outside groups will serve as effective instruments of restraint upon a government agency may be somewhat illusory. But the public pressure which has periodically brought about reduction in defense spending, and which forced American withdrawal from Vietnam, suggests that not even a strong oligopoly like the military-industrial complex is altogether immune to outside controls.

If there is one factor that contributes more than any other to bureaucratic dominance in the political system, it is inattention by the other actors or participants in policy making, who have at least the potential capacity to limit the influence bureaucrats can exert over government actions or decisions.

This inattention may result from the practice of secrecy that executive agencies so often follow on policy decisions or deliberations, especially in national security affairs. People can hardly be attentive to matters about which they are allowed to know nothing. Secrecy may thus serve bureaucratic power by enforcing inattention to important policy issues on the part of other participants in political life. Though this secrecy has been reduced by enactment of freedom of information or "sunshine" legislation, it has not been — nor could it be — eliminated. As the exemptions in the freedom of information acts clearly imply, there are many legitimate reasons for maintaining the confidentiality of some kinds of government records.

The complexity of many of the issues with which bureaucracies deal may also reduce if not foreclose attention by other political actors. It is difficult for many of these actors to invest the time needed to understand the issues that executive agencies commonly confront, and complexity is increasingly characteristic of the policy issues that arise in politics today. Both secrecy and complexity thus work in much the same way to curtail the attention other participants in the policy process can give to decisions that bureaucratic organizations may be making.

A crisis in policy makes dramatically clear how bureaucratic power thrives on the inattention of other participants in the policy process. In a crisis both the president and Congress may give close and continuous attention to what bureaucrats are doing, and even the public may be momentarily aroused and pay uncommonly close attention to a policy issue. And in a crisis many decisions that are ordinarily left to bureaucrats are taken out of their hands altogether. This happened in the Cuban missile crisis, for example, when decisions on the disposition and use of Navy ships in the Caribbean were made in the Office of the Secretary of Defense, in close consultation with the White House. When the Social Security Administration faced a financial crisis in the early 1980s, both Congress and the president began to give intense scrutiny to an agency they had previously allowed operate as virtually a self-directing organization. Of course, the crisis atmosphere eventually recedes, and as policy making falls back into obscurity, it may once again be dominated by the routines of bureaucracy. When that happens, an agency like the Social Security Administration soon regains control over its program.

The future will thus present a continuing challenge to maintain effective oversight over the exercise of bureaucratic power. In the past, democratic societies have exhibited impressive powers of invention for this purpose, and we have shown that this inventive capacity is still very strong in the United States. Old mechanisms for controlling bureaucratic behavior and decision have been strengthened, and new ones have been developed. Although bureaucratic rather than party politics is now the dominant theater of decision in the modern state, many players other than professional bureaucrats may have a deciding role.

Throughout this discussion we have strongly emphasized the necessity of having an extensive network of public controls over bureaucratic behavior and decision in a democratic society. Without such controls democracy becomes technocracy, as power over decision comes to rest in the hands of nonelected experts in bureaucratic organizations. Elections and the other avenues through which citizens influence the conduct and character of government policy then become meaningless rituals.

At the same time bureaucratic organizations are established to achieve specified public goals, and attainment of such objectives often requires that these organizations be given sufficient freedom of action to cope with the task. From the public's point of view the best administrative organizations are those which do very well the things they are charged with doing, and the American experience often suggests that the best performances are turned in by agencies that enjoy by law or political custom a large measure of autonomy in the way in which they do business.

The roster of national agencies whose successful performance has been linked to their autonomous status is impressive. It includes the TVA, the Peace Corps, the Federal Reserve, the Bureau of Labor Statistics, and NASA. At lower levels of government, state colleges and universities also enjoy an independence designed to enhance their effectiveness, as do the numerous public authorities set up to achieve many varieties of community purposes.[31] Such agencies are commonly staffed by professional groups who themselves enjoy long autonomy in the practice of their craft. The concept of public control over bureaucracy is thus not incompatible with the idea and practice of administrative autonomy-giving administrative agencies the elbow room they require to record the achievements expected of them by the public.

Moreover, public control over bureaucracy is consistent with providing abundant opportunities for career civil servants to have an impact on their own agencies' policies. Recent years have seen a growing tendency to "politicize" the upper ranks of government employment, filling these slots with political appointees. This trend partly reflects an effort to strengthen political control over bureaucracy, but partly also it is intended to "presidentialize" policy making within executive agencies. Presidentializing policy making may be sharply distinguished from political control over bureaucracy, because it often requires agencies to defer in their decisions not to the imperatives of the laws they are administering but to the ideological tilt of the White House.

The result in any event may be a bureaucracy so overloaded at the top with political appointees that little opportunity is left for meaningful participation in major policy decisions by career civil servants.[32] When pursuit of the goal of political control over bureaucracy has this effect, it undermines efforts to recruit talented young people into the public service, and it encourages career professionals to leave government employment for more challenging responsibilities in the private sector. More than that, it diminishes the input into policy of professional skills and judgments that may be vital for its success. Professional talent is essential in the conduct of governmental activities, and to the extent the excessive politicization of bureaucracy significantly reduces the contribution that skilled professionals can make to executive policy making, it threatens the viability of democratic government itself. The "energy in the executive" that Alexander Hamilton long ago saw as essential to free government depends upon the detached expertise of the bureaucrat as well as the political zeal of a chief executive's appointees.

# *Notes*

1. For an analysis of some of the early literature bearing on this problem, see Dwight Waldo, *The Administrative State* (New York: Ronald Press, 1948), pp. 89–103. For a recent picture of the menacing features of bureaucracy, see Ralph P. Hummel, *The Bureaucratic Experience*, 2nd ed. (New York: St Martin's Press, 1982).
2. The exaggerated forms this fear can take are closely and clearly examined in Herbert Kaufman, "Fear of Bureaucracy: A Raging Pandemic," *Public Administration Review* 41 (January/February 1981): 1–9.
3. See pp. 92–93, 102.
4. David Riesman, *The Lonely Crowd* (New Haven: Yale University Press, 1950), p. 252.
5. See J. Leiper Freeman, *The Political Process: Executive Bureau — Legislative Committee Relations*, rev. ed. (New York: Random House, 1965), pp. 80–81.

6. In this connection, see the account of the career of Representative Carl Vinson of Georgia in David B. Truman, *The Governmental Process* (New York: Alfred A. Knopf, 1951), p. 424.

7. For a discussion of some of the strains in the president's relationship with the bureaucracy, see Francis E. Rourke, "Grappling with the Bureaucracy," in Arnold J. Meltsner, ed., *Politics and the Oval Office* (San Francisco: Institute for Contemporary Studies, 1981), pp. 123–140.

8. For an analysis of the role of private business organizations in framing public policy in the United States, see Mark V. Nadel, "The Hidden Dimension of Public Policy: Private Governments and the Policy Making Process," *Journal of Politics* 37 (February 1975): 2–34.

9. See, in this connection, Douglass Cater, *The Fourth Branch of Government* (Boston: Houghton Mifflin, 1959).

10. Russell Baker, *An American in Washington* (New York: Alfred A. Knopf, 1961), pp. 198–199.

11. Analyses of the many-sided relationship between executive agencies and the press may be found in Cater, *The Fourth Branch of Government,* Bernard Cohen, *The Press and Foreign Policy* (Princeton: Princeton University Press, 1963), Leon V. Sigal, *Reporters and Officials* (Lexington, Mass.: Lexington Books, 1973), Michael B. Grossman and Martha J. Kumar, *Portraying the President* (Baltimore: Johns Hopkins University Press, 1981), and Stephen Hess, *The Washington Reporters* (Washington, D.C.: Brookings Institution, 1981).

12. Delmer D. Dunn, *Public Officials and the Press* (Reading, Mass.: Addison-Wesley, 1969).

13. See also the discussion of this point on pp. 39–40.

14. See Joseph Tanenhaus, "Supreme Court Attitudes Toward Federal Administrative Agencies," *Journal of Politics* 22 (August 1960): 513. Of 243 decisions involving federal agencies, 168 were favorable to them.

15. For a very interesting analysis of these developments, see David H. Rosenbloom, "The Judicial Response to the Rise of the American Administrative State," *American Review of Public Administration* 15 (Spring 1981): 29–51.

16. See James O. Freedman, *Crisis and Legitimacy* (Cambridge: Cambridge University Press, 1978).

17. See Donald L. Horowitz, *The Courts and Social Policy* (Washington, D.C.: Brookings Institution, 1977).

18. For an informative account of the role of lawyers in bureaucratic policy making, see Victor A. Thompson, *The Regulatory Process in OPA Rationing* (New York: Columbia University Press, 1950), esp. pp. 207–222. For a more recent study, see Donald L. Horowitz, *The Jurocracy: Government Lawyers, Agency Programs and Judicial Decisions* (Lexington, Mass.: Lexington Books, 1977).

19. See Samuel P. Huntington, *The Common Defense* (New York: Columbia University Press, 1961), pp. 371–372, 113–115.

20. See, in this regard, William R. Emerson, "F.D.R.," in Ernest R. May, ed., *The Ultimate Decision: The President as Commander in Chief* (New York: George Braziller, 1960), pp. 135–177.

21. See James Q. Wilson and Patricia Rachal, "Can Government Regulate Itself?" *The Public Interest* 47 (March 1977): 3–14.

22. The role of the ombudsman has attracted much attention in the literature of comparative administration. See especially Walter Gellhorn, *Ombudsman and Others: Citizens' Protectors in Nine Countries* (Cambridge: Harvard University Press, 1967), and Donald C. Rowat, *The Ombudsman Plan: Essays on the Worldwide Spread of an Idea* (Toronto: McClelland and Stewart, 1973).

23. The term role is here used in the sense of forms of behaviors expected of, or considered suitable for, individuals occupying a certain position or performing a particular function in an organization. See Abraham Zaleznik, "Interpersonal Relations in Organizations," in James March, ed., *Handbook of Organizations* (Chicago: Rand McNally, 1965), pp. 589–590.

24. One survey of bureaucrats found, however, that about one-third of them agreed with a variety of antidemocratic statements on, for example, freedom of speech. See Bob L. Wynia, "Federal Bureaucrats' Attitudes Toward a Democratic Ideology," *Public Administration Review* 34 (March/April 1974): 156–162.

25. The concept of "anticipated reactions" to describe the way in which public opinion is built into the original design of policy comes from Carl Friedrich, "Public Policy and the Nature of Administrative Responsibility," in Carl J. Friedrich and Edward S. Mason, eds., *Public Policy* (Cambridge: Harvard University Press, 1940), pp. 15–16.

26. See, for example, the description of the "trustee" relationship between administrative officials and their publics in Robert S. Friedman, Bernard W. Klein, and John H. Romani, "Administrative Agencies and the Publics They Serve," *Public Administration Review* 26 (September 1966): 195: "a trustee . . . is satisfied with the knowledge that his constituents are supportive of his decisions and is likely to read the absence of complaints by constituents as support or acceptance."

27. See Friedrich, *op. cit.*

28. Herman Finer, "Administrative Responsibility in Democratic Government," *Public Administration Review* I (Summer 1941): 336–337.

29. See Roy P. Fairfield, ed., *The Federalist Papers* (Garden City, N.Y.: Doubleday Anchor edition, 1961), p. 160.

30. For a discussion of these trade-offs as they have occurred in a number of societies, see Samuel Krislov, *Representative Bureaucracy* (Englewood Cliffs, N.J.: Prentice-Hall, 1974), esp. pp. 82–103. Cf. also V. Subramanian, "Representative Bureaucracy: A Reassessment," *American Political Science Review* 61 (December 1967): 1010–1019.

31. For an excellent analysis of the current status of public authorities in the United States, see Jameson W. Doig, " 'If I See a Murderous Fellow Sharpening a Knife Cleverly . . .': The Wilsonian Dichotomy and the Public Authority Tradition," *Public Administration Review* 43 (July/August 1983): 292–304.

32. For some thoughtful comments on this problem, see Hugh Heclo, *A Government of Strangers: Executive Politics in Washington* (Washington, D.C.: Brookings Institution, 1977). Cf. also Herbert J. Storing, "Political Parties and the Bureaucracy," in Robert A. Goldwin, ed., *Political Parties, U.S.A.* (Chicago: Rand McNally, 1964).

# Selected Bibliography

Aberbach, Joel D., Robert D. Putnam, and Bert A. Rockman. *Bureaucrats and Politicians in Western Democracies.* Cambridge: Harvard University Press, 1981.
————, and Bert A. Rockman. "Clashing Beliefs within the Executive Branch: The Nixon Administration Bureaucracy." *American Political Science Review* 70 (June 1976): 456–468.
Albrow, Martin. *Bureaucracy.* New York: Praeger, 1970.
Allison, Graham T. *Essence of Decision: Explaining the Cuban Missile Crisis.* Boston: Little, Brown, 1971.
Altshuler, Alan A. *Community Control.* New York: Pegasus, 1970.
Anderson, James E. *Public Policy-Making,* 3rd ed. New York: Holt, Rinehart and Winston, 1984.
Anderson, Patrick. *The Presidents' Men.* New York: Doubleday, 1969.
Argyris, Chris. *Personality and Organization: The Conflict between System and the Individual.* New York: Harper, 1957.
Arnold, R. Douglas. *Congress and the Bureaucracy: A Theory of Influence.* New Haven: Yale University Press, 1979.
Ascher, William. *Forecasting: An Appraisal for Policy-Makers and Planners.* Baltimore: Johns Hopkins University Press, 1978.
Bachrach, Peter, and Morton S. Baratz. *Power and Poverty.* New York: Oxford University Press, 1970.
Banfield, Edward C. *Political Influence.* New York: Free Press, 1961.
Barber, Bernard. "Control and Responsibility in the Powerful Professions." *Political Science Quarterly* 93 (Winter 1978–79): 599–615.
Bardach, Eugene. *The Implementation Game: What Happens after a Bill Becomes a Law.* Cambridge: MIT Press, 1977.
Bell, Daniel. *The Coming of Post-Industrial Society.* New York: Basic Books, 1973.
Benjamin, Gerald. *Race Relations and the New York City Commission on Human Rights.* Ithaca, N.Y.: Cornell University Press, 1974.

218                                                     *Selected Bibliography*

Bennis, Warren G. *Changing Organizations*. New York: McGraw-Hill, 1966.

Benveniste, Guy. *The Politics of Expertise*. Berkeley: Glendessary Press, 1972.

———. *Bureaucracy*. San Francisco: Boyd and Fraser, 1977.

Berger, Raoul. *Executive Privilege: A Constitutional Myth*. Cambridge: Harvard University Press, 1974.

Berman, Larry. *The Office of Management and Budget and the Presidency, 1921–1979*. Princeton: Princeton University Press, 1979.

———. *Planning a Tragedy: The Americanization of the War in Vietnam*. New York: W. W. Norton, 1982.

Bernstein, Barton J. "The Cuban Missile Crisis: Trading the Jupiters in Turkey?" *Political Science Quarterly* 95 (Spring 1980): 97–125.

Bernstein, Marver H. *Regulating Business by Independent Commission*. Princeton: Princeton University Press, 1955.

———. *The Job of the Federal Executive*. Washington, D.C.: Brookings Institution, 1958.

Berry, Jeffrey M. *Lobbying for the People: The Political Behavior of Public Interest Groups*. Princeton: Princeton University Press, 1977.

Braybrooke, David, and Charles E. Lindblom. *A Strategy of Decision*. New York: Free Press, 1963.

Brown, Lawrence D. *New Policies, New Politics: Government's Response to Government's Growth*. Washington, D.C.: Brookings Institution, 1983.

Brown, Roger. "Party and Bureaucracy from Kennedy to Reagan." *Political Science Quarterly* 97 (Summer 1982): 279–294.

Bryner, Gary. "Congress, Courts and Agencies: Equal Employment and the Limits of Policy Implementation." *Political Science Quarterly* 96 (Fall 1981): 411–430.

Caiden, Gerald E. *Administrative Reform*. Chicago: Aldine, 1969.

Callahan, North. *TVA: Bridge over Troubled Waters*. South Brunswick, N.J.: A. S. Barnes, 1980.

Cater, Douglass. *The Fourth Branch of Government*. Boston: Houghton Mifflin, 1959.

Chandler, Alfred D. *The Visible Hand: The Managerial Revolution in American Business*. Cambridge: Harvard University Press, 1977.

Chittick, William O. *State Department, Press, and Pressure Groups: A Role Analysis*. New York: John Wiley, 1970.

Clark, Burton R. "Organizational Adaptation and Precarious Values: A Case Study." *American Sociological Review* 21 (June 1956): 327–336.

Cleveland, Harlan. *The Future Executive: A Guide for Tomorrow's Managers*. New York: Harper & Row, 1972.

Cohen, Bernard. *The Press and Foreign Policy*. Princeton: Princeton University Press, 1963.

Cole, Richard L., and David A. Caputo. "Presidential Control of the Senior Civil Service: Assessing the Strategies of the Nixon Years." *American Political Science Review* 73 (June 1979): 399–413.

Corson, John J., and R. Shale Paul. *Men Near the Top.* Baltimore: Johns Hopkins Press, 1966.

Crenson, Matthew A. *The Unpolitics of Air Pollution.* Baltimore: Johns Hopkins Press, 1971.

———. *The Federal Machine: Beginnings of Bureaucracy in Jacksonian America.* Baltimore: Johns Hopkins Press, 1975.

———. "Urban Bureaucracy in Urban Politics." In J. David Greenstone, ed., *Public Values and Private Power in American Politics.* Chicago: University of Chicago Press, 1982.

Cronin, Thomas E., and Sanford D. Greenberg, eds. *The Presidential Advisory System.* New York: Harper and Row, 1969.

Crozier, Michel. *The Bureaucratic Phenomenon.* Chicago: University of Chicago Press, 1964.

Dahl, Robert A. *Who Governs?* New Haven: Yale University Press, 1961.

———. *Modern Political Analysis,* 3rd ed. Englewood Cliffs, N.J.: Prentice-Hall, 1976.

———, and Charles E. Lindblom. *Politics, Economics, and Welfare.* New York: Harper, 1953.

Davidson, Roger H. "Congress and the Executive: The Race for Representation." In Alfred DeGrazia, coord., *Twelve Studies of the Organization of Congress.* Washington, D.C.: American Enterprise Institute for Public Policy Research, 1966.

Davis, David. *How the Bureaucracy Makes Foreign Policy: An Exchange Analysis.* Lexington, Mass.: Lexington Books, 1972.

Davis, James W., Jr., and Kenneth Dolbeare. *Little Groups of Neighbors: The Selective Service System.* Chicago: Markham, 1968.

Davis, Kenneth C. *Discretionary Justice.* Baton Rouge: Louisiana State University Press, 1969.

Derthick, Martha. *Policymaking for Social Security.* Washington, D.C.: Brookings Institution, 1979.

———, with Gary Bombardier. *Between State and Nation: Regional Organizations of the United States.* Washington, D.C.: Brookings Institution, 1974.

Destler, I. M. *Presidents, Bureaucrats, and Foreign Policy.* Princeton: Princeton University Press, 1972.

———. "National Security Management: What Presidents Have Wrought." *Political Science Quarterly* 95 (Winter 1980–81): 573–588.

Divine, Robert A. *Blowing on the Wind: The Nuclear Test Ban Debate, 1954–1960.* New York: Oxford University Press, 1978.

Dodd, Lawrence C., and Richard L. Schott. *Congress and the Administrative State.* New York: John Wiley, 1979.

Doig, Jameson W. " 'If I See a Murderous Fellow Sharpening a Knife Cleverly . . . ': The Wilsonian Dichotomy and the Public Authority Tradition." *Public Administration Review* 43 (March/April 1983): 292–304.

Downs, Anthony. *Inside Bureaucracy.* Boston: Little, Brown, 1967.

———. "Up and Down with Ecology — the Issue Attention Cycle," *The Public Interest* 28 (Summer 1972): 38–50.

Dror, Yehezkel. "Muddling Through — 'Science' or Inertia?" *Public Administration Review* 24 (September 1964): 153–157.

———. "Policy Analysts: A New Professional Role in Government Service." *Public Administration Review* 27 (September 1967): 197–203.

Dunn, Delmer D. *Public Officials and the Press.* Reading, Mass.: Addison-Wesley, 1969.

Dvorin, Eugene P., and Robert H. Simmons. *From Amoral to Humane Bureaucracy.* San Francisco: Canfield Press, 1972.

Edelman, Murray. *The Symbolic Uses of Politics.* Urbana: University of Illinois Press, 1964.

Edwards, George C., III. *Implementing Public Policy.* Washington, D.C.: Congressional Quarterly Press, 1980.

Eisenstadt, Samuel N. "Bureaucracy and Bureaucratization." In *Essays on Comparative Institutions.* New York: John Wiley, 1965, pp. 175–271.

Elmore, Richard F. *Complexity and Control: What Legislators and Administrators Can Do about Implementing Public Policy.* Seattle, Wash.: Institute for Public Policy and Management, 1979.

———. "Backward Mapping: Implementation Research and Policy Decisions." *Political Science Quarterly* 94 (Winter 1979–80): 601–616.

Etzioni, Amitai. *A Comparative Analysis of Complex Organizations.* New York: Free Press, 1961.

———. *Modern Organizations.* Englewood Cliffs, N.J.: Prentice-Hall, 1964.

———. "Mixed-Scanning: A 'Third' Approach to Decision-Making." *Public Administration Review* 27 (December 1967): 385–392.

Fainsod, Merle. "Some Reflections on the Nature of the Regulatory Process." In Carl J. Friedrich and Edward S. Mason, eds., *Public Policy,* vol. I. Cambridge: Harvard University Press, 1940.

Falk, Stanley L. "The National Security Council under Truman, Eisenhower, and Kennedy." *Political Science Quarterly* 79 (September 1964): 403–434.

Feit, Edward. *The Armed Bureaucrats.* Boston: Houghton Mifflin, 1973.

Fenno, Richard F. *The President's Cabinet.* Cambridge: Harvard University Press, 1959.

———. *The Power of the Purse.* Boston: Little, Brown, 1966.

Ferkiss, Victor C. *Technological Man.* New York: George Braziller, 1969.

Fesler, James W. "Politics, Policy, and Bureaucracy at the Top." *Annals* of the American Academy of Political and Social Science 466 (March 1983): 23–41.

Finer, Herman. "Administrative Responsibility in Democratic Government." *Public Administration Review* I (Summer 1941): 335–350.

Fiorina, Morris P. *Congress: Keystone of the Washington Establishment.* New Haven: Yale University Press, 1977.

Fisher, Louis. *President and Congress.* New York: Free Press, 1972.

———. "A Political Context for Legislative Vetoes." *Political Science Quarterly* 93 (Summer 1978): 241–254.

———, and Ronald C. Moe. "Presidential Reorganization Authority: Is It Worth the Cost?" *Political Science Quarterly* 96 (Summer 1981): 301–318.

Flash, Edward S., Jr. *Economic Advice and Presidential Leadership.* New York: Columbia University Press, 1965.

Foss, Phillip O. *Politics and Grass.* Seattle: University of Washington Press, 1960.

Fox, Douglas M. *The Politics of City and State Bureaucracy.* Pacific Palisades, Calif.: Goodyear, 1974.

Franck, Thomas M., and Edward Weisband, eds. *Secrecy and Foreign Policy.* New York: Oxford University Press, 1974.

Freedman, James O. *Crisis and Legitimacy: The Administrative Process and American Government.* Cambridge: Cambridge University Press, 1978.

Freeman, J. Leiper. "The Bureaucracy in Pressure Politics." *Annals* of the American Academy of Political and Social Science 319 (September 1958): 10–19.

———. *The Political Process: Executive Bureau–Legislative Committee Relations,* rev. ed. New York: Random House, 1965.

Friedman, Robert S. *Professionalism: Expertise and Policy Making.* New York: General Learning Press, 1971.

———, Bernard W. Klein, and John H. Romani. "Administrative Agencies and the Publics They Serve." *Public Administration Review* 26 (September 1966): 192–204.

Friedrich, Carl J. "Public Policy and the Nature of Administrative Responsibility." In Carl J. Friedrich and Edward S. Mason, eds., *Public Policy.* Vol I. Cambridge: Harvard University Press, 1940.

Fritschler, A. Lee. *Smoking and Politics: Policymaking and the Federal Bureaucracy,* 3rd ed. Englewood Cliffs, N.J.: Prentice-Hall, 1983.

Gawthrop, Louis C. *Administrative Politics and Social Change.* New York: St. Martin's Press, 1971.

Gelb, Leslie H., with Richard K. Betts. *The Irony of Vietnam: The System Worked.* Washington, D.C.: Brookings Institution, 1979.

Gellhorn, Ernest. "Adverse Publicity by Administrative Agencies," *Harvard Law Review* 86 (June 1973): 1380–1441.

Gellhorn, Walter. *Ombudsman and Others: Citizens' Protectors in Nine Countries.* Cambridge: Harvard University Press, 1967.

George, Alexander M. "The Case for Multiple Advocacy in Making Foreign Policy." *American Political Science Review* 66 (September 1972): 751–785.

Gerth, H. H., and C. Wright Mills, eds. *From Max Weber: Essays in Sociology.* New York: Oxford University Press, 1946.

Gilb, Corinne L. *Hidden Hierarchies.* New York: Harper and Row, 1966.

Gilbert, Charles E. "The Framework of Administrative Responsibility." *Journal of Politics* 21 (August 1959): 373–407.

———, ed. "Implementing Governmental Change." *Annals* of the American Academy of Political and Social Science 466 (March 1983).

Gilmour, Robert S. "Central Legislative Clearance: A Revised Perspective." *Public Administration Review* 31 (March/April 1971): 150–158.

Gilpin, Robert, and Christopher Wright, eds. *Scientists and National Policy-Making.* New York: Columbia University Press, 1964.

Green, Philip. "Science, Government and the Case of RAND: A Singular Pluralism." *World Politics* 20 (January 1968): 301–326.

Greenberg, Daniel S. *The Politics of Pure Science.* New York: New American Library, 1968.

Greider, William. "The Education of David Stockman." *Atlantic Monthly* (December 1981).

Grossman, Michael B., and Martha J. Kumar. *Portraying the President: The White House and the News Media.* Baltimore: Johns Hopkins University Press, 1981.

Haar, John E. *The Professional Diplomat.* Princeton: Princeton University Press, 1969.

Halberstam, David. *The Best and the Brightest.* New York: Random House, 1972.

Hale, George E., and Marion Lief Palley. *The Politics of Federal Grants.* Washington, D.C.: Congressional Quarterly Press, 1981.

Halperin, Morton H. "The Gaither Committee and the Policy Process." *World Politics* 13 (April 1961): 360–384.

———. *Bureaucratic Politics and Foreign Policy.* Washington, D.C.: Brookings Institution, 1974.

Hammond, Paul Y. "The National Security Council as a Device for Interdepartmental Coordination." *American Political Science Review* 54 (December 1960): 899–910.

———. "Foreign Policy-Making and Administrative Politics." *World Politics* 17 (July 1965): 656–671.

Hardin, Charles M. *The Politics of Agriculture.* Glencoe, Ill.: Free Press, 1952.

Hargrove, Erwin C. *The Missing Link: The Study of the Implementation of Social Policy.* Washington, D.C.: Urban Institute, 1975.

Harris, Joseph P. *Congressional Control of Administration.* New York: Doubleday Anchor edition, 1965.

Heclo, Hugh. "OMB and the Presidency: The Problem of Neutral Competence." *The Public Interest* 38 (Winter 1975): 80–98.

———. "Political Executives and the Washington Bureaucracy." *Political Science Quarterly* 92 (Fall 1977): 395–424.

———. *A Government of Strangers: Executive Politics in Washington.* Washington, D.C.: Brookings Institution, 1977.

———. "Issue Networks and the Executive Establishment." In Anthony King, ed., *The New American Political System.* Washington, D.C.: American Enterprise Institute for Public Policy Research, 1978.

———. "One Executive Branch or Many?" In Anthony King, ed., *Both Ends of the Avenue: The Presidency, the Executive Branch, and Congress in the 1980s.* Washington, D.C.: American Enterprise Institute for Public Policy Research, 1983.

———, and Lester M. Salamon, eds. *The Illusion of Presidential Government.* Boulder, Colo.: Westview Press, 1981.

Heidenheimer, Arnold J., Hugh Heclo, and Carolyn Teich Adams. *Comparative Public Policy: The Politics of Social Change in Europe and America,* 2nd ed. New York: St. Martin's Press, 1983.

Held, Virginia. "PPBS Comes to Washington." *The Public Interest* 4 (Summer 1966): 102–115.

Herring, E. Pendleton. *Public Administration and the Public Interest.* New York: McGraw-Hill, 1936.

Hershey, Gary. *Protest in the Public Service.* Lexington, Mass.: Lexington Books, 1973.

Hess, Stephen. *The Washington Reporters.* Washington, D.C.: Brookings Institution, 1981.

Hirschman, Albert O. *Exit, Voice, and Loyalty.* Cambridge: Harvard University Press, 1970.

Hofstadter, Richard. *The Age of Reform: From Bryan to F.D.R.* New York: Alfred A. Knopf, 1955.

Holden, Matthew, Jr. " 'Imperialism' in Bureaucracy." *American Political Science Review* 60 (December 1966): 943–951.

Holtzman, Abraham H. *Legislative Liaison: Executive Leadership in Congress.* Chicago: Rand McNally, 1970.

Horowitz, Donald L. *The Courts and Social Policy.* Washington, D.C.: Brookings Institution, 1977.

———. *The Jurocracy: Government Lawyers, Agency Programs and Judicial Decisions.* Lexington, Mass.: Lexington Books, 1977.

Huddleston, Mark W. "The Carter Civil Service Reforms: Some Implications for Political Theory and Public Administration." *Political Science Quarterly* 96 (Winter 1981–82): 607–621.

Hummel, Ralph P. *The Bureaucratic Experience,* 2nd ed. New York: St. Martin's Press, 1982.

Huntington, Samuel P. "The Marasmus of the I.C.C.: The Commission, the Railroads, and the Public Interest." *Yale Law Journal* 61 (April 1952): 467–509.

———. *The Soldier and the State.* Cambridge: Harvard University Press, 1957.

———. *The Common Defense: Strategic Programs in National Politics.* New York: Columbia University Press, 1961.

Jacob, Herbert, and Kenneth N. Vines, eds. *Politics in the American States,* 3rd ed. Boston: Little, Brown, 1976.

Janis, Irving L. *Groupthink,* 2nd ed. Boston: Houghton Mifflin, 1982.

Janowitz, Morris. *The Professional Soldier.* New York: Free Press, 1960.

Jennings, M. Kent. *Community Influentials.* New York: Free Press, 1964.

———, Milton C. Cummings, Jr., and Franklin P. Kilpatrick. "Trusted Leaders: Perceptions of Appointed Federal Officials." *Public Opinion Quarterly* 30 (Fall 1966): 368–384.

Jones, Charles O. "The Limits of Public Support: Air Pollution Agency Development." *Public Administration Review* 32 (September/October 1972): 502–508.

———. *Clean Air: The Policies and Politics of Pollution.* Pittsburgh: University of Pittsburgh Press, 1975.

———. *An Introduction to the Study of Public Policy,* 2nd ed. North Scituate, Mass.: Duxbury Press, 1977.

Kaufman, Herbert. "Emerging Conflicts in the Doctrines of Public Administration." *American Political Science Review* 50 (December 1956): 1057–1073.

———. *The Forest Ranger: A Study in Administrative Behavior.* Baltimore: Johns Hopkins Press, 1960.

———. *The Limits of Organizational Change.* University, Ala.: University of Alabama Press, 1971.

———. *Administrative Feedback: Monitoring Subordinates' Behavior.* Washington, D.C.: Brookings Institution, 1973.

———. *Are Government Organizations Immortal?* Washington, D.C.: Brookings Institution, 1976.

———. *Red Tape: Its Origins, Uses, and Abuses.* Washington, D.C.: Brookings Institution, 1977.

———. "Reflections on Administrative Reorganization." In Joseph A. Peckman, ed., *Setting National Priorities: The 1978 Budget.* Washington, D.C.: Brookings Institution, 1977.

———. *The Administrative Behavior of Federal Bureau Chiefs.* Washington, D.C.: Brookings Institution, 1981.

———. "Fear of Bureaucracy: A Raging Pandemic." *Public Administration Review* 41 (January/February 1981): 1–9.

Kessel, John H. *The Domestic Presidency: Decision-Making in the White House.* North Scituate, Mass.: Duxbury Press, 1975.

Kissinger, Henry A. *American Foreign Policy,* expanded ed. New York: W. W. Norton, 1974.

Knorr, Klaus. "Failures in National Intelligence Estimates: The Case of the Cuban Missiles." *World Politics* 16 (April 1964): 455–467.

Kohlmeier, Louis M. *The Regulators.* New York: Harper and Row, 1969.

Krasnow, Erwin G., Lawrence D. Longley, and Herbert A. Terry. *The Politics of Broadcast Regulation,* 3rd ed. New York: St. Martin's Press, 1982.

Krislov, Samuel. *Representative Bureaucracy.* Englewood Cliffs, N.J.: Prentice-Hall, 1974.

Lambright, W. Henry. *Governing Science and Technology.* New York: Oxford University Press, 1976.

Landau, Martin. "Redundancy, Rationality, and the Problem of Duplication and Overlap." *Public Administration Review* 29 (July/August 1969): 346–358.

La Palombara, Joseph, ed. *Bureaucracy and Political Development.* Princeton: Princeton University Press, 1963.

Leiserson, Avery. "Scientists and the Policy Process." *American Political Science Review* 59 (June 1965): 408–416.

Levine, Charles H., ed. *Managing Fiscal Stress: The Crisis in the Public Sector.* Chatham, N.J.: Chatham House, 1980.

Levine, Sol, and Paul E. White. "Exchange as a Conceptual Framework for the Study of Interorganizational Relationships." *Administrative Science Quarterly* 5 (March 1961): 583–601.

Levitan, Sar A., and Robert Taggart. "The Great Society Did Succeed." *Political Science Quarterly* 91 (Winter 1976–77): 601–618.

Lewis, Eugene. *American Politics in a Bureaucratic Age: Citizens, Constituents, Clients and Victims.* Cambridge: Winthrop, 1977.

———. *Public Entrepreneurship: Toward a Theory of Bureaucratic Political Power.* Bloomington: Indiana University Press, 1980.

Lindblom, Charles E. "Policy Analysis," *American Economic Review* 48 (June 1958): 298–312.

———. *The Intelligence of Democracy.* New York: Free Press, 1965.

Long, Norton. *The Polity.* Chicago: Rand McNally, 1962.

———. "Bureaucracy, Pluralism and the Public Interest." Paper delivered at the annual meeting of the American Political Science Association, 1979.

Lowi, Theodore J. "American Business, Public Policy, Case Studies, and Political Theory." *World Politics* 16 (July 1964): 677–715.

———. *The End of Liberalism,* rev. ed. New York: W. W. Norton, 1979.

Lynn, Laurence E. *Managing the Public's Business: The Job of the Government Executive.* New York: Basic Books, 1981.

Maass, Arthur. *Muddy Waters.* Cambridge: Harvard University Press, 1951.

————. "Benefit-Cost Analysis: Its Relevance to Public Investment Decisions." *Quarterly Journal of Economics* 80 (May 1966): 208–226.

McConnell, Grant. *Private Power and American Democracy.* New York: Alfred A. Knopf, 1966.

Mann, Dean E. "The Selection of Federal Political Executives." *American Political Science Review* 58 (March 1964): 81–99.

March, James G., ed. *Handbook of Organizations.* Chicago: Rand McNally, 1965.

————, and Johan P. Olson. "What Administrative Reorganization Tells Us about Governing." *American Political Science Review* 77 (June 1983): 281–296.

————, and Herbert A. Simon. *Organizations.* New York: John Wiley, 1958.

Marini, Frank, ed. *Toward the New Public Administration: The Minnowbrook Perspective.* Scranton, Pa.: Chandler, 1971.

Marvick, Dwaine. *Career Perspectives in a Bureaucratic Setting.* Ann Arbor: University of Michigan Press, 1954.

Mayhew, David R. *Congress: The Electoral Connection.* New Haven: Yale University Press, 1974.

Mazmanian, Daniel A., and Jeanne Nienaber. *Can Organizations Change?* Washington, D.C.: Brookings Institution, 1979.

Meier, Kenneth J. "Representative Bureaucracy: An Empirical Analysis." *American Political Science Review* 69 (June 1975): 526–542.

————. *Politics and the Bureaucracy: Policymaking in the Fourth Branch of Government.* North Scituate, Mass.: Duxbury Press, 1979.

————. "Executive Reorganization of Government: Impact on Employment and Expenditures." *American Journal of Political Science* 24 (August 1980): 396–412.

Meltzner, Arnold J. *Policy Analysts in the Bureaucracy.* Berkeley: University of California Press, 1976.

Moos, Malcolm, and Francis E. Rourke. *The Campus and the State.* Baltimore: Johns Hopkins Press, 1959.

Mosher, Frederick C. *Democracy and the Public Service,* 2nd ed. New York: Oxford University Press, 1982.

Moynihan, Daniel P. *Maximum Feasible Misunderstanding: Community Action in the War on Poverty.* New York: Free Press, 1970.

Muir, William Ker. *Police: Streetcorner Politicians.* Chicago: University of Chicago Press, 1977.

Nadel, Mark V. *The Politics of Consumer Protection.* Indianapolis: Bobbs-Merrill, 1971.

————. "The Hidden Dimension of Public Policy: Private Governments and the Policy Making Process." *Journal of Politics* 37 (February 1975): 2–34.

————, and Francis E. Rourke. "Bureaucracies." In Fred I. Greenstein and Nelson W. Polsby, eds., *Handbook of Political Science*. Vol. 5. Reading, Mass.: Addison-Wesley, 1975.

Nathan, Richard P. *The Administrative Presidency*. New York: John Wiley, 1983.

————. "The Reagan Presidency in Domestic Affairs." In Fred I. Greenstein, ed., *The Reagan Presidency: An Early Assessment*. Baltimore: Johns Hopkins University Press, 1983.

Nelson, Michael. "A Short Ironic History of American National Bureaucracy." *Journal of Politics* 44 (August 1982): 747–778.

Nelson, William E. *The Roots of American Bureaucracy, 1830–1900*. Cambridge: Harvard University Press, 1982.

Neustadt, Richard E. "Presidency and Legislation: The Growth of Central Clearance." *American Political Science Review* 48 (September 1954): 641–671.

————. "Presidency and Legislation: Planning the President's Program." *American Political Science Review* 49 (December 1955): 980–1021.

————. "Approaches to Staffing the Presidency: Notes on FDR and JFK." *American Political Science Review* 57 (December 1963): 855–864.

————. "White House and Whitehall." *The Public Interest* 2 (Winter 1966): 55–69.

————. *Presidential Power: The Politics of Leadership from FDR to Carter*. New York: John Wiley, 1980.

Niskanen, William A. *Bureaucracy and Representative Government*. Chicago: Aldine Atherton, 1971.

Ogul, Morris S. *Congress Oversees the Bureaucracy: Studies in Legislative Supervision*. Pittsburgh: University of Pittsburgh Press, 1976.

Ostrom, Vincent. *The Intellectual Crisis in American Public Administration*. University, Ala.: University of Alabama Press, 1971.

Owen, Marguerite. *The Tennessee Valley Authority*. New York: Praeger Publishers, 1979.

Peabody, Robert L., and Francis E. Rourke. "Public Bureaucracies." In James G. March, ed., *Handbook of Organizations*. Chicago: Rand McNally, 1965.

Penniman, Clara. "Reorganization and the Internal Revenue Service." *Public Administration Review* 21 (Summer 1961): 121–130.

Peters, B. Guy. *The Politics of Bureaucracy: A Comparative Perspective*. New York: Longman, 1978.

Pipe, G. Russell. "Congressional Liaison: The Executive Branch Consolidates Its Relations with Congress." *Public Administration Review* 26 (March 1966): 14–24.

Polsby, Nelson W. *Congress and the Presidency*, 3rd ed. Englewood Cliffs, N.J.: Prentice-Hall, 1976.

————. "Presidential Cabinet Making: Lessons for the Political System." *Political Science Quarterly* 93 (Spring 1978): 15–25.

————. *Political Innovation in America: The Politics of Policy Innovation.* New Haven: Yale University Press, 1984.

Porter, Roger B. *Presidential Decision Making: The Economic Policy Board.* Cambridge: Cambridge University Press, 1980.

Pressman, Jeffrey L., and Aaron Wildavsky. *Implementation,* 2nd ed. Berkeley: University of California Press, 1979.

Presthus, Robert. *The Organizational Society: An Analysis and a Theory.* New York: Alfred A. Knopf, 1962.

Price, Don K. *Government and Science.* New York: New York University Press, 1954.

————. *The Scientific Estate.* Cambridge: Harvard University Press, 1965.

Pye, Lucian W. *Aspects of Political Development.* Boston: Little, Brown, 1966.

Quirk, Paul J. *Industry Influence in Federal Regulatory Agencies.* Princeton: Princeton University Press, 1981.

Randall, Ronald. "Presidential Power versus Bureaucratic Intransigence: The Influence of the Nixon Administration on Welfare Policy." *American Political Science Review* 73 (September 1979): 795–810.

Ransom, Harry Howe. *Can American Democracy Survive Cold War?* Garden City, N.Y.: Doubleday Anchor Books, 1964.

Reagan, Michael D. "The Political Structure of the Federal Reserve System." *American Political Science Review* 55 (March 1961): 64–76.

Redford, Emmette S. *Ideal and Practice in Public Administration.* University, Ala.: University of Alabama Press, 1958.

————, and Marlan Blissett. *Organizing the Executive Branch: The Johnson Presidency.* Chicago: University of Chicago Press, 1981.

Reedy, George E. *The Twilight of the Presidency.* New York: World, 1970.

Rehfuss, John. *Public Administration as Political Process.* New York: Charles Scribner's Sons, 1973.

Relyea, Harold C. "Opening Government to Public Scrutiny: A Decade of Federal Efforts." *Public Administration Review* 35 (January/February 1975): 3–10.

Riggs, Fred W. "Bureaucracy and Political Development: A Paradoxical View." In Joseph La Palombara, ed., *Bureaucracy and Political Development.* Princeton: Princeton University Press, 1963.

Ripley, Randall B., and Grace A. Franklin. *Congress, the Bureaucracy, and Public Policy,* rev. ed. Homewood, Ill.: Dorsey Press, 1980.

Rogers, David. *110 Livingston Street.* New York: Random House, 1968.

Rose, Richard. *Managing Presidential Objectives.* New York: Free Press, 1976.

Rosenbaum, Walter A. *The Politics of Environmental Concern.* New York: Praeger, 1973.

Rosenbloom, David H. "The Judicial Response to the Rise of the American Administrative State." *American Review of Public Administration* 15 (Spring 1981): 29–51.

Rourke, Francis E. *Secrecy and Publicity: Dilemmas of Democracy.* Baltimore: Johns Hopkins Press, 1961.

———. *Bureaucracy and Foreign Policy.* Baltimore: Johns Hopkins University Press, 1972.

———. "Bureaucratic Secrecy and Its Constituents." *The Bureaucrat* 1 (Summer 1972): 116–121.

———. "Executive Fallibility: Presidential Management Styles." *Administration and Society* 6 (August 1974): 171–177.

———. "Grappling with the Bureaucracy." In Arnold J. Meltsner, ed., *Politics and the Oval Office.* San Francisco: Institute for Contemporary Studies, 1981.

———. "The Presidency and Bureaucracy: Strategic Alternatives." In Michael Nelson, ed., *The Presidency and the Political System.* Washington, D.C.: Congressional Quarterly Press, 1984.

———, and Glenn E. Brooks. *The Managerial Revolution in Higher Education.* Baltimore: Johns Hopkins Press, 1966.

Rowat, Donald C. *The Ombudsman Plan: Essays on the Worldwide Spread of an Idea.* Toronto: McClelland and Stewart, 1973.

Sabatier, Paul. "Social Movements and Regulatory Agencies: Toward a More Adequate — and Less Pessimistic — Theory of Clientele Capture." *Policy Sciences* 6 (September 1975): 301–342.

Salamon, Lester B., and Gary L. Wamsley. "The Federal Bureaucracy: Responsive to Whom?" In Leroy N. Rieselbach, ed., *People vs. Government: The Responsiveness of American Institutions.* Bloomington: Indiana University Press, 1975.

Sayre, Wallace, ed. *The Federal Government Service.* Englewood Cliffs, N.J.: Prentice-Hall, 1965.

———, and Herbert Kaufman. *Governing New York City.* New York: Russell Sage Foundation, 1960.

Schaller, Lyle E. "Is the Citizen Advisory Committee a Threat to Representative Government?" *Public Administration Review* 24 (September 1964): 175–179.

Schattschneider, E. E. *The Semisovereign People.* New York: Holt, Rinehart and Winston, 1960.

Scher, Seymour. "Congressional Committee Members as Independent Agency Overseers: A Case Study." *American Political Science Review* 54 (December 1960): 911–920.

————. "Regulatory Agency Control through Appointment: The Case of the Eisenhower Administration and the NLRB." *Journal of Politics* 23 (November 1961): 667–688.

Schick, Allen. "A Death in the Bureaucracy: The Demise of Federal PPB." *Public Administration Review* 33 (March/April 1973): 146–156.

————. *Congress and Money: Budgeting, Spending, and Taxing.* Washington, D.C.: Urban Institute, 1980.

————. "The Problem of Presidential Budgeting." In Hugh Heclo and Lester M. Salamon, eds., *The Illusion of Presidential Government.* Boulder, Colo.: Westview Press, 1981.

Schiff, Ashley L. *Fire and Water: Scientific Heresy in the Forest Service.* Cambridge: Harvard University Press, 1962.

Schilling, Warner R. "The H-Bomb Decision: How to Decide without Actually Choosing." *Political Science Quarterly* 76 (March 1961): 24–46.

————. "Scientists, Foreign Policy, and Politics." In Robert Gilpin and Christopher Wright, eds., *Scientists and National Policy-Making.* New York: Columbia University Press, 1964.

Schlozman, Kay Lehman, and John T. Tierney. "More of the Same: Washington Pressure Group Activity in a Decade of Change." *Journal of Politics* 45 (May 1983): 351–377.

Schubert, Glendon. *The Public Interest.* New York: Free Press, 1960.

Schulman, Paul R. *Large-Scale Policy Making.* New York: Elsevier, 1980.

Scott, Andrew M. "Environmental Change and Organizational Adaptation." *International Studies Quarterly* 14 (March 1970): 85–94.

Sears, David O., and Jack Citrin. *Tax Revolt: Something for Nothing in California.* Cambridge: Harvard University Press, 1982.

Seidman, Harold. *Politics, Position, and Power: The Dynamics of Federal Organization,* 3rd ed. New York: Oxford University Press, 1980.

Selznick, Philip. *TVA and the Grass Roots.* Berkeley: University of California Press, 1949.

————. *Leadership in Administration.* Evanston, Ill.: Row, Peterson, 1957.

Shapiro, Martin. *The Supreme Court and Administrative Agencies.* New York: Free Press, 1968.

Sharkansky, Ira. "Four Agencies and an Appropriations Subcommittee: A Comparative Study of Budget Strategies." *Midwest Journal of Political Science* 9 (August 1965): 254–281.

————. "An Appropriations Subcommittee and Its Client Agencies: A Comparative Study of Supervision and Control." *American Political Science Review* 59 (September 1965): 622–628.

Shefter, Martin. "New York City's Fiscal Crisis." In Charles H. Levine, ed., *Managing Fiscal Stress.* Chatham, N.J.: Chatham House, 1980.

Sigal, Leon V. *Reporters and Officials: The Organization and Politics of Newsmaking.* New York: D. C. Heath, 1973.

Simon, Herbert A. *Models of Man: Social and Rational.* New York: John Wiley, 1957.

———. *The New Science of Management Decision.* New York: Harper & Row, 1960.

———. *Administrative Behavior: A Study of Decision-Making Processes in Administrative Organizations,* 3rd ed. New York: Free Press, 1976.

———, Donald W. Smithburg, and Victor Thompson. *Public Administration.* New York: Alfred A. Knopf, 1950.

Sjoberg, Gideon, Richard A. Brymer, and Buford Farris. "Bureaucracy and the Lower Class." *Sociology and Social Research* 50 (April 1966): 325–337.

Skocpol, Theda, and Kenneth Finegold. "State Capacity and Economic Intervention in the Early New Deal." *Political Science Quarterly* 97 (Summer 1982): 255–278.

Skolnick, Jerome. *Justice without Trial.* New York: John Wiley, 1966.

Skowronek, Stephen. *Building a New American State: The Expansion of National Administrative Capacities, 1877–1920.* New York: Cambridge University Press, 1982.

Smith, Bruce L. R. *The Rand Corporation: Case Study of a Nonprofit Advisory Corporation.* Cambridge: Harvard University Press, 1966.

Snow, C. P. *Science and Government.* Cambridge: Harvard University Press, 1961.

Sorauf, Frank J. "The Public Interest Reconsidered." *Journal of Politics* 19 (November 1957): 616–639.

Sorensen, Theodore C. *Decision-Making in the White House.* New York: Columbia University Press, 1963.

Stein, Harold, ed. *Public Administration and Policy Development.* New York: Harcourt Brace, 1952.

Steiner, Gilbert Y. *Social Insecurity: The Politics of Welfare.* Chicago: Rand McNally, 1966.

Steinfels, Peter. *The Neoconservatives: The Men Who Are Changing America's Politics.* New York: Simon and Schuster, 1979.

Stillman, Richard J. "Woodrow Wilson and the Study of Administration: A New Look at an Old Essay." *American Political Science Review* 67 (June 1973): 582–588.

Storing, Herbert J. "Political Parties and the Bureaucracy." In Robert A. Goldwin, ed., *Political Parties, U.S.A.* Chicago: Rand McNally, 1964.

Subramanian, V. "Representative Bureaucracy: A Reassessment." *American Political Science Review* 61 (December 1967): 1010–1019.

Szanton, Peter, ed. *Federal Reorganization: What Have We Learned?* Chatham, N.J.: Chatham House, 1981.

Tanenhaus, Joseph. "Supreme Court Attitudes toward Federal Administrative Agencies." *Journal of Politics* 22 (August 1960): 502–524.

Thayer, Frederick C. *An End to Hierarchy! An End to Competition!* New York: New Viewpoints, 1973.

Theoharis, Athan G. "The FBI's Stretching of Presidential Directives, 1936–1953." *Political Science Quarterly* 91 (Winter 1976–77): 649–672.

Thomas, Norman C., and Harold L. Wolman. "The Presidency and Policy Formulation: The Task Force Device." *Public Administration Review* 29 (September/October 1969): 459–471.

Thompson, James D., and William J. McEwen. "Organizational Goals and Environment: Goal-Setting as an Interaction Process." *American Sociological Review* 23 (February 1958): 23–31.

Thompson, Victor A. *The Regulatory Process in OPA Rationing.* New York: Columbia University Press, 1950.

———. *Modern Organization.* New York: Alfred A. Knopf, 1961.

Thomson, James C. "How Could Vietnam Happen? An Autopsy." *The Atlantic* 221 (April 1968): 47–53.

Tierney, John T. *Postal Reorganization: Managing the Public's Business.* Boston: Auburn House, 1981.

Truman, David B. *The Governmental Process.* New York: Alfred A. Knopf, 1951.

Vogel, David. "The Public-Interest Movement and the American Reform Tradition." *Political Science Quarterly* 95 (Winter 1980–81): 607–627.

Waldo, Dwight. *The Administrative State.* New York: Ronald Press, 1948.

Walker, Jack L. "The Origins and Maintenance of Interest Groups in America." *American Political Science Review* 77 (June 1983): 390–406.

Wamsley, Gary L., and Mayer N. Zald. *The Political Economy of Public Organizations.* Lexington, Mass.: Lexington Books, 1973.

Weisband, Edward, and Thomas M. Franck. *Resignation in Protest.* New York: Grossman, 1975.

Weiss, Carol H., and Allen H. Barton, eds. *Making Bureaucracies Work.* Beverly Hills, Calif.: Sage Publications, 1980.

Wengert, Norman. *Natural Resources and the Political Struggle.* Garden City, N.Y.: Doubleday, 1955.

Wildavsky, Aaron. *Dixon-Yates: A Study in Power Politics.* New Haven: Yale University Press, 1962.

———. *The Politics of the Budgetary Process,* 3rd ed. Boston: Little, Brown, 1979.

Wilensky, Harold L. *Organizational Intelligence.* New York: Basic Books, 1967.

Wilson, Graham K. "Are Department Secretaries Really a President's Natural Enemies?" *British Journal of Political Science* 7 (July 1977): 273–299.

———. *Special Interests and Policymaking: Agricultural Policies and Politics in Britain and the United States of America, 1956–70.* New York: John Wiley, 1977.

Wilson, James Q. "Innovation in Organization: Notes toward a Theory." In James D. Thompson, ed., *Approaches to Organizational Design.* Pittsburgh: University of Pittsburgh Press, 1966.

———. "The Bureaucracy Problem." *The Public Interest.* 6 (Winter 1967): 3–9.

———. *Varieties of Police Behavior.* Cambridge: Harvard University Press, 1968.

———. *Political Organizations.* New York: Basic Books, 1973.

———. *The Investigators: Managing F.B.I. and Narcotics Agents.* New York: Basic Books, 1978.

———, ed. *The Politics of Regulation.* New York: Basic Books, 1980.

———, and Patricia Rachal. "Can Government Regulate Itself?" *The Public Interest* 46 (Winter 1977): 3–14.

Wilson, Woodrow. "The Study of Administration." *Political Science Quarterly* 2 (June 1887): 197–222.

Witte, Edwin E. "The Preparation of Proposed Legislative Measures by Administrative Departments." In U.S. President's Committee on Administrative Management, *Report with Special Studies.* Washington, D.C.: U.S. Government Printing Office, 1937.

Wofford, Harris. *Of Kennedys and Kings: Making Sense of the Sixties.* New York: Farrar, Straus, Giroux, 1980.

Wynia, Bob L. "Federal Bureaucrats' Attitudes toward a Democratic Ideology." *Public Administration Review* 34 (March/April 1974): 156–162.

Wyszomirski, Margaret J. "The De-Institutionalization of Presidential Staff Agencies." *Public Administration Review* 42 (September/October 1982): 448–458.

Yates, Douglas. *Bureaucratic Democracy: The Search for Democracy and Efficiency in American Government.* Cambridge: Harvard University Press, 1982.

Yin, Robert K., William A. Lucas, Peter L. Szanton, and J. Andrew Spindler. *Citizen Organizations: Increasing Client Control over Services.* Santa Monica, Calif.: Rand Corporation, 1973.

Zeigler, Harmon. *Interest Groups in American Society.* Englewood Cliffs, N.J.: Prentice-Hall, 1972.

# Index

*Index*